NIXON AND THE DRAGON LADY

Did Richard Nixon Conspire with Anna Chennault in 1968 to Destroy Peace in Vietnam?

Evan Edward Laine

NIXON AND THE DRAGON LADY

Did Richard Nixon Conspire with Anna Chennault in 1968 to Destroy Peace in Vietnam?

Evan Edward Laine

COMMON GROUND PUBLISHING 2015,

First published in 2015 in Champaign, Illinois, USA
by Common Ground Publishing LLC
as part of the New Directions in the Humanities book imprint

Library of Congress Cataloging-in-Publication Data

Laine, Evan Edward, author.
  Nixon and the Dragon Lady : did Richard Nixon conspire with Anna Chennault in 1968 to destroy peace in Vietnam? / Evan Edward Laine.
      pages cm
  Includes bibliographical references and index.
  ISBN 978-1-61229-795-8 (pbk : alk. paper) -- ISBN 978-1-61229-796-5 (pdf)
  1. Vietnam War, 1961-1975--Peace. 2. Vietnam War, 1961-1975--Diplomatic history. 3. Nixon, Richard M. (Richard Milhous), 1913-1994. 4. Chennault, Anna. I. Title.
  DS559.7.L36 2015
  959.704'32--dc23
                        2015023774

To my wife Michele, whose support and devotion have allowed me to chase and catch my dreams.

Table of Contents

ACKNOWLEDGEMENTS

I would like to thank Phillip Scranton P.H.D., my mentor at_Rutgers University for all his much needed help and guidance.

Foreword

Characters *in Nixon and the Dragon Lady* include powerful countries, famous world leaders, upstart nations and questionable personalities; however, the primary character in this book is you, the reader. You will be actively charged to determine whether in 1968, candidate for President Richard Nixon conspired to effectively destroy a realistic opportunity for peace in the Vietnam War for the purpose of getting elected. Using an interdisciplinary approach, employing the fields of history, political science, law, social science and psychology, you will be provided with a wide range of evidence. As a member of that hypothetical civil jury, you will weigh that evidence for the purposes of rendering a "historical" verdict. In a simple word, you are charged with deciding the "truth." This task is far from simple. As a lawyer for 28 years, I took thousands of statements and prepared countless witnesses for their eventual testimony. I examined and cross-examined doctors, politicians, scientists, electricians, engineers, plumbers, teachers, and grocery clerks, and came away from these experiences with one conclusion; there is no "THE TRUTH." Of course, there are clear undisputed facts. World War II did occur, the Towers did fall on 9/11, and the Boston Red Sox lost the World Series to the New York Mets in 1986. Nevertheless, the clarity of an event dissipates when we seek the identity of its relevant actors, and why and how they acted. My denial of "THE TRUTH" is not meant in an existential manner. I am a pragmatist and do not involve myself much in philosophy. Instead, my experiences have been that when the whos, hows and whys are scrutinized, what emerges are versions of events given by those who experience them firsthand, second hand or through rumor or fantasy. Therefore, as an aide to the reader in performing their task in ultimately rendering a verdict, I offer in this foreword a lesson in what I deem "versionology."

First, the basics. There are reasonable, logical versions and there are those that are unreasonable, illogical, ridiculous and nonsensical, but versions all the same. The proposition that one report may seem more reasonable than another does not mean that it is more credible or reliable. I have come to understand a version is usually an individual's good faith perception of what happened in his environment and what his/her behavior was in that system. I found it is very rare that witnesses lie intentionally as part of some dark plot; rather they see the facts through filters of protection, self-interest, prejudice, and stupidity. Thus, our lesson plan will explore the common pitfalls of our new science. We will begin with the illusion of the "big lie." There is a maxim in law, "Lie in one, lie in all."

Judges often instruct a jury that they are to consider that maxim when evaluating the credibility of a witness. The big *Kahuna of* cross-examination is to catch a witness in a lie, or what is perceived to be a lie. If you are lucky enough to accomplish this feat, the effect is as if a Monty Pythonesqe giant foot comes out of the sky and squashes the witness along with whatever negative aspects that witness shed on your case. Another bonus; that squashing weakens your opponent's entire case, even affecting his credible witnesses. Sounds great, right? Nevertheless, it is rarely that simple, and instead of yielding clarity of thought, the "big lie" frequently leads to lazily determined conclusions based on parlor tricks designed to make versions much easier to choose. Many times among the lies there are very substantial truths or vice versa. Sifting through the chaff to find the wheat is arduous but necessary. One cannot stop at the first sign of chaff!

In this book, almost all the major witnesses substantially differ in their versions of events among each other and with themselves. The stakes are indeed high because the ramifications of a Nixon led conspiracy that actually destroyed a realistic opportunity for peace in 1968, is measured in thousands of lives. Therefore, to help the reader wade through the morass of confusion and contradictions, I attempt to deconstruct every witness by exposing their motivations, their relevant backstories and their reputations for truthfulness. I will also apply the same analysis to all other evidence, whether it is recorded conversations, recreations of events through memory, expert opinions, or the results of official investigations or reports. When analyzing all evidence you should not only weigh their credibility, but also ponder alternative explanations for their findings or observations and always scrutinize their logic. In your search for "THE TRUTH," I caution that you cannot simply conclude a lie! AH HA a lie! and come to simple broad conclusions. Rather you must determine why that particular version was told and even if you determine there is some untruth, you must decide whether that untruth squashes the witness, dents them a little or may even be inconsequential.

I have warned you about the problems of lies, now I warn about "good faith." Beware any predisposition you have that humans make good recording devices of their surrounding events. During the process of preparing witnesses for statements or testimony, I learned that their versions are rarely rock solid; rather they are like sand dunes shifting and changing due to their internal and external conditions. Indeed, if there were truly a reliable lie detector machine, many witnesses to the same event would pass while giving contradictory versions of that event because they firmly believed in their version for whatever reason.

Our exercise in versionology must include analysis of those factors affecting the "sand dune." External factors are critical, such as whether the witness was in a position to accurately receive and interpret the evidence. Were they in the loop, did they play a small or substantial part, must be accounted for in your analysis. A witness's internal factors, including how their experiences, biases and prejudices, and what they were trying to protect, what they had lost or what they are trying to gain back, are critical in judging credibility. All the above are essential elements in deciding what to accept or reject from each individual witness. Also, be warned that as a presenter of the facts, your attorney in this case, I also have filters. I will, of course, attempt objectivity and avoid intentionally steering you to believe in a certain way. In a nutshell, this is what I have told you. Those who tell lies may, in the end, be believed, and those exercising good faith, may not be believed. Evidence that appears clear may not be. You will meet many characters in this book, but the most important character will be yourselves. In the end, the point of this book is to have the readers, after a meticulous examination of the evidence, make their own conclusions as to what, if anything happened. You will be the ultimate arbiter interpreting these versions, selecting among and within them what you believe.

Introduction

This is a tale of espionage, sabotage, mystery, the hope of peace versus the misery of continued brutal war, deceit, betrayal, famous powerful men and a beautiful inscrutable woman. This is not fiction. Rather, it is the saddest story of all, one of possible lost opportunity to prevent or lessen the pain and destruction of a national tragedy that, to this very day, haunts the nation's psyche and policy. This story is about the war in Vietnam. From 1964 until 1973, the United States battled with North Vietnam over the political future of that fledgling nation. In October of 1968, through an amalgamation of various trajectories and different gravity fields, something miraculous occurred; the stars supporting peace aligned. Despite this extraordinary opportunity, this prospect for peace failed. How this accumulation of events occurred and how the personal ambition of one man may have led to their unraveling, is the heart of this matter. The actors in this drama, iconic and mundane, include President Lyndon Johnson, Presidential candidate Richard Nixon, Secretary of Defense Clark Clifford, President of South Vietnam Nguyen Van Thiệu, South Vietnamese Ambassador to the United States Bui Diem, Premier of the Soviet Union Alexey Kosygin and, of course, the "Dragon Lady" herself, Anna Chennault, widow of the famous General Claire Chennault and leader of the "China lobby."

Our story centers on the 1968 presidential election between Richard Nixon, Hubert Humphrey, and third party candidate George Wallace. Johnson withdrew his hat from the ring during his famous March 1968 speech where he dedicated himself to seeking an honorable solution to the war, which had effectively destroyed his presidency. Although formal peace discussions began in May of 1968, the talks were nothing more than a frustrating exercise in propaganda, accomplishing little more than stalemate. June of 1968 brought a change; the stalemate started to ease and then dramatically broke in October. The North Vietnamese, for the first time, demonstrated a willingness to make major implicit concessions in exchange for an "unconditional" bombing halt of their territory by the United States. To the surprise of many, there was actual light in the peace process. Real peace negotiations, to take place in Paris, suddenly became a distinct possibility. One of the key sources of the prior stalemate was the North Vietnamese insistence that they would never negotiate with the US "puppet" government of South Vietnam headed by President Nguyen Van Thiệu. Nevertheless, this resistance dissolved and momentum towards peace started to roll forward. The bombing halt was scheduled to commence on October 31, 1968.

On November 2, 1968, three days before the presidential election, the United States, Hanoi, the National Liberation Front, and Saigon, were to begin negotiations to discuss substantive issues. Hope was so high that the most powerful leaders of the United States and the Soviet Union exchanged optimistic letters touting the end of the war. US negotiators in Paris actually had champagne on ice ready to celebrate the imminent honorable negotiated peace.

Yet, in any good story, where there is light, there must also be dark. Republican candidate Richard Nixon, allegedly tipped off by his spies within the White House and Paris, learned about the peace initiatives. So concerned was he that the breakout of peace in Vietnam would wreck his candidacy, Nixon, along with his chief accomplices Anna Chennault and South Vietnamese Ambassador Bui Diem, allegedly conferred to sabotage this fledgling initiative by convincing South Vietnam not to attend the election eve meeting in exchange for a "better deal" if Nixon was elected president.[1] On November 1, 1968, President Thiệu shocked the Johnson administration when he declared he would not be a part of the peace process, although he previously confirmed his participation on three separate occasions. The fallout was toxic and the chance for meaningful talks fell apart. The South Vietnamese eventually did show up after the election, but peace failed and the war raged on for several more years causing tens of thousands of American deaths and countless other costs.

The possibility of peace denied because of the personal ambitions of one man, no doubt an interesting, if not appalling story. However, if true, does this drama arise to one of historical impact? The conceit here will be that the reader will judge all the major factors as if they were participating in a civil trial jury approaching a verdict. The verdict sheet will present four separate questions, all of which must be answered affirmatively to establish that the Nixon conspiracy effectively destroyed an early peaceful resolution of the Vietnam War. This task is best explained by the analogy to a hurdles race with each separate verdict question serving as an individual hurdle. In this track contest, it doesn't matter if the runner clears each hurdle by 1 inch or 3 feet, to win he must successfully clear all hurdles. Our race, though, is unique because as it is occurring, individuals from outside and within engage in either raising or lowering the hurdles. Watching the runners alone is not sufficient; we must also study the spectators because their reactions affect the runner's desire and ability to struggle onward.

---

[1] A caveat, however, from this author to the reader, descriptions of events hereafter may be couched with the passive words of "allegation," "possibility," and the like, because little in this story is without controversy. I am not without my own opinions, but the goal of this exercise is for you to develop your opinion on what happened. With the purpose of all this passivity explained, we move on to what "allegedly" happened.

The structure of our analysis, however, will not be linear, but rather an exploration of parts, all transpiring within the same relative time span. Staying within our race analogy, instead of viewing classic beginning to end action, our camera will pan to the crowd reactions, the behind the scenes reports, the character's back stories, and expert analysis, all while the race is ongoing. At the end of the event, we then turn to the usual post game analysis of the results.

Now at the starting line we discover that our race consists of four hurdles; their height each determined by the controversies, contradictions, and confusions comprising them. We approach the first hurdle where we must determine the sincerity of the North Vietnamese, the Soviets, the Chinese and the United States toward the peace process. Are the North Vietnamese, a) stung by devastating losses in the January 1968 Tet Offensive, b) weakened by the failure of their subsequent fall and spring attacks, c) surprised by the increasing fighting ability of the South Vietnamese army, d) wounded by US bombing and e) pressured towards peace by their allies, the Soviet Union and China, genuinely interested in obtaining de-escalation or peace? On the other hand, were their efforts nothing more than callous manipulations of the United States' presidential election and the United States citizenry's opposition to an increasingly unpopular war? Since it would be impossible to calculate the sincerity of the North Vietnamese without understanding how and why they reached their position, critical to our conclusions will be an analysis of the development of their attitude and behaviors between 1964 and October 1968.

Integral to this analysis are the ramifications of the Sino-Soviet conflict for communist dominance. How their differing strategies concerning the American presence in Indochina influenced, if at all, the profoundly independent North Vietnamese government's stance on negotiating an end to hostilities with the United States will be a focus of our study. The Chinese, North Vietnam's initial ally in the conflict, considered the United States as their enemy since it represented the major obstacle to their global revolutionary plan. Strong believers in protracted war theory, where weaker countries engage a larger more powerful one in guerrilla war, the Chinese consistently encouraged the North Vietnamese never to negotiate with the United States. Further, a protracted war in Vietnam was politically advantageous for China's Leader Mao Zedong and his struggle to control the communist world and his need to quell his own domestic problems. Finally, we will explore the effect of the 1968 Soviet invasion of Czechoslovakia and how that may have influenced a last-minute drastic policy change in the Chinese position on negotiations with the United States.

Regarding the Soviets, did their shifting position between indifference to actively promoting negotiation represent a sincere desire for a resolution of the conflict between Vietnam and the United States or were they primarily interested in manipulating the 1968 US election against Richard Nixon, an avowed anti-Communist. The consequences of the Soviet's very public failure in their attempt to place missiles in Cuba in 1962, the change of regime from Khrushchev to Kosygin in 1964, their concern over the Mao-led Chinese government and their desire to court the United States as an ally, all will be significant factors in our analysis.

For US President Lyndon Johnson, we must determine whether his attempt at peace in Paris constituted a true effort to end an unpopular war and preserve his personal legacy, or a charade, a mere cynical political ploy, created to strengthen the electoral chances of Vice President Hubert Humphrey or even his own. After all, optimism for a peace nights before an election, an October surprise, if you may, would certainly benefit the vice-president. The president's motivation for removing himself from reelection in March of 1968, his aborted comeback, and his political and personal relationship with Hubert Humphrey and Richard Nixon during the election campaign, and Johnson's actual efforts to bring about peace during the critical period of June through November 5 (Election Day) 1968, are all critical items of evidence for our analysis.

Our first hurdle serves as a foundation for the entire race. If you find reasonable sincerity on part of all the major participants in the peace process, you will go to the verdict sheet for question #1 select YES, and continue with your deliberation. If you conclude the parties were not reasonably sincere, the foundation fails and you vote NO on the verdict sheet and the race stops. Of course, you keep reading since you can change your minds at any time.

If the first hurdle is cleared, then we run full speed towards the question concerning the alleged conspiracy. [2] Was there solid evidence that Nixon

---

[2] The term "conspiracy" defines a constellation of acts that amount to a legal wrong under either the criminal and/or civil codes. There, very well, could be an argument here that, if proven, the acts of Nixon and others amounted to crimes under the Logan Act, 18 U.S. Code § 953, which forbids unauthorized citizens from negotiating with foreign governments. Both Nixon and Chennault were obviously unauthorized because the position of candidate for President did not grant Nixon any power or privileges. It should be noted that to present date, there have been no prosecutions under the Act. Nevertheless, it is not the purpose of this work to analyze whether there was a technical violation of a Federal Act or a commission of another criminal act or civil wrong. The prevention of peace for personal gain is a greater, if not unspeakable crime. If Nixon authored a conspiracy to defeat the prospects of peace, then he set in motion events possibly causing the unnecessary deaths of soldiers and civilians in the tens of thousands. If such an event occurred, reducing it to fodder for technical legal argument only lessens its impact.

promulgated a conspiracy to sabotage the November 1968 peace conference by convincing the South Vietnamese not to attend at a critical stage? If so, what did he promise the Saigon government? We will discover how this conspiracy was allegedly organized, promulgated, and eventually discovered by the Johnson administration. Central to our discussion will be a controversy concerning whether Nixon's alleged main conduit to President Thiệu, Anna Chennault, acted upon Nixon's or his lieutenant's instructions, or operated on her own furthering her own agenda. Without Nixon as the main prognosticator, our race, although entertaining, does not merit "Olympic" proportions.

To facilitate our analysis, the personalities and motivations of the primary players, Richard Nixon, Anna Chennault, Clark Clifford, Bui Diem, and others will come under the microscope. We will examine Anna Chennault's lifelong quest for validation, her obsession to fight communism and avenge the bitter defeat of the Chinese Nationalists to Mao, all in the light of her questionable credibility. Critical advisor and member of the Johnson administration Clark Clifford, was a material witness to all areas of this controversy often giving contradictory opinions and conclusions. We will explore just how his need for personal and professional redemption generated his puzzling credibility. Alleged co-conspirator Ambassador Bui Diem's almost pathetic attempts at exculpation are helpful because they prove the workings of the conspiracy. Finally, our examination turns to Richard Nixon. We will study if such a conspiracy was consistent with the character of this man who exhibited a "win at any costs" strategy in previous elections before 1968. Further, relevant direct and/or circumstantial evidence that allegedly directly link him to the conspiracy will be debated. Once again, you will be asked to answer a question, now #2, on the verdict sheet, asking whether you believe there is sufficient evidence of a Nixon led conspiracy. If you answer YES, you move on to question #3.

Assuming the sincerity of all the above parties and a Nixon centered conspiracy, we now approach the next two hurdles, which are the highest, because they pose the proverbial "so what" predicament. In the third hurdle, the question becomes whether the alleged Nixon conspiracy influenced South Vietnam's late entry to the peace talks or were they already predetermined not to attend despite these alleged acts. Thus, the dilemma posed here is how to decide responsibility when there are multiple possible causative factors acting either

---

Therefore, when the term "conspiracy," or its equivalent, is used throughout this book, it does not refer to a violation of the criminal or civil law, but rather it refers to its common definition of an evil, unlawful, treacherous, or surreptitious plan formulated in secret by two or more persons. See Dictionary.com, "Definition of Conspiracy" http://dictionary.reference.com/browse/conspiracy. (accessed November 29, 2007)

alone or in tandem in producing a result. To facilitate decision-making in this section, I will borrow the concept of "proximate cause" from the civil law. Under this doctrine, legal responsibility is founded even if there are other explanations for an ultimate harm, as long as the alleged acts of the wrongdoer were not a deminimus or inconsequential cause of the outcome in question.

As we approach this third hurdle, we must examine the difference between preference and available choice. Stated simply as possible, I always hated math. I never wanted to go to any math classes; nevertheless, I suffered through three years of high school math because it was mandated. In my senior year, math became an elective, which I enthusiastically declined. In the first three years of my high school career, despite my preferences wants and desires, I had no available options. Given a reasonable alternative in my senior year, I was able to make a choice. Therefore, desire, itself, is not where our analysis ends. Many individuals and entities act in modes contrary to their preference if there are no other reasonable opportunities or alternatives available. Therefore, we will go beyond desire and explore what options were originally open to President Thiệu and whether or not the alleged Nixon conspiracy created new ones, originally unavailable, allowing a reasonable choice when once there was none. The fact that Saigon had a pre-existing mindset not to attend the talks does not rule out liability under proximate cause analysis. If you find that this predisposition and the Nixon conspiracy worked together to produce the ultimate result, proximate cause is still founded and you vote YES on question #3 on the verdict sheet. It is not necessary that the Nixon conspiracy be the primary moving force, as long as you do not decide that the effect of the conspiracy was deminimus.

In the alternative, Saigon may have never intended to attend the conferences whether or not there was a Nixon conspiracy. Nations do not always make decisions based upon reason. The ultimate decisions of South Vietnamese President Thiệu may have been based on his enormous ego, personal hatred of Democratic Presidential candidate Hubert Humphrey, stupidity, corrupt nature, greed, or paranoia. If you find Saigon's non-attendance was a foregone conclusion despite the whispers and promises of the alleged Nixon conspiracy, proximate cause is not found, the runner trips over this hurdle and you vote No to Question #3.

We approach the final and fourth hurdle confronted with the issue of the impact, if any, of South Vietnam's decision to initially avoid the peace conference. It is well known that once negotiations finally started, they were a study in abject failure. Instead of conducting serious negotiations, delegates wasted countless hours deciding the size of the conference room table and the placement of flags. It was not until five years thereafter, that the Nixon administration negotiated the end of the war. Nevertheless, did the failure of the South Vietnamese to timely attend the peace conferences make any real difference? As in hurdle three, we are once again faced with the "so what" question. This query, though, differs in that our focus is not on whether "A" caused "B," but rather, did the failure result in a missed opportunity for peace. Once again, we will turn to civil law to aid us in our decision-making. When a claim for damages is based on a missed opportunity in a civil action, the doctrine of "increased risk of harm" may be applicable. This theory, detailed herein, essentially sets forth that when there are lost opportunities, due to the actions or omissions of others, we calculate the implication, if any, of those acts by asking the question of whether they significantly increased the risk of the ultimate harm. If the actions of the conspirators significantly increased the risk of the ultimate failure of the Paris peace negotiations, then we successfully meet the dictates of this hurdle then you will vote YES to question #4 on the verdict sheet and, of course, NO if you do not so find. Note that we employ this type of analysis because when there is a lost opportunity, we can never, with any reasonable degree of certainty, determine what could have happened, because it did not happen. Simple example: A woman falls off a cruise ship. One of the ship's security officers notices her floating off into the Atlantic. The officer has a life preserver in his hand, but the woman is some distance from the ship. He does not throw the life preserver and the woman drowns. Was she close enough to make a toss of the preserver successful? Had she successfully grabbed it, would she have drowned anyway because of the waves, her poor swimming ability, sharks, or other risks? None of these questions can be answered because the man did not throw it. We just do not know. Therefore, the law in such a scenario examines whether or not, in light of all the circumstances, his failure increased the risk that she would die.

In our attempt to answer this question, we will explore the relevance of several factors set in motion by the South Vietnamese actions, which may or may have not increased the risk that the conferences would fail. These factors include, 1) The change in "playing field" caused by the acrimony between the United States and Saigon when the South Vietnamese did not timely appear at the peace talks as promised, 2) The loss of momentum in the peace process and 3) The United States' loss of face with the North Vietnamese and the effect of that on the negotiation process in general.

Within each of the succeeding chapters, we will discover that motivations of the parties were very rarely singular, linear, or rational. The evidence for our review consists of Department of State memoranda, actual transcripts of recorded conversations of United States Security Council, direct statements by the involved parties, including their autobiographies and personal interviews, FBI surveillance, CIA reports, documents from the Soviet Union, North Vietnam, China, the opinions of other authors, some more respected than others, and numerous other sources. The race to discover significance within this fascinating story will be an arduous one, but, if accomplished, well worth the effort. You have now been sworn/affirmed as a juror. As a juror, you are the judge of the facts, but in determining what actually happened, remember your verdict must be solely upon the evidence, without prejudice or sympathy.[3] Counsel is ready to proceed.

---

[3] Loosely based upon "N.J.S.A 2B:23-6 Oath of Jurors,"
http://www.judiciary.state.nj.us/essex/jury/ (accessed December 27,2014)

CHAPTER 1

The Long March Forward

It was 1968. North Vietnam, a fledgling Asian country, engaged in a steadily escalating war with the United States, the greatest superpower of the time. Despite all its military might, the United States could not see victory on the horizon and the North Vietnamese position defined intransigence. Initially, when the war began in earnest in 1964, the North Vietnamese refused to discuss an end to the conflict unless it was on their terms, without conditions, without reciprocity, without any assurances for the safety of the United States soldiers and without the involvement of the "puppet" Saigon regime. Meanwhile, 30,000 American soldiers died, with hundreds of thousands already wounded, and countless dollars already spent.[1]

Yet, as the years progressed Hanoi's position eventually evolved. In May 1968, the United States and North Vietnam began a negotiation process in Paris, but little was accomplished and prospects looked bleak. However, from June through October, intransigence yielded to flexibility. Hanoi, for the first time, indicated a willingness to give implicit assurances for the safety of both the United States soldiers and South Vietnam cities and to negotiate with the Saigon government in exchange for a United States bombing halt. At this point, twenty two thousand additional American GIs had not yet died, several hundred thousand more had not yet been wounded, and billions more dollars had not yet been spent. It was an optimistic time. "A final compromise between the delegations appears to be within reach," proclaimed Valentin Oberemko, of the Soviet Embassy in Paris.[2] United States Secretary of State Dean Rusk, enthusiastically declared, in regard to the ten steps necessary towards peace, that the North Vietnamese "have taken eight, and we have taken two."[3] The American negotiation team in Paris broke out bottles of champagne to celebrate what they hoped would be an impending peace.[4]

---

[1] References to Hanoi, the capital of North Vietnam, from now on in will be synonymous with its government.

[2] Ilya Gaiduk, *The Soviet Union and the Vietnam War* (Chicago, IL: Ivan Dee, 1966), 184.

[3] Ibid., 185.

[4] Daniel I. Davidson (member of United States negotiation team assistant to April Harriman), interview by author, August 14, 2007

Despite the good feeling, not all were convinced of the sincerity of North Vietnam's recent concessions and many remained suspicious of their motives and intentions. Echoing this sentiment, Walter Rostow, President Lyndon Johnson's (LBJ) Special Assistant for National Security Affairs, declared, "I've learned this rule-if something unexpected happens, stop in your tracks and ask this question: what has been wrong in my picture of the situation, which led to the unexpected event?"[5] Our purpose here, as Rostow suggested, is to stop in our tracks and determine why and if something unexpected actually happened and if indeed, our picture of the situation is clear. We, of course, know now that the optimism dissolved in nothing but bitter disappointment. We know now that the war would go on for five more years. Nevertheless, we cannot judge what happened then by what we know now. Instead, we must freeze our frame to that period focusing on what was known or should have been known, as the future was still undetermined.

A CALCULATED MOVE, OR IS ALL LBJ IS SAYING IS GIVE PEACE A CHANCE?

On March 31, 1968, President Johnson was about to deliver the most important speech of his political life. To that point, his nation had been involved in a steadily escalating bloody war, which became a frustrating deadly quagmire. The unanimous advice of his staff concluded that the American people, and the Congress, demanded a dramatic change in the nation's approach to the war, yet, the question remained, in what direction? Acrimonious debate within the administration filled the weeks leading up to his speech. Those in LBJ's cabinet led by Secretary of Defense Clark Clifford represented the "doves" and those led by Secretary of State Dean Rusk, represented the "hawks." The "doves" encouraged Johnson to take all necessary reasonable steps to end the war through negotiation.[6] The "hawks," holding the contrary position, supported a militant

---

[5] United States. Department of State Office of Historian, *Foreign Relations, 1964-1968 Volume VII, Vietnam, September 1968-January 1969*, section 59, http://www.state.gov/r/pa/prs/ps/2003/22465.htm (accessed November 26, 2007) (Hereinafter referred to as DOS)

[6] "The dove's career as a symbol of peace is even older, dating back at least to the *Epic of Gilgamesh* and the Old Testament—both Gilgamesh and Noah send out a dove to look for dry land in a flood. It wasn't until the Cuban missile crisis, though, that journalists began invoking the dove as the opposite of the hawk. The first usage... appears in the *Saturday Evening Post* in 1962 where it was written the hawks favored an air strike to eliminate the Cuban missile bases... The doves opposed the air strikes and favored a blockade." See Alice Robb, "Let's Kill All the Hawks and Doves! As Lazy Metaphors, That Is,"

approach directed at winning the war. [7] Originally, according to Johnson's speechwriter Harry McPherson, Johnson prepared his speech adopting the "hawk" view aimed at rallying the country around the flag for victory. [8] Nevertheless, shortly before he would speak to the nation, he presented his advisers another version adopting the "dove" standpoint. It was not certain which speech he would give. Even his closest advisers did not know that the end of the speech hid a surprise. Before we analyze Johnson's words, it is first necessary to understand the man.

Lyndon Johnson was born on August 27, 1908, in central Texas. In 1934, he married the former Claudia "Lady Bird" Taylor. During World War II, he served in the Navy as a lieutenant commander, winning a Silver Star. After spending six terms in the House of Representatives, Johnson was elected to the United States Senate in 1948. In 1953, he became the youngest Minority Leader in Senate history, and in the following year, when the Democrats won control, he reached the powerful position of Senate Majority Leader. [9] In 1960, he became Vice-President, serving with President John Kennedy; and upon Kennedy's assassination, in 1963, took over the reins of government. In 1964, he reached the pinnacle of his ambitions when President defeating Republican Barry Goldwater in a landslide. An impressive resume, no doubt, but what of the man?

According to Joseph A. Califano, a close Johnson adviser:

> No one could work for Johnson (or listen to the Johnson tapes) without being astounded by his relentless energy, his demanding, overbearing personality...brave and brutal, compassionate and cruel, incredibly intelligent and infuriatingly insensitive...[man]... with a shrewd and uncanny instinct for the jugular of his allies and adversaries. [10]

An evaluation of Johnson requires an understanding that as a big man both physically and in personality; he had a unique approach to negotiation. If he

---

http://www.newrepublic.com/article/115734/hawks-doves-origins-metaphors-war-peace-supporters. (accessed December 23, 2014)

[7] "According to the *Oxford English Dictionary*, the term "war hawk," to mean "one who is eager for the fray," first appeared in a letter Thomas Jefferson wrote to James Madison in 1798, to describe Federalists who wanted to go to war with France." Ibid.

[8] Larry Addington, *America's War in Vietnam: A Short Narrative History* (Bloomington, IN: Indiana Press, 2000), 122-33.

[9] United States. The White House. *Presidents: Johnson*
http://www.whitehouse.gov/history/presidents/lj36.html (accessed November 26, 2007)

[10] Joseph A. Califano, Jr. *The Triumph & Tragedy of Lyndon Johnson: The White House Years* (Texas: Texas A&M University Press, 2000), 398. Califano served as special assistant to the United States Secretary of Defense, and Deputy Secretary.

wanted another Congressman or Senator to vote his way, Johnson would actually grab them by the lapels, physically intimidating them to adopt his position. Journalists Rowland Evans and Robert Novak aptly describe this method, known as "The Treatment," as consisting of:

> Supplication, accusation, cajolery, exuberance, scorn, tears, complaint, the hint of threat. It was all these together. It ran the gamut of human emotions. Its velocity was breathtaking, and it was all in one direction. Interjections from the target were rare. Johnson anticipated them before they could be spoken. He moved in close, his face a scant millimeter from his target, his eyes widening and narrowing, his eyebrows rising and falling. From his pockets poured clippings, memos, statistics. Mimicry, humor, and the genius of analogy made "The Treatment" an almost hypnotic experience and rendered the target stunned and helpless.[11]

If physical intimidation did not work, Johnson, a master of Senate protocol, adeptly used procedure to push his political agenda. Johnson was not above using his ability to grant or deny plum Senate positions as devices to "persuade" his colleagues to vote for his programs.[12] He was not used to losing. His domestic accomplishments as president can only be described as impressive. In the period from 1965 to 1967, Johnson was responsible for the passage of the social reform program, dubbed the "Great Society." This program introduced Medicare providing medical assistance to the elderly through the Social Security system. LBJ enacted extensive new programs of federal aid to education and housing to deprived areas. The Voting Rights Act, mandating federal intervention to ensure the voting rights of black citizens, became law in 1965 under his stewardship.[13] Perhaps his greatest accomplishment was the passage of the 1964 Civil Rights Act, which outlawed discrimination from public accommodations in hotels and restaurants to hiring in the workplace. The Act even gave the federal government new power to enforce school desegregation through the aid to education it

---

[11] Robert Dallek, "Character Above All,"
http://www.pbs.org/newshour/character/essays/johnson.html. (accessed November 26, 2007)
[12] Robert A Caro, *Master of the Senate: The Years of Lyndon Johnson* (New York, NY: Alfred a Knopf Inc., 2002)
[13] Lyndon Johnson's "Great Society" http://www.ushistory.org/us/56e.asp. (accessed December 5, 2014)

provided. In a country scarred by enduring segregation the passing of the Act required all of Johnson's skills.[14]

In addition to his impressive political skills, Johnson also displayed talent as a skillful and unabashed liar. If Johnson, instead of George Washington, chopped down the proverbial cherry tree, he would blame it on an opponent and sell the wood for profit, but only after harsh negotiations. Powerful Washington insider and Secretary of Defense, Clark Clifford, who knew Lyndon Johnson from 1946 until his death in 1973, described his relationship with the President as developing from a "casual relationship to close associate and intimate adviser."[15] Commenting on LBJ's credibility, in his autobiography, Clifford related an incident concerning whether Bobby Kennedy would run with Johnson as vice-president during the 1964 election. LBJ met with Kennedy and informed him that he would not choose him and Kennedy assumed that the meeting would be confidential. Johnson, ignoring even the pretense of privacy, immediately informed reporters about the meeting, even mimicking Kennedy's reaction to the rejection. When Kennedy found out about the leak, he was furious and called the president to protest. According to Clifford who witnessed the call, "Johnson said he hadn't told anyone about the meeting and Bobby bluntly called him a liar. Johnson retreated a bit, saying, well, maybe there was a conversation he had forgot."[16]

In *Means of Ascent* Johnson's biographer Robert Caro, in meticulous fashion, dissects and attacks Johnson credibility during his detailed analysis of LBJ's claimed World War II war record and the "Box 13" incident. The story of Johnson's war heroism arose from his June 6, 1942 visit to a US Air Force base in Melbourne Australia. At that point, the then Texas Congressman, anxious for some wartime "cred" from the folks back at home, finagled an observation seat on a bombing run. During this mission, the plane was fired upon and chased, undoubtedly subjecting its occupants to some harrowing moments. Despite the drama, the bomber managed to return to base without any further incident.[17] Yet, "nothing about Johnson's war service was more revealing than the way he came to portray it."[18] During the election campaign, this one flight grew into dozens!

---

14 "Robert Caro: LBJ and the Civil Rights Act of 1964 (Interview of Robert Caro)"
http://thedianerehmshow.org/shows/2014-06-30/robert-caro-lbj-and-civil-rights-act-1964
(accessed December 5, 2014)
[15] Clark Clifford and Richard Holbrooke, *Counsel to the President: A Memoir* (New York, NY: Random House, 1991), 385
[16] Ibid. 392.
[17] Robert Caro, *The Years of Lyndon Johnson, Means of Ascent* (New York, NY: Knopf, 1990), 335-53
[18] Ibid. 46.

LBJ's rhetoric grew to such an absurd height that Johnson claimed he had flown thousands of miles engaging in numerous conflicts "earning" the status of a "war –scarred veteran."[19] He even displayed phony medals with great "humility." To put it bluntly, on countless occasions Johnson blatantly lied about his war service.

While Johnson's service record fabrications retain some comical element, the "Box 13" incident serves as a grim example of his dark nature. During 1948, Johnson and popular former Texas Governor Coke Stevenson engaged in a battle for the democratic nomination for United States Senate. The close results of the initial Democratic primary required a second runoff election. During this nomination battle, Johnson engaged in criminal fraud, rumor mongering, vote buying, vote creation and a systematic strategy of outright lying about Stevenson's character and record.[20] Yet the most shocking example of Johnson's criminality occurred during the "Box 13 incident," which concerned the votes of Precinct 13 in Jim Wells County Texas. Despite Johnson's extraordinary efforts to gain the nomination, both legitimate and illegitimate, after the vote counting, Johnson trailed Stevenson by a scant 86 votes. The story however, did not end there, on election night Precinct 13 of Jim Wells County reported 726 votes for Johnson, yet, four days after the election a startling change in the vote tally occurred when that number changed to 926 in favor of LBJ. In a scenario rivaling a Clint Eastwood movie, Caro described how armed *pistoleros* and a notoriously corrupt county boss, who was clearly in Johnson's pocket, deliberately changed the number seven to the number nine upon his Johnson's direct request. Due to Johnson's legal wrangling and corruption, the majority tally stood and Johnson received the Democratic nomination and ultimately the post of United States Senator from Texas. Perhaps the most telling element of the story occurred when Johnson, in the proper mood, without compunction, actually bragged about his misdeeds during the 1948 election. The point here is not to delve into the numerous machinations of that election, which indeed serves as fascinating reading, but rather to warn the reader that Lyndon Johnson's relationship to the truth was remote at best.

Johnson's usual success in negotiations and ability to bend the truth as he saw fit did not transfer to the North Vietnamese. Unlike his previous opponents, they were not easily bullied, or forced into making compromises. This war was

---

[19] Ibid. 48.
[20] Ibid. 269-350. With superb clarity Caro proves that Johnson mastermind a campaign replete with diabolical and criminal intentions. Distinction between vote buying and vote creation is that in the buying scenario individuals were given cash for their votes. In the vote creation scenario, voting records were deliberately altered to reflect tallies that bore no semblance to the actual vote.

not going well and despite all its domestic policy accomplishments, the Johnson presidency was in trouble.[21]

We are back then to March 31, 1968, and Johnson is about to address the nation. As he spoke, it soon became evident that he had adopted the Clifford "dove" position, concluding that peacefully settling the Vietnam War served America's best interests. In typical Johnson style, he figuratively grabbed the lapel of the North Vietnamese by announcing a unilateral pause in the bombing north of the 20th Parallel.[22] In response to this action, the president requested from the North Vietnamese, "that talks begin promptly, they be serious talks on the substance of peace. We assume that during those talks Hanoi will not take advantage of our restraint."[23] He warned North Vietnam, "Even this very limited bombing of the North could come to an early end--if our restraint isn't matched by restraint in Hanoi. But I cannot in good conscience stop all bombing so long as to do so would immediately and directly endanger the lives of our men and our allies."[24]

Although he halted the bombing, he dropped a bomb of his own declaring,

> I have concluded that I should not permit the presidency to become involved in the partisan divisions that are developing in this political year. With America's sons in the fields far away, with America's future under challenge right here at home, with our hopes and the world's hopes for peace in the balance every day, I do not believe that I should devote an hour or a day of my time to any personal partisan causes or to any

---

[21] According to the Gallup poll his approval ratings in 1964 were 80%, by 1968 they were lower than 40%. "LBJ & Public Opinion Polls," http://ows.edb.utexas.edu/site/natalies-site/lbj-public-opinion. (accessed December 24, 2014)

[22] The 19th parallel refers to a location on the map of North Vietnam. A line connecting all the points with the same latitude value is called a line of latitude. This term is usually used to refer to the lines that represent values in whole degrees. All lines of latitude are parallel to the Equator, and they are sometimes referred to as parallels. Parallels are equally spaced. There are 90 degrees of latitude going north from the Equator, and the North Pole is at 90 degrees N. There are 90 degrees to the south of the Equator, and the South Pole is at 90 degrees S. When the directional designators are omitted, northern latitudes are given positive values and southern latitudes are given negative values. See National Atlas. "Where we are: Latitude," http://www.nationalatlas.gov/articles/mapping/a_latlong.html. (accessed November 26, 2007)

[23] Lyndon Baines Johnson Library and Museum. "President Lyndon B. Johnson's Address to the Nation Announcing Steps To Limit the War in Vietnam and Reporting His Decision Not To Seek Reelection March 31, 1968" http://www.lbjlib.utexas.edu/johnson/archives.hom/speeches.hom/680331.asp. (accessed November 7, 2007) (Hereinafter referred to as LBJ Library).

[24] Ibid.,

duties other than the awesome duties of this office--the presidency of
your country. Accordingly, I shall not seek, and I will not accept, the
nomination of my party for another term as your president. [25]

Johnson's announcements direct us onto two separate paths of study. First, we
need to determine whether his attempts to energize the peace process were
political moves designed to aid the Democratic Party's candidate in the upcoming
electoral process or whether they represented a sincere dedication to the
nonpartisan cause of seeking peace in Vietnam. Our second path, the efficacy of
these actions in the peace process, we will travel in later chapters.

LBJ AND HHH, BROTHERS IN ARMS?

Republican leaders alleged that Johnson's attempts at peace, which started in
March of 1968, and climaxed in the period of September to November, were
designed to aid the presidential aspirations of his Vice President, Hubert
Humphrey who had been chosen as the Democratic candidate succeeding LBJ
during the infamous Chicago Convention. [26] [27] Leaving no doubt as to the
republican's allegation of Johnson's lack of sincerity, Nixon in his memoirs
declared his belief that Johnson's attempt at peace before the election amounted to
nothing more than a ploy to get Humphrey elected.[28] Nixon claimed he knew
Johnson "well enough to know that everything he did was weighed a second time
on a strictly political scale."[29] President Thiệu of South Vietnam, echoing the
Republican position, expressed fears that the North Vietnamese were giving
nothing in return for the US bombing halt. He had concern that "the US
government wished to do something dramatic in order to help Humphrey on five
November [Election Day]."[30] Author Jonathan Aitken, a well-known Nixon

---

[25] Ibid. See also DOS, section 166. Note, lost in all the excitement was Johnson's response
to the army's original request for an additional 200,000 troops. Johnson did agree to an
escalation of only 13,500 troops even less than that recommended by his Defense
Secretary Clifford.

[26] DOS, section 70.

[27] Thousand rioted outside the Convention Center as the democrat's debated strategy
concerning the Vietnam War. "When the convention was finally over, the Chicago police
reported 589 arrests had been made and 119 police and 100 protesters were injured." See
"Brief History of Chicago's 1968 Democratic Convention,"
http://www.cnn.com/ALLPOLITICS/1996/conventions/chicago/facts/chicago68/index.sht
ml (accessed December 5, 2014)

[28] Richard Nixon, *RN: The Memoirs of Richard Nixon* (New York, NY: Touchstone,
1978), 326

[29] Ibid., 327.

[30] DOS, section144.

apologist, predictably reinforced the Republican conclusion.[31] However, when historian Stephen Ambrose, hardly known for having sympathy for Nixon, backed this political conclusion, then attention has to be paid to this allegation, especially in light of the fact that most of the "peace" action took place in the weeks leading up to Election Day.[32]

Integral to the allegation against Johnson's sincerity, is whether in fact he favored Humphrey. Indeed, at least until the end of October 1968, there was strong evidence that Johnson hardly enamored with Hubert Humphrey might have even favored Nixon in the election. In a conversation with Clifford regarding Humphrey's character, LBJ "doubted Humphrey had the ability to be president "and he would have respected him more if he "showed he had some balls."[33] Humphrey's campaign adviser James Rowe, a friend of LBJ's, requested that the president make speeches supporting his candidate in New Jersey and other states. Johnson refusing to campaign on Humphrey's behalf told Rowe, "You know that Nixon is following my policies more closely than Humphrey."[34] Further, Johnson significantly hindered the Humphrey campaign by personally withholding $700,000 in much needed funds that the Democratic Party raised earlier in 1965.[35] Humphrey obviously was furious with Johnson's obstructionism. At another point, Larry O'Brien, Humphrey's campaign manager, passed along information to the Justice Department that Greek military rulers "donated" $500,000 towards Nixon's campaign.[36] Such a story, if credible, would have generated favorable press fodder for the Humphrey campaign. However, despite Humphrey's request, "Johnson would not ask CIA Director Richard Helms to verify the report, or should it be true, consider leaking it to the press."[37]

Johnson demonstrated a certain fondness, if not admiration, for Nixon. During the election campaign, Reverend Billy Graham carried a message to

---

[31] Aitken described that Johnson's effort to stop the bombing "was to ensure that the negotiations would have maximum impact on the presidential election." Jonathan Aitken, *Nixon a Life* (Washington , D.C.: Regnery Publishing, Inc., 1994), 362

[32] Ambrose takes the position that Johnson was playing a high-stakes politics "poker" game aimed at making Humphrey the winner of the 1968 United States Presidential election. Stephen Ambrose, *Nixon: The Triumph of a Politician, 1962-1972* (New York, NY: Simon & Schuster, 1989), 207.

[33] Clifford, 571.

[34] Robert Dallek, *Nixon and Kissinger: Partners in Power* (New York, NY: HarperCollins, 2007), 66

[35] Penn Kemble, "The Democrats After 1968," http://www.commentarymagazine.com/article/the-democrats-after-1968/#1 (accessed December 5, 2104)

[36] Dallek, 66.

[37] Ibid.

Johnson from Nixon promising a warm and respectful relationship after the election if Nixon won. Johnson was very pleased and touched by this memo.[38] However, when Humphrey insisted on a slightly different platform than Johnson's on Vietnam policy during the Democratic convention, Johnson felt betrayed. In addition to this annoyance, Johnson later was furious with Humphrey over the contents of his Salt Lake City campaign speech, which Johnson believed impeded the peace process.[39] According to Clifford, "his anger at Humphrey led him toward his old adversary, Richard Nixon."[40] Johnson later told Clifford and Dean Rusk "when he (Nixon) gets the nomination he may prove to be more responsible than the Democrats. He says he is for our position in Vietnam."[41] Thus "began a relationship between Johnson and Nixon, in which Nixon skillfully promoted himself as more sympathetic to the president's position in Vietnam than Humphrey."[42]

Anxious to warm up their chilly relationship, Humphrey went to see Johnson to work out their differences. His attempt was hardly a resounding success. Humphrey arrived just meager minutes late to the meeting because he was coming from a campaign rally and wanted to clean up before the seeing the president. Using this "lateness" as an excuse, Johnson refused to see him. Humphrey, enraged by this obvious disrespect, shouted to LBJ's White House

---

[38] Ibid.

[39] In September 1968, Humphrey gave a speech in Salt Lake City, Utah defining his position on the Vietnam War. Although, his words were essentially the same as in LBJ's March 1968 speech, Johnson believed Humphrey managed to convey his readiness to take greater risks to settle the war. See, Time Magazine. "Some Forward Motion for H.H.H," (October 11, 1968) http://www.time.com/time/magazine/article/0,9171,902365-2,00.html (accessed November 26, 2007). In a conversation with Johnson, Humphrey was questioned on whether a stoppage of bombing, as he promised in his speech, was unconditional. Humphrey answered that he placed key importance on evidence, whether direct or indirect, or by word or by deed, of the communist's willingness to restore the DMZ between the North and South. The President reminded the Vice President of the three factors, including South Vietnamese participation at the proposed negotiations. The vice president admitted that DMZ restoration was a condition, but he did not state whether South Vietnamese participation or a stoppage of the shelling of South Vietnam's cities would be a specific condition, although he stated the North Vietnamese have to be in good faith and he defined a stoppage of the attack on the cities as part of good faith. In any event, Johnson believed that Humphrey's speech undermined his position with the North Vietnamese. Note that after the Salt Lake speech, Humphrey, who was doing poorly in the polls, started to rally and he attracted significant new funding. See DOS, section 29.

[40] Clifford, 563.

[41] Ibid.

[42] Ibid.

aide Jim Jones, "that bastard Johnson... I saw him sitting in his office." He then instructed Jones, "You tell the president he can cram it up his ass."[43]

Johnson, nobody's fool, was well aware of the potential allegation that political favoritism served as the motivation behind his actions towards attempting a peace in Vietnam. Not until the very end of the presidential campaign, after the alleged Nixon-Chennault conspiracy became evident to him, did Johnson show any hint of favorable treatment to his vice-president. When it appeared in October that peace might be at hand, Johnson simultaneously called the three major presidential candidates to brief them as to progress.[44] According to his biographer Carl Solberg, Humphrey "was crushed" by the arm's length treatment, "his fidelity to the president, his position as the administration's candidate, seemed at that moment to count for nothing."[45] Daniel Davidson, assistant to Averill Harriman, chief negotiator at Paris, was then and remains to present day convinced that aiding the Humphrey campaign was definitely not the purpose of Johnson's actions. He related that if there were references or even a mention in the records of this alleged political motivation, "Cyrus Vance would keep it out fearing that Johnson would be so angered by these claims, that this would adversely affect the peace process."[46]

Before we canonize Johnson as a selfless apostle of peace dedicating himself to the cause in absence of personal gain, his rejection of the Democratic Party's nomination may not have been what it seemed. In August 1968, credible evidence indicated that Johnson secretly attempted to arrange a draft for his nomination at the Democratic convention. Very close associate and friend of LBJ's, former Texas Governor John Connolly alleged, "I can make a very strong case that, notwithstanding his statement of withdrawal, he (Johnson) very much hoped he would be drafted by the convention in 1968." Indeed LBJ "did send White House aide Martin Watson to assess the possibility of the success of a draft. When the chances of success were seen as slim, it was withdrawn."[47] Was the dramatic March 1968 withdrawal from the race sincere or was it a calculated political move to create the scenario for a convention draft with the Democratic Party turning to its president after positive news regarding a possible peace in Vietnam? The answer to this question cannot be known, but Johnson's actions remain

---

[43] Carl Solberg, *Hubert Humphrey, a Biography* (St Paul, MN: Borealis Books, 2003), 392.
[44] Hubert Humphrey represented the Democratic Party, Richard Nixon represented the Republican Party and George Wallace represented the American Independent Party.
[45] Solberg, 391.
[46] David Danielson, interview.
[47] Dallek, *Nixon and Kissinger: Partners in Power*, 62.

troubling. What we do know, however, is that throughout his long political career, Johnson was a winner, unaccustomed to defeat. His actions in halting the bombing in March 1968 and his subsequent efforts to bring about peace up and through election day, may have been a product of his pure intentions to end a horrible war, his desire to bolster his legacy, his need to satisfy his ego, or even a calculated move designed to support a run for another term of office. However, it is logical to conclude that based upon the evidence, helping Humphrey did not rise to the top of Johnson's list.

There remains another possible explanation for Johnson's choices. It is reasonably possible that he was playing poker with the North Vietnamese, bluffing them believing they would not call his cards. Johnson, faced with an unruly citizenry that demanded that he act towards peace, needed to make a move. If North Vietnam rejected his peace proposal, then LBJ could turn to the public claiming he had done everything possible. Thus, it was the North Vietnamese, not the United States, who were warmongers. LBJ may have preferred a North Vietnamese rejection of his olive branch because this might take the steam out of the antiwar movement. Indeed, according to historian George Herring, "Hanoi's positive response to the American overture caught Washington by surprise."[48] This concept gets some traction when you consider that when explaining the partial bombing halt to the embassy in Saigon, "the State Department indicated that Hanoi would probably 'denounce' it and thus free our hand after a short period."[49] Nevertheless, the North Vietnamese did respond positively and the game was on. Once in the game, with his bluff called by the North Vietnamese, "the circumstances in which the March decisions were made and the conciliatory tone of Johnson's speech, made it difficult, if not impossible, for him to change course."[50]

KNOW THY ENEMY OR I HAVE NO STRINGS

Having examined Johnson's sincerity, we turn next to analyzing the sincerity of his primary partner in the peace process, the North Vietnamese. To understand Hanoi's response to Johnson's throwing of the gauntlet in March 1968, it is first necessary to explore not only where the North Vietnamese stood on that date, but also where they came from to get there. By no means is the following a comprehensive history of Vietnam, however it is offered to give foundational

---

[48] George C. Herring, *America's Longest War: the United States in Vietnam, 1950-1975* (New York, NY: John Wiley & Sons, 1979), 207.
[49] Ibid., 205.
[50] Ibid.

basis to determine the level of their sincerity in the peace process. If their position evolved from intransigence to flexibility, it is imperative that we investigate the precipitating factors to determine their authenticity. It is not reasonably possible to calculate all the dynamics influencing a foreign government over 40 years ago, yet it is helpful to focus on three major elements, which were relevant: the Sino-Soviet conflict and competition for North Vietnamese alliance, the military situation of the war, and the 1968 United States presidential elections.

In the 1960s, two powerful countries dominated the communist world, the People's Republic of China and the Soviet Union. Despite the simplistic idea of a red vs. blue world often put forth in the propaganda of the day, their perceived shared communist economic system did not automatically lead to a sharing of purpose. Rather the Soviets and the Chinese were often in conflict, especially on the issue of which country would prevail in the battle to establish international communist leadership and policymaking. This conflict between powers would often center on what each country thought was best for the North Vietnamese and what was best for themselves.

In the early portion of the decade, the North Vietnamese embraced China as their ally. As the years progressed, they steadily shifted their allegiance to the Soviet Union. Under whose influence the North Vietnamese found themselves and whether that influence substantially influenced their approach to negotiations to end their war with the United States becomes critical to our analysis. Therefore, when assessing the sincerity of the North Vietnamese towards peace, it is enlightening to understand how each country weighed, if at all, upon Hanoi's ultimate decisions. When determining the efficacy of that influence, we must always be aware of the ramifications of the "Pinocchio syndrome." I will explain; here the master of the puppet, or client state, pulls strings while pretending to others and to the puppet, that the master desires the puppet to become a "real boy." Sometimes, to the surprise and often dismay of the master, the puppet does become "a real boy" making its own free movements and decisions. To understand how this syndrome applies to Vietnam is important to study the prior history of the region.

Before World War II, Vietnam was a French colony. Because of Nazi Germany's invasion of France, French control of Vietnam essentially terminated. Sensing an opportunity, the Japanese claimed Vietnam allowing only a remaining puppet French government to rule.[51] In March 1945, the Viet Minh working with the Americans "waged intensive an effective guerrilla war against their new

---

[51] Marvin E. Gettleman, *Vietnam and America: A Documented History* (New York, NY: Grove Press 1995), 4.

colonial masters," the Japanese.[52] In a word, the United States and Ho Chi Minh, the guerrilla leader, were allies. President Franklin D Roosevelt was hardly enthusiastic about the French retaking their colonial possession in the future. Even before the defeat of the Japanese, Roosevelt declared,

> I [have] for over a year expressed the opinion that Indochina should not go back to France but that it should be administered by an international trusteeship. France has had the country-30 million inhabitants-for nearly one hundred years, and the people are worse off than they were at the beginning.[53]

When Japan surrendered to the US and withdrew from Vietnam in August 1945, the Viet Minh stepped into the power vacuum and declared control over the decreed independent state of Vietnam. Pronouncing his nationalist fervor, on Sept. 2, 1945, Ho Chi Minh, stood under his country's flag, and read an announcement affirming: "All men are created equal. They are endowed by their Creator with certain inalienable rights; among these are life, liberty and the pursuit of happiness."[54] [55] For Ho Chi Minh, who would lead North Vietnam in its eventual war with the United States, "It was a declaration of independence and the proclamation of a new republic in Vietnam."[56]

Yet as with all issues concerning Vietnam, events became complicated. The French government, now restored after the defeat of Hitler by the Allies, once again claimed their former possession much to the chagrin of the Viet Minh who demanded independence. The United States government found itself caught between two interests. Initially, President Harry Truman stayed true to FDR's opposition to French colonization of Indochina and supported the Vietnam independence movement. However, after the war, larger issues concerning the threat of Soviet world dominance became paramount. Warned by moderate

---

[52] Herring, 4.

[53] The Choices Program Vietnam, http://www.choices.edu/resources/supplemental_fogofwar_vietnam.php (accessed November 19, 2014)

[54] Iver Peterson, "The Long War in Vietnam: A History" (May 1, 1975), http://partners.nytimes.com/library/world/asia/050175vietnam-history-ip.html (accessed November 26, 2007)

[55] Immediately prior to the speech Ho Chi Minh actually conferred with agent of the Office of Strategic Services (OSS), a United States intelligence agency formed during World War and a predecessor of the Central Intelligence Agency (CIA). Interview with Archimedes L. A. Patti, http://openvault.wgbh.org/catalog/vietnam-bf3262-interview-with-archimedes-l-a-patti-1981 (Accessed November 19, 2014)

[56] Peterson

French politicians that outside interference in colonial matters would play into the hands of the French communist party and push France into the Soviet corner, the United States chose to support the French claim of power over the region to retain France as an ally.[57] The United States broke its promise to Ho Chi Minh and the Vietnamese people and this would not be the first time.

We now turn to 1954. After years of struggle, Ho Chi Minh defeated the US supported French colonists at the decisive and humiliating battle of Dien Bien Phu. The parties chose Geneva Switzerland for the location of the peace conference. In addition to the warring parties, the Soviets, the Communist Chinese and the United Kingdom were also present. Although President Eisenhower carefully monitored the talks, officially the United States refused to participate in the conference. On April 27, 1954, the Conference produced a declaration, known as the "Geneva Accords" granting Indochina its independence from France. This agreement, however, contained a provision that temporarily separated Vietnam into northern and southern regions. The purpose of the split was to facilitate the orderly withdrawal of French troops from the southern region. Upon the completion of the French military pullout, a supervised free election was to be held to decide the ultimate form of government for the united Vietnam. This election was planned to occur on or about July 1956. The Vietnamese, considering themselves victorious against the French and entitled to the spoils of war, strongly disliked the terms "but Moscow prevailed upon Hanoi to accept the ostensibly temporary partition on the ground that a Vietminh victory at the polls and reunification were assured."[58] Despite the terms of the Accords, the reunification vote evaporated because Ngo Dinh Diem, serving as a US proxy claiming leadership of the southern region of Vietnam at that critical juncture, announced that because he had not signed the Geneva Accords, they would not bind him.[59] The United States understanding that a unification vote would end in the election of Ho Chi Min who was now labeled as a communist, strongly opposed the election agreed upon in the Accords. Eisenhower, like Diem claimed he was not bound by them since the US were not signers of the Accords.[60] The domino theory is widely [61]accepted as a motivation behind US decision making regarding Vietnam. This strategy of containment demanded the U.S. stop

---

[57] Herring, 7.
[58] Ibid. Note the term Vietminh applies to the Vietnamese rebel fighters against the French colonialists
[59] Herring, 55.
[60] Ibid.
[61] "The Domino Theory," http://www.globalsecurity.org/military/ops/vietnam2-domino-theory.htm. (accessed December 28, 2104)

communist progression into Southeast Asia. The domino theory stated if one new country went communist in Asia then it would begin a chain reaction, like falling dominos that would cause several more Southeast Asian countries to fall under communist domination.

With dreams of a united free Vietnam squashed by the obvious actions of the US, the North Vietnamese, in response, eventually resorted to a military solution to reestablish a united Vietnam, which eventually evolved into Vietnam's full-scale conflict with the United States in 1964. The principal participants in this war were the North Vietnamese (NVN or DRV); the National Liberation Front (NLF) a North Vietnamese controlled semi-entity consisting of North Vietnamese soldiers and South Vietnamese partisans, commonly referred to as the Viet Cong; and the South Vietnamese controlled by the Saigon government (GVN) and supported by the United States. (See Appendix I for reference concerning abbreviations of the various sovereignties.)

Ho Chi Minh's Vietnam, short of supplies, needed a benefactor; the most likely sources were the Soviet Union and/or the People's Republic of China. There was reciprocal benefit on behalf of the communist superpowers because both desired Vietnam as an ally in their battle for dominance.[62] The point here is that the leaders of the Vietnamese independence movement, although communist, were nationalists first. Vietnam was not a domino; it was a country with its own interests and dreams.[63] It cannot be forgotten that the US and Ho Chi Minh were once allies. One must be very careful in making concrete decisions that their interests would necessarily be the same as China's or the Soviet's just because they shared a similar political/economic system.[64]

The Vietnamese were nobody's puppet. Thus, we must always approach every question concerning influence with the understanding that the North Vietnamese considered themselves free agents, always looking for a better deal serving their own natural interests. Additionally, we cannot be caught up in the

---

[62]United States of America. Central Intelligence Agency (C.I.A.), *Intelligence Study, the Positions of Hanoi, Peking, and Moscow on the issue of Vietnam negotiations: 1962 to 1966 (reference title: ESAU -66), p-3,* http://www.foia.cia.gov/document/intelligence-study-positions-hanoi-peking-and-moscow-issue-vietnam-negotiations-1962-1966 (accessed December 23, 2014)

[63] Johnson's Secretary of Defense Robert McNamara says now, "I think we were wrong. I do not believe that Vietnam was that important to the communists. I don't believe that its loss would have lead - it didn't lead – to Communist control of Asia." David Brown, "The Fall of Vietnam Would Not Have Led to Communist Control of Asia" *The Christian Science Monitor* 28 (April, 1995): 18.

[64] Herring, 4. Susheela Kaushik, The Agony Of Vietnam (New Delhi, Sterling Publishing, 1972), 215-16

debates about communism versus capitalism, because nationalism often trumped either of these dynamics in controlling North Vietnam's ultimate policy dynamic.[65] Thus began the interesting dance of three participants, North Vietnam, the USSR and China, each having distinct interests, where partners shifted, the lead was in flux and the music was dynamic. The problem for those watching these dancers was how to interpret their moves.

CHINA HAS THE REAR BUT WHO SUPPORTS THE FRONT?

In the spring of 1962, China was at a crossroads regarding its foreign policy. Its leader, Mao Zedong, considered the United States his enemy, yet now there were hints of reconsideration among other leadership. At that point, an important discussion arose concerning whether the communist Chinese should peacefully coexist with capitalist countries or throw their support behind global national liberation movements.[66] Wang Jiaxiang, Director of the International Liaison Department of the Chinese Central Committee advised that other Chinese leaders overrated the danger of world war and underestimated the possibility of peaceful coexistence with imperialist countries. "In terms of support for national liberation movements, Wang emphasized restraint, calling attention to China's own economic problems and limitations in resources."[67] When addressing the subject of Vietnam, he warned against a Korea-style war created by the American imperialists and against the Soviets trapping them into such a war. [68] Wang's theories, however, were condemned and rejected by Mao as "revisionist." Historian Qiang Zhai theorized, "Mao felt the need to rekindle class struggle in order to maintain a revolutionary momentum. He decided to use the struggle against US imperialism, the conflict with 'Soviet revisionism,' and support for national liberation movements to give publicity to his political views in China and to overcome domestic obstacles to his program of continuous revolution."[69]

In addition to furthering its political agenda, China also feared that the United States would back a Taiwanese invasion against the current Chinese government. The large presence of American military forces, allied with Taiwan, so near its borders, could not give China much comfort.[70] Responding to its

---

[65] Jeffrey Record, "The Wrong War Why We Lost in Vietnam,"
http://www.nytimes.com/books/first/r/record-war.html (accessed December 24, 2014)
[66] Quang Zhai, *China and Vietnam Wars, 1960-1975* (Chapel Hill, NC: University of North Carolina Press, 2000), 114.
[67] Ibid.
[68] Ibid.
[69] Ibid., 115.
[70] Ibid., 140.

interests, in 1964 Mao assured the North Vietnamese that "our two parties and two countries must cooperate and fight the enemy together. Your business is my business and my business is your business."[71] China advised North Vietnam that they should confront the United States' military presence in South Vietnam by utilizing Mao's small war theory and should demand immediate US withdrawal. The small war theory argued that a weaker country could successfully defeat a superpower by utilizing guerrilla tactics over a protracted period. Continuous warfare served the purpose of "destroying the will of the enemy to persist without military defeat"[72] Further, the United States with its resources bogged down in Southeast Asia, would be unable to send its troops to suppress other liberation movements around the world. More important, the US would be too engaged to invade China.[73] Thus, as of 1964, China remained a strong supporter of continued Vietnamese engagement with the Americans, and China's influence over their North Vietnamese allies at this point was paramount to the Soviets.

There were many reasons why North Vietnam chose to initially ally itself with the Communist Chinese over the Soviets. Perhaps it was the prior camaraderie between Ho Chi Minh and Mao. Perhaps it was due to Ho's disenchantment with Russian advice during the Geneva Accords along with the perceived Russia's indifference to his conflict with the United States. Maybe the similarity in Chinese and Vietnamese cultures brought the two countries together, whatever the reason when faced with a choice of contrasting options; the North Vietnamese allied themselves with the Chinese position. This relationship was not without complications. Although Hanoi readily accepted guns, money, supplies, and even soldiers from China, it did not readily receive advice, instruction, or dictates from its Chinese benefactors. "Vietnamese historical pride and cultural sensitivity was one major factor that complicated Beijing-Hanoi interactions."[74] Up to and through 1964, the Chinese continued to urge the Vietnamese to continue their guerrilla style war against the United States, making it very clear that negotiation was not an option. Adopting the Chinese position,

---

[71] Xue Mouhong and Pei Jianzhang, Dangdai, Zhonggou waijiao, 159: Qu Aiguo, Bao Ming-rong, and Xiao Zuyao, Yuan Yue KangMei, 8. Quoted in Zhai, 13.
[72] United States of America. Central Intelligence Agency (CIA). *The Attitudes of North Vietnamese Leaders Towards Fighting and Negotiating (reference title:esau xxxvii) (March 28, 1968)*, http://www.foia.cia.gov/CPE/ESAU/esau-36.pdf, 2 (accessed November 26, 2007). See also Dr. Charles A. Russell and Major Robert F. Hildner, "Revolutionary War a Comparison of Chinese Communist and North Vietnamese Strategy and Tactics," htpp://www.airpower.maxwell.af.mil/airchronicles/aureview/1973/jan-feb/russell.html (accessed November 39, 2007)
[73] Zhai, 166
[74] Ibid..152

the only alternative for the end of hostilities voiced by Hanoi was total United States withdrawal from Vietnam, preceding internal elections on the fate of South Vietnam. However, significant events unfolding in 1968 may very well have created an attitude change on behalf of the Chinese.

FROM RUSSIA WITH INDIFFERENCE

Early in the decade, the Soviets under Khrushchev had different purposes than the Chinese and advised the North Vietnamese to avoid a direct confrontation with the United States.[75] According to CIA analysis, the reasons for the Soviet's lack of interest in Vietnam, at that time, was strategic. In the spring of 1962, Khrushchev "was already engaged in his major effort to deceive Washington about the Soviet intentions to put strategic missiles in Cuba and he was careful not to alarm the United States by taking a hard line on Vietnam, which at that time was an area of only marginal importance to him."[76] After his failure in Cuba, Khrushchev, anxious to avoid other confrontations with the United States, remained indifferent to the Indochina conflict and pursued a strategy of peaceful coexistence with the United States until the end of his reign in October 1964.[77] For whatever reason, in the early years of the conflict, the Soviets did not see it in their best interest to support a protracted war between the United States and Vietnam.

KEEPING OPTIONS OPEN

Despite its alliance with the Chinese, North Vietnam never shy to ask for support, continued to engage the Soviet Union. In 1964, the North Vietnamese visited

---

[75] United States of America. Central Intelligence Agency (CIA), *The Attitudes of North Vietnamese Leaders Toward Fighting And Negotiating (Reference Title: Esau Xxxvii); Subchapter-The Attitudes of North Vietnamese Leaders Toward The Conduct of The War, 3,* http://www.foia.cia.gov/sites/default/files/document_conversions/14/esau-36.pdf (accessed December 8, 2014)

[76] United States of America. Central Intelligence Agency (CIA), *The Positions Of Hanoi, Peking, and Moscow on the Issue of Vietnam Negotiations: 1962 To 1966(Reference Title : Esau Xxxx-66) Subchapter: Sino-Vietnamese Agreement On Nature And Timing Of International Negotiations As Khrushchev Stands Aside, 3,* http://www.foia.cia.gov/sites/default/files/document_conversions/14/esau-29.pdf (accessed December 8, 2014)

[77] Zhai, 122. The Cuban missile crisis concerned a show down between the Kennedy administration and Soviets led by Khrushchev. Upon the US' discovery of a secret soviet installed missile base in Cuba, the soviets buckled to US pressure and removed the missiles. For a complete discussion of the matter see Robert F. Kennedy, *Thirteen Days: A Memoir of the Cuban Missile Crisis* (New York, NY: W. W. Norton & Company, 1999)

Khrushchev, who again urged them to be cautious in their war with the United States. Clearly disappointed with the Soviets' position, even moderates in the Vietnamese Politburo openly criticized Khrushchev.[78] Taking advantage of the rift between the Soviets and the North Vietnamese, the Chinese quickly increased their support for North Vietnam in June of 1964.[79]

When the Khrushchev government fell that October 1964, the North Vietnamese perceived an opportunity and went to Moscow, again seeking aid. The new Soviet government led by Alexei Kosygin, also seeing an opportunity for a new relationship, agreed to supply military and political support, but there was a price. The North Vietnamese had to agree to a private statement confirming Moscow's preference for a negotiated settlement of the war.[80] The Chinese learned of Hanoi's agreement and were greatly disturbed. The mere mention of negotiation conflicted with Mao's protracted war theory triggering, of course, sharp Chinese opposition and concern over what they perceived as "a trace of flexibility in Hanoi's attitude."[81] The Chinese not only urged Hanoi to reject negotiations categorically but also incited the North Vietnamese to conduct a large-scale attack across the 17th parallel.[82] Whether the North Vietnamese were showing flexibility or providing mere lip service to receive much-needed supplies is open to interpretation. Nonetheless, this "private statement" with the Soviets created a fissure in the North Vietnamese - Chinese relationship.

SO WE CHANGE PARTNERS, TIME TO CHANGE PARTNERS

In April 1965, North Vietnam proposed its "four points" which dictated its preconditions for any negotiations with the United States to end the war. Briefly, this plan demanded, 1) US withdrawal, 2) abstention of North and South from military alliances, 3) settlement of affairs in the south in accordance with National Liberation Front's program, and 4) reunification. The withdrawal of US troops did not need to take place prior to negotiations; rather a promise for later

---

[78] CIA: The Positions Of Hanoi, Peking, and Moscow on the Issue of Vietnam Negotiations: 1962 To 1966(Reference Title: Esau Xxxx-66) 9, 10.
[79] Ibid., 6.
[80] A private agreement is one held confidentially between the parties and not published to outside sources or entities
[81] Ibid., 25.
[82] United States of America. Central Intelligence Agency (CIA) *The Sino-Vietnamese Effort To Limit American Actions In The Vietnam War (Polo Xx), 16 & 24* http://www.foia.cia.gov/sites/default/files/document_conversions/14/polo-11.pdf. (accessed December 8, 2014)

action would suffice.[83] The "four points" in and of themselves were nothing new, but according to the Bureau of Intelligence and Research (INR), " the way in which they were presented meant that, for the first time, Hanoi officially sanctioned that the conflict could end in a political settlement and provided terms for it."[84] Beijing strongly criticized the North Vietnamese position as showing weakness not in line with protracted war theory.

The Chinese, none too happy with the new cozying up between the North Vietnamese and the Soviets, reacted by blocking the supplies shipment sent to Vietnam from Moscow.[85] According to CIA analysis, in April 1965, the North Vietnamese reacted angrily to this obstruction by replacing a pro-Chinese Foreign Minister with one less sympathetic.[86] This move can be read in two ways: first disenchantment with China or second that North Vietnam cleverly, but dangerously, played China versus Russia to increase supplies from both.

Moscow, believing that North Vietnam's growing rift with Peking made them the lead partner, pushed their negotiation strategy by calling upon the United States to implement a cessation of the bombing, which they assured would be a precondition for negotiations. Despite North Vietnam's four conditions, the Soviets, relying on the private statements of the North Vietnamese Prime Minister, Pham van Dong, believed that a bombing halt might be the only precondition for talks. Based upon Soviet assurances, the Johnson administration suspended bombing in May 1965. The Soviets, unfortunately, misread their new "partner" and the "week long pause in the bombing in mid-May did not make Hanoi any more forthcoming."[87] Obviously, Moscow miscalculated the North Vietnamese stance and overestimated their actual degree of influence over them. This mistake not only highlighted their inability to appreciate their new partner's independence, but also led to serious ramifications in 1968. Johnson once burned by Soviet assurances on North Vietnamese intentions would be reluctant to trust them again. Thus, quite opposite to what the Soviets believed, in 1965, the North

---

[83] Ibid., 9.

[84] The National Security Archive. (INR) *Intelligence and Vietnam: The Top Secret 1969 State Department Study; Thematic Summary C (IV):Prospects for Beginning Talks and Negotiating a Settlement,* http://www.gwu.edu/~nsarchiv/NSAEBB/NSAEBB121/C-IV.pdf, 2,3 (accessed November 26, 2007)

[85] China dismissed the Soviet suggestion asserting "that China's argument with the Soviet Union would continue for another 9000 years" Cong Jin, Quzhe fazhan de suiyue , 607. Quoted in Zhai. 153.

[86] CIA (reference title:esau xxxvii), 10.

[87] Ibid.

Vietnamese, "probably were not interested in negotiations or even in entangling Washington in protracted contacts."[88]

At the end of the year, although nothing changed regarding the composition of the North Vietnamese Politburo, their leader's positions shifted away from extreme pro-Chinese positions of non-negotiation to the more flexible Soviet stance. According to CIA analysis, "All of the primary figures apparently were moving towards a rough agreement to undertake talks if the US was willing to make an important concession (at the very least the cessation of the bombing) to get them."[89]

In January 1966, the United States offered their "14 point statement" towards ending the conflict. The North Vietnamese quickly denounced the plan, yet they interpreted it as a tacit acceptance of three of their four points, thus having gone far towards Hanoi's conditions for negotiations. [90] The point not accepted concerned the United States' refusal to recognize the National Liberation Front (NLF) as the sole representative for the South Vietnamese people.[91] The North Vietnamese remained adamant that they would not ever negotiate with the "puppet" Saigon government. Interpreting their reactions to the US proposal as an encouraging sign, a Soviet delegation traveled to Hanoi with the purpose of encouraging them to begin negotiations. Again, Moscow misread the North Vietnamese who proved more concerned with the United States refusal regarding sole NLF recognition.

A CRACK IN THE ICE?

In June of 1966, the North Vietnamese proposed that they would engage with the United States in peace discussions in exchange for an unconditional and permanent cessation of bombing. Further, they suggested that in exchange for the bombing halt, North Vietnam would halt the movements of Northerners into the South and would not demand Communist domination of the government in the south, Further; Hanoi representatives expressed a willingness to accept international supervision of an election to determine the South's destiny.[92] Note that this is the first time we see anything looking like concessions by the North Vietnamese. It is no surprise that the Chinese strongly attacked the negotiations or even possibilities of talks.

---

[88] INR, C. (IV), 4.
[89] CIA (reference title:esau xxxvii), 13.
[90] Ibid., 14.
[91] Ibid.
[92] Ibid., 18.

THE REAL BOY?

Responding to competing pressures placed upon them by the Soviets and the Chinese, in late 1966, the North Vietnamese once again declared their independence from their supposed masters by proclaiming, "They would not let Peking formulate Hanoi's foreign policy, and that they would enter into negotiations if and when they decide it was in their interest."[93] Li Daun, a pro-Chinese member of the North Vietnamese government, gave a speech attacking Mao's Cultural Revolution in China and proclaimed Ho as the true communist leader. The North Vietnamese Politburo adopted a resolution taking a neutral position in the Sino-Soviet dispute and emphasized the need for Hanoi to "manage the war independently of Russian and Chinese positions." The Politburo further claimed that Hanoi would "no longer be deterred by Peking from acting on its desire for a negotiated settlement." [94] These bold statements of independence by an emerging country deserve admiration; but North Vietnam, involved in a costly and bloody war with the United States, needed food for their people, bullets for their guns and supplies for its armies. It is fair to state that provisions usually do not come without cost.

By late January 1967, according to the CIA analysis, Hanoi seemed more forthcoming about negotiations than it had been at any other time since autumn 1964. Representatives of their government publicly stated that talks, although not technically negotiations could follow cessation of the bombing and other acts of war. Although official Hanoi public statements indicated positive movements, after making claims that an unconditional bombing halt was their sole condition, the NVN gave no further ground remaining "highly suspicious, distrustful of US actions, and concerned over their ability to gain much through negotiations."[95] Despite all the rhetoric, they did offer a significant concession. The earlier requirement that the bombing halt be permanent was no longer mentioned. [96] Nevertheless, the requirement that the United States recognize the NLF as the only representative of the South Vietnamese people, remained.

LBJ, HE WROTE HO A LETTER

In February 1967, Hanoi publicly and privately assured the US that its January offer of talks was genuine. Moscow, pleased with this negotiation's momentum,

---

[93] Ibid., 19.
[94] Ibid., 21.
[95] INR, C. (IV), 4.
[96] CIA (reference title:esau xxxvii), 24.

encouraged Washington to accept. Of course, the Chinese strongly criticized Hanoi's stance. In response to this apparent opening, on February 8, 1967, Johnson sent a letter to Ho Chi Minh, indicating his willingness to order a bombing halt and stall a proposed US troop buildup if he were assured that the North Vietnamese would stop the infiltration of troops into the South. In addition, Johnson included an ultimatum in his letter, which declared that the US would wait until February 14 for a reply from the North Vietnamese government. As a sign of good faith, the United States halted the bombing. The Chinese, ever hostile to any negotiation attempt, criticized the president's proposal and urged the North Vietnamese to ignore it.[97] On February 14, due to the lack of a reply within Johnson's prescribed time limit, the bombing resumed. Maddeningly, Ho Chi Minh did reply one day after the ultimatum. However, "Ho's reply ignored the President's call for a halt in infiltration and reiterated that Hanoi would enter into talks only if there was an unconditional cessation of the bombing."[98]

SOME MOVEMENT ON THE NLF ISSUE

In April 1967, a North Vietnamese delegation traveled to Moscow with the mission to secure increased military aid. The Soviets informed them that they would support the military effort, but only if the North Vietnamese recognized that the Soviets desired a negotiated settlement to the war. Further, the Soviet government did "not believe that a military victory was possible."[99] On or about this time, another major change occurred when the North Vietnamese modified the fourth point of their plan. They dropped the requirement that the United States politically recognize the NLF. However, the demand that the NLF be the sole representative of the South Vietnamese people remained intact. [100] The participation of the Saigon government in the negotiation process, however, remained unacceptable.

THIS IS WHERE WE ARE

As of spring of 1967, whether they were cozying up to the Chinese or the Russians, we are back to the same old ground; Hanoi would give nothing, agree to nothing, and supply no assurances in exchange for negotiations. However, on the positive end, the NVN, at least, considered the possibility of negotiations. In

---

[97]Ibid., 25.
[98]Ibid., 26.
[99]Ibid.
[100]Ibid., 27.

addition, there was progress when Hanoi dropped its demand that the United States recognize the NLF as a political entity. Further, the unconditional bombing halt they demanded of the United States need not be permanent. This concession had special importance because it allowed the United States some implicit assurances. That is, if the North Vietnamese did take advantage of the bombing halt by attacking South Vietnamese cities and United States troops, the United States retained the ability to reinstate the bombing without breaking an agreement. As we will discover, one word can make an enormous difference within the dynamics of negotiations.

WELCOME TO THE FACTS OF LIFE-PART I

On August 25, 1967, President Johnson announced that the United States would halt the bombing if assured that prompt and productive discussions would follow and that the North Vietnamese would not take military advantage. Johnson left it unclear whether the United States would assume that the North Vietnamese would not take military advantage or whether the United States needed direct assurances. If Johnson could assume that the North Vietnamese would perform in a certain way, then this operated as a clever strategy to avoid the unconditional language they required. However, if Johnson demanded express assurances, then that amounted to a condition and the North Vietnamese requirements for negotiation remained unmet.

On September 29, 1967, President Johnson gave a seminal policy speech in San Antonio, Texas. Here he reiterated his August statements offering to stop the bombing if it would lead promptly to productive discussions, and he stated that the US would **assume** that Hanoi would not take military advantage.[101] Johnson now made it clear that he was making assumptions and not demanding assurances. His approach would lead later to the "Facts of Life" doctrine. This device operated as follows; neither side had to give assurances to the other, however, both sides understand implicitly how the other side would respond to their behavior as a "Facts of Life." For example, if the Vietnamese would cross the border and attack the US soldiers after a bombing halt, it is simply a "Facts of Life" that the United States would reemploy the bombing. If both parties understood the "Facts of Life," or the consequences of their actions, express assurances were not required. This face saving device would later function as a critical tool furthering the negotiating process.

---

[101] Ibid., 34. (Emphasis added)

The North Vietnamese, to the surprise the United States government, rejected Johnson's initiative. According to CIA analysis, this rejection, at a time when the US was unusually forthcoming, could have several possible explanations, including, "(a) Hanoi had never been serious about negotiations, or (b); Hanoi did not want to prejudice the chance of an unconditional cessation by showing interest in a lesser offer; or (c); Ho Chi Minh was incapacitated and party leadership had fallen to militants opposed to negotiations."[102] In an after-the-fact analysis, the CIA, weighing the options, concluded that Johnson's offer did not significantly show that the US's will was broken, and they wanted to await the success of the upcoming Tet Offensive.[103] Further, an unrelated phenomenon manifesting at this of time bears mentioning since it affected the negotiating strategy of the North Vietnamese. In the summer of 1967, race riots in Detroit, Milwaukee, and Newark, plagued the United States. North Vietnamese leaders were optimistic that the struggle of Negro Americans might instigate a revolution diverting America attention from Vietnam. Therefore, the North Vietnamese, in no rush towards negotiations, believed that if they remained patient, they might become unintended beneficiaries of the violence. [104] Finally, the North Vietnamese interpreted the San Antonio speech as requiring conditions for a bombing halt. Perhaps at that point, they did not understand the "Facts of Life."

Johnson, in his January 17, 1968 State of the Union address, affirmed his message from San Antonio, but inexplicably he backed away from the novel "Facts of Life" approach and proclaimed that "North Vietnam must not take advantage" of the bombing halt. The "Facts of Life" doctrine may have been initially short lived but was not quite dead yet. To the astonishment of few, the North Vietnamese interpreted Johnson's movement away from assumption towards assurances language as conditional and rejected it outright.

THE TET OFFENSIVE OR HOW TO WIN BY LOSING

January 30 1968 was *Tết Nguyên Đán*, the opening day of the lunar New Year, the most sacred Vietnamese holiday. On that day the NLF and North Vietnamese mounted a country-wide simultaneous assault upon the South, attacking more than 100 towns and cities, including 36 of 44 provincial capitals, five of the six autonomous cities, 72 of 245 district towns, and the national capital of Saigon

---

[102] Ibid.

[103] This is a large-scale attack by the NVN and the NLF on southern positions, which will be discussed in detail in Chapter 14, herein.

[104] Ibid., 33.

including a 6 1/2 hour siege of the United States Embassy.[105] These attacks, which represented the largest military operation conducted by either side, resulted from Hanoi's "serious hope, if not a firm belief, that the military pressure would bring an early and decisive turn in the conflict." [106] It was clear that the "real boy" was acting out. Ignoring the Soviet's opinion that they could not win the war militarily, the North Vietnamese were taking their best shot at victory, or in the alternative setting up very favorable negotiating conditions. This large-scale military attack seeking quick victory could not please the Chinese, as they were determined to help the North Vietnamese "fight until the generation of their (North Vietnamese) sons and grandsons." [107] Since the preparations for the offensive did not take place overnight, the North Vietnamese while discussing negotiation, actually prepared for a major assault. Therefore, any representations they made before the attack could be seen as nothing more than a smokescreen successfully designed to keep the United States off the trail. This smokescreen worked very well, although some claim, including Johnson in his own memoirs, that they saw the Tet offensive coming. According to Clark Clifford (presidential adviser and later Secretary of Defense), that was not true. Clifford argued that Johnson and Westmoreland read reports of the possibility of an offense in early 1968. However, "neither man, nor anyone else in the American intelligence community predicted a force or anything approaching the extraordinary size and scope or having the impact of the Tet Offensive."[108] Indeed, only four days before the Tet Offensive took place US General William Westmoreland (commander of all U.S. military operations in the Vietnam War from 1964 to 1968), reported to the president that, "in many areas the enemy has been driven away from the population centers... the year ended with the enemy increasingly resorting to desperation tactics... and has experienced only failure in these attempts."[109]

Any fair interpretation must include that the Tet Offensive meant that the Communists were not interested in talks on any terms. However, the CIA dismissed this position, arguing that the offensive represented the NVN's attempt to get negotiations on what they deemed fair terms. The offensive "(was) undertaken as part of a scenario in which the Communists envisaged successful

---

[105] Howard Schaffer, *Ellsworth Bunker: Global Trouble Shooter, Vietnam Hawk* (Chapel Hill, NC: University of North Carolina Press, 2003), 195.

[106] DOS, section 37.

[107] Li Ke and Hao Shengzhang, Wehahu dagemeing zhong de renmin jeifangjun, 341-42. Quoted in Zhai, 171.

[108] Clifford, 467.

[109] Neil Sheehan, Hendrick Smith, E. W. Kentworthy, and Fox Butterfield, *The Pentagon Papers: As Published By The New York Times* (New York, NY: Quadrangle Books, 1971), 606.

attacks as leading to American acceptance of communist terms for negotiations as well as American acceptance of any kind of coalition the communists might proclaim." [110] In other words, the NVN planned to end run the Saigon government, by conquering the countryside and establishing an "independent" coalition of these newly freed areas with which the North Vietnamese would directly negotiate. Such strategy, if successful, would accomplish a takeover of South Vietnam without technically defeating the Saigon government.

Militarily, the Tet Offensive failed. Although the Americans and the South Vietnamese together lost approximately 9,000 soldiers, the estimated Communist losses were over 58,000 men. In fact, the Communists failed to hold any of the major cities except Hue, for more than a few days." [111] Hanoi, which had hopes for mass defections of South Vietnamese armed forces and pro-communist uprisings in some of the cities saw their hopes amount to dismal failure. The NLF, in particular, suffered severe damage. "Its regular units were destroyed and would never totally recover, and its political infrastructure incurred heavy losses." [112] To the surprise of North Vietnam, the South Vietnamese Army fought and fought well, which must have been a sobering discovery. North Vietnamese *Commentaries and Journals*, hardly the bastion of independent news, publicly recognized the failure of the mission, when they reported on February 11, 1968, that whereas the Tet Offensive had achieved a "marvelous victory, the American will to persist was not yet broken... The Americans, basically stubborn, would pour in more troops and money." [113]

Did North Vietnam, with its devastating loss of men and the complete failure in their mission objectives, gain from the Tet Offensive? Contrary to the US military victory serving as a clarion call for its citizen's support of the war; it became fodder for the growing antiwar movement. How could that be? The answer lies in the disinformation served to the American public by the military and the Johnson administration. Just three months before the assault, the Pentagon was touting that the North Vietnamese military strength was weakening and the U.S. forces were making "solid progress." [114] According to Clark Clifford, Tet "was a turning point in the war. Its size and scope made mockery of what the American military had told the public about the war and devastated administration credibility." [115] Due to the numerous optimistic official reports

[110] CIA (reference title:esau xxxvii), 42.
[111] Clifford, 473. Note, The city of Hue was later recaptured
[112] Zhai, 179.
[113] CIA (reference title:esau xxxvii), 46.
[114] Clifford, 468.
[115] Clifford, 473.

delivered to the public prior to the Tet Offensive, US citizens were unprepared for the ferocity of the North Vietnamese attacks. Popular television newscaster Walter Cronkite best summed up the Nation's emotions when he declared, "What the hell is going on? I thought we were winning this war!"[116] The irony that their defeat could actually contribute to the breaking of their enemy's will, must have given Hanoi great solace. Thus, in our mission to determine the evolution and the sincerity, if any, of the North Vietnamese October of 1968 proposal, the Tet Offensive weighs on both sides of our scale.

What can be deduced for the above is that the North Vietnamese, freely moving on their own, devised a mixed strategy between the Chinese and Russian positions. This approach allowed them to continue to receive support from both the Chinese and the Soviets, while confusing the United States with contradictory signals. Nevertheless, there was movement in a definitive positive direction. Originally within China's sphere of influence, Hanoi shifted its alliance to the Soviets. At the same point, Hanoi went from a position of no negotiations to one of discussing conditions for negotiations. Intransigence was yielding to flexibility, but whether it had any real significance would depend not on North Vietnam's words but on its deeds. It is certain that Hanoi vehemently opposed recognizing the Saigon government in any manner, asserting that the NLF was the sole representative of the South Vietnamese people. Therefore, flexibility in these areas would provide a true litmus test as to their sincerity for the peace process.

THE NORTH VIETNAMESE RESPONSE OR THE BEGINNING OF THE END OR END OF THE BEGINNING

We return to Johnson's speech of March of 1968. In typical Johnson style, the President seized the initiative. On April 3, 1968, over Radio Hanoi, the North Vietnamese broadcasted, a statement proclaiming that:

> While Hanoi recognized that the United States had not unconditionally stopped the bombing of its territory, it was ready to make a move as well. .. for its part, the Government of the Democratic Republic of Vietnam declares its readiness to appoint its representative to contact the US representative with a view to determining with the American side the unconditional cessation of the U.S. bombing raids and all other acts of

---

[116] Herring, *America's Longest War*, 188.

war against the Democratic Republic of Vietnam so that talks may start.[117]

After hearing Hanoi's announcement, Zhou Enlai, Premier of the People's Republic of China, immediately questioned Ho Chi Minh, who was in Beijing for medical treatment, as to its meaning. Ho said, "He knew nothing about it."[118] "Clearly in making the decision to begin negotiations with the United States, the VWP Politburo under Le Daun's leadership had neither reported to Ho in Beijing nor consulted with the Chinese." [119] This lack of communication started a controversy that would endure, concerning just who was running the show. Due to Hanoi's positive response, Johnson pledged that the United States would establish contact with North Vietnamese representatives anytime, anyplace.[120]

The North Vietnamese, who previously demanded an unconditional, permanent total bombing cessation as a precondition of the negotiations, were now agreeing to discussions based upon a conditional, temporary, partial bombing halt. Asked to postulate as to the possible reasons for this change, the CIA concluded: "One reason may have been that Hanoi may have been fearful of even larger scale attack if the North Vietnamese did not respond promptly. Second, North Vietnam might have been attempting, to influence US public opinion, or create divisions between Washington and Saigon, and to undermine the South Vietnamese morale."[121] On April 8, the president and his top foreign policy advisers received a more detailed analysis of Hanoi's motives. It postulated three new possibilities. One; the North Vietnamese leadership was "highly optimistic" in believing that the tide of the war had turned in its favor and thus would "begin talking while still fighting." Two; perhaps the North Vietnamese were "uncertain" and thus "the President's initiative offered an opportunity-- though not an ideal one--to give greater emphasis to the political aspects of the struggle." Three; the North Vietnamese might have appraised the situation as "pessimistic" due to the losses they suffered at Tet and therefore "the President's statement provided a way out."[122] Other contingencies the memorandum explored included possible domestic turbulence inside North Vietnam or a struggle among

---

[117] DOS, Section 175. Editorial Note http://2001-
2009.state.gov/r/pa/ho/frus/johnsonlb/vi/14368.htm (accessed December 22, 2014)
[118] Hoang Van Hoan, "Distortion Of Facts About Militant Friendship Between Vietnam And China Is Impermissible." *Beijing Review* (December 7, 1978): 11-25, 18. Quoted in Zhai, 172.
[119] Zhai, 172.
[120] Ibid.
[121] DOS, *Section 175*
[122] Ibid.

the top leadership. This suggestion gains credibility in light of Ho Chi Minh's ignorance of Le Daun's decision. Further, given Ho's death later in October, it is reasonable to conclude that his health was poor. In conclusion, the CIA memorandum argued, "Hanoi considers that it can register further military successes at costs it can afford to bear, even if it would prefer not to, that it believes the will to persist is beginning to crumble on the US/GVN side, and that hard bargaining combined with continued military pressure can bring a favorable outcome."[123]

Despite their detailed analysis, the CIA may have missed several essential motivating factors for North Vietnamese actions, the first of which was the effect and ramifications of the United States bombing of their territory. In February 13, 1968, Under Secretary of the Air Force Townsend Hoopes reported to Secretary of Defense Clifford on the possibility of US victory in Vietnam. Referring to the bombing, he concluded that it had caused "heavy damage to North Vietnam's economy and society, but Hanoi's allies had more than made up for the damage with foreign aid. Hanoi's capacity to wage war on whatever level they wish had not been seriously impaired."[124] What we gain from Hoopes' observations is that without foreign aid, Hanoi's capacity to wage war would have been seriously compromised, therefore Hanoi had become heavily dependent on foreign subsidy due to US bombing. With Hanoi absolutely requiring outside supplies, this Pinocchio, under the right circumstances, may have some dances left for his master/benefactor. Because the Soviets now acted as North Vietnam's primary ally, their desire for a negotiated end to the war would have greater weight than ever before.

We must allow for still another possibility that explains the North Vietnamese actions. Hanoi, cognizant of the growing protest against the war within the US, was adept at manipulating these sentiments for the purpose of weakening its enemy's resolve. These psychological games were not without risk and those who attempted manipulation could become victims of their own machinations. North Vietnam could not risk appearing as the aggressor, having to that point enjoyed the fruits of the victim role. If they turned down serious peace initiatives, then they could jeopardize what they had gained in the psychological war. Therefore, the North Vietnamese, while not desiring negotiations, may have allowed themselves little room to reject them.

No matter what the opposition's intentions, Johnson took a step towards negotiations and Hanoi responded positively. Nonetheless, two critical points

---

[123] Ibid.
[124] Clifford, 478.

remained, would the North Vietnamese take advantage of the limited halt and when and where the talks would take place. With respect to the first question, US intelligence revealed shortly after Johnson's speech that the North Vietnamese were engaged in a massive effort to bring additional military forces into South Vietnam.[125] This information could hardly have encouraged LBJ as to North Vietnam's sincerity. With respect to the second objective, after a month-long exhaustive exchange concerning the location for the talks, and despite Johnson's original promise to meet anywhere, Paris was finally selected as a mutually agreeable site. After four agonizing years of repeated disappointments, on May 13, 1968, the peace process finally began.

It would soon be abundantly clear that actors not sitting at any of the tables would have a significant impact on the success or failure of the fledgling talks. As they had been all along, the People's Republic of China and the Soviet Union would remain major players in the prosecution and/or resolution of this war. For its part, Moscow displayed great optimism for these talks, as expressed through the extensive coverage and positive statements published in *Pravda*, the official publication of the Soviet government.[126] The Chinese, staying true to form, reacted with extreme negativity to the negotiation process, rejecting its mere existence. They heavily criticized the North Vietnamese involvement and were quick to remind them of their previous failures in negotiations by making easy concessions.[127] The Chinese were so intent in their opposition that they created various difficulties for the North Vietnamese. "They upset the delivery of Soviet aid to the DRV, organizing provocations against Soviet ships that came to Chinese ports in route to North Vietnam."[128] A Soviet Embassy report documented that in May and June, the Chinese detained a hundred railroad cars meant to go to the North Vietnamese with arms and other military equipment. "The harassment of Soviet shipments to Vietnam was accompanied by agitation on the Soviet Chinese border, where such incidences increased from 90 in January-February 1968 to 164 in May."[129]

After all these years, negotiations finally transpired, but not without ominous signs. For his part, Johnson was skeptical. "I am glad we're going to talk," he told US chief negotiator Averell Harriman and other members of the delegation, "but

---

[125] DOS, section 197.

[126] Gaiduk, 158.

[127] A clear reference to the trust they placed in the Soviet's assurance during the Geneva Accords.

[128] Soviet Embassy in Beijing, Political report for 1968. SCCD, F.5, op. 60, d. 367, p.89. Quoted in Gaiduk, 168.

[129] Foreign Policy and International Relations of the PRC, 131. Quoted in Gaiduk, 169.

I'm not overly hopeful.[130] The North Vietnamese appointed Xuan Thuy as their head negotiator. Thuy's pro-Chinese leanings were well known. He had been previously removed from a prominent position in the North Vietnamese government when China became unpopular. His selection, an obvious act to placate the Chinese, telegraphed North Vietnam's lack of optimism for these negotiations and signaled that the Chinese still had some influence upon them.[131]

Harriman, receiving very narrow instructions from Washington, articulated the United States position that a full bombing halt would occur only if Hanoi would agree to respect the demilitarized zone, not increase the movement of troops from North Vietnam to South Vietnam and agree to the South Vietnamese government participation in discussions.[132] Hanoi rejected Harriman's three points, reiterating its position that the talks would discuss substantive matters only upon an unconditional bombing halt. The talks quickly degenerated into a stalemate with both sides making speeches with nobody listening. The initial excitement became disillusionment especially on the part of the Soviets. Because of the lack of progress, on May 17, Pravda criticized the United States as being responsible for dragging out negotiations to "win time for the preparation of military operations of much larger scale."[133] Moscow feared that a deadlock in negotiations could lead to the breakdown of the whole process of finding a peaceful settlement in Vietnam. "Although publicly Moscow could blame the Americans, Soviet leaders were aware that Hanoi shared the responsibility for lack of progress." [134] The situation required creative thinking and Averill Harriman, the old negotiator, had a good idea. Sensing that the Soviet Union maintained a strong interest in the success of these talks, he set up a process where he could recruit them to act as a broker between the United States and North Vietnam. Harriman took it upon himself to act as a liaison between the American delegation and the Soviet Embassy.[135] One important proviso: for his plan to work, he had to be right about the level of Soviet interest.

---

[130] Gaiduk, 156.

[131] Ibid., 156-7.

[132] Instructions to Governor Harriman, Draft. Harriman Papers, Special Files: Public Service, Subject File, Paris Peace Talks, box 557. Quoted in Gaiduk, 157.

[133] Pravda, May 17, 1968. Quoted in Gaiduk, 158.

[134] Gaiduk, 158.

[135] Ibid., 159.

BACK IN THE USSR OR FROM RUSSIA WITH PEACE

The North Vietnamese clearly showing themselves to be independent operators not easily persuaded by even their most essential allies could not close their eyes to reality. Supplies were desperately needed and the influence of the USSR and China could not be absolutely ignored. Significant world events would soon cause major changes in USSR and Chinese policy. In 1968, in addition to political differences, the Soviets were becoming increasingly wary of the Chinese. Leading up to this period, China experienced its "Cultural Revolution," during which it was estimated hundreds of thousands, perhaps millions, perished in violence.[136] Mao, informed of such losses, particularly that people were driven to suicide, blithely commented, "People who try to commit suicide - don't attempt to save them! . . . China is such a populous nation, it is not as if we cannot do without a few people"[137] A nation indifferent to the deaths of its own citizens, certainly becomes a serious international threat in the nuclear era. Soviet Ambassador Anatoly Dobrynin, expressing his nation's concern over the Chinese, confided to White House Special Assistant Walter Rostow that in their dealings with Moscow, the Chinese Communists often took positions "that made absolutely no sense to the Russian mind... They did not mind a nuclear war. This would wipe out most of the Soviet population and a high proportion of the Chinese population, but would leave them with 200 or 300 million Chinese."[138] Having more in common with the United States' western mind and a mutual distrust in and concern over China, Russia sought the United States as a tactical ally. For the USSR, the Vietnam War was a nuisance that interfered with an alliance, which concerned the greater issue of Soviet security.

Harriman, cognizant of the current state of Sino-Soviet relations, believed that "Moscow's influence had brought Hanoi to Paris against the wishes of Beijing, and if talks were broken off it would be a defeat for Moscow and a

---

[136] Initiated by the Chairman of the Communist Party of China Mao Zedong, on May 16, 1966, the Cultural revolution, which lasted through 1969 concerned a struggle for power within the Communist Party of China that manifested itself wide-scale social, political, and economic chaos, to such a degree that the nation was on the brink civil war. Roderick MacFarquhar and Michael Schoenhals, *Mao's Last Revolution* (Cambridge, MA: Harvard University Press, 2006).

[137] Ibid, 1100.

[138] DOS, section 9. Note that the unidentified quote upon the behalf of the Chinese may be nothing more than the Ambassador's general impression, but remains important because this was the belief of a high-ranking Russian, whether the Chinese believed this or not, cannot be verified.

feather in Beijing's cap." [139] We have here a high stakes game, with Russia throwing the dice at a point where they needed very much to win. Harriman wisely stated, "There were certain common objectives among the Soviet Union, the DRV, and the United States. All three wanted North Vietnam free of Peking domination." [140] Therefore, we know where the Soviets stood. However, were there any remaining strings still connected to Pinocchio? Without influence over the North Vietnamese, Soviet desires lose relevance.

HARRIMAN'S IDEA TREE BEGINS TO BEAR FRUIT

In late spring of 1968, after a series of discussions between Harriman and Soviet ambassadors Zorin and Oberemko, the Soviets met with the North Vietnamese to weigh options. Shortly thereafter, ambassador Zorin voiced his personal opinion to Harriman that the character of the talks might eventually change in favor of real progress. However, this opinion was most likely not personal, but rather an expression of official Soviet policy. As pointed out by author Ilya Gaiduk, Soviet ambassadors, and especially Zorin, did not have personal opinions, and everything they said originated from the Soviet hierarchy. [141] Zorin was right, the North Vietnamese, in a decision, which very well "might have been a result of pressure on the DRV leadership from its Moscow colleagues," decided to replace Thuy and send Le Duc Tho to Paris as its chief negotiator. [142] This was no mere appointment. Tho, a very powerful member of the North Vietnamese government possessed the authority to render on the spot decisions. His selection demonstrated that the North Vietnamese might be more interested in peace negotiations than appeasing Communist China. Expressing an optimistic vision, Gaiduk, argues: "Contrary to the initial purpose to hold talks about talks, the Vietnamese Communists now intended to transform the meetings from exercises in suggest and reject... into occasions for give and take." [143] However, the appointment this new powerful negotiator could be just as much a show for the Russians as the appointment of Thuy was a show for the Chinese. After four years of bloody war, the time for words had passed, and now only actions had weight. The North Vietnamese would have to give up something substantial to prove their sincerity in the peace process and that would have to be recognition of

---

[139] Memorandum of conversation, Zorin -Harriman, June 13, 1968. Harriman papers, Special Files: Public Service, subject file, box 559. Quoted in Gaiduk, 170.
[140] Gaiduk, 170.
[141] Ibid., 162.
[142] Ibid., 163.
[143] Ibid., 169.

the security assurances demanded by the United States and negotiations with the GVN at the table.

MAY 1968, MORE VIETNAMESE DEFEAT

Despite their defeat during the Tet Offensive, the North Vietnamese continued to press on militarily. In May of 1968, they launched another offensive. This attack coincided with a major change in American military leadership as Deputy Chief of Staff Creighton Abrams replaced William Westmoreland as Commander of Forces. Hanoi's new offensive failed and General Abrams new leadership played a large role in spoiling their operations. According to Secretary Clifford, the North Vietnamese losses were substantial; he questioned whether the North Vietnamese could carry on in light of the high rates of casualties.[144] During a National Security Council meeting on September 4, 1968, General Wheeler (Chairman of the Joint Chiefs of Staff) opined:

> General Abrams is confident that we can handle anything the enemy tries to do to us. We can not only keep up with the enemy but also get ahead of him. General Abrams is right when he says that South Vietnamese units have performed well--some with distinction. The improvement in the performance of the ARVN is a very hopeful sign for the future.[145]

General Abrams remarks must be read in light of previous overly optimistic reports from the military. Nevertheless, a September 17, 1968 CIA study, to some extent, backed Wheeler's statement when they concluded the third Communist offensive fell "well short of its advanced billing" and credited "the increasingly effective Allied spoiling operations for the failure."[146] The study did add the cautionary statement that it is their belief "that the Communists have now made a strategic decision to conserve their forces. In terms of manpower and material, communist forces are still capable of a formidable effort, however, not without extremely high costs."[147] Therefore, the North Vietnamese suffered two consecutive significant military losses. The United States Army had new purpose and new effective leadership. The South Vietnamese army showed continued improvements in performance. The NLF had not recovered to its pre-Tet strength.

---

[144] DOS, section 3.
[145] Ibid.
[146] DOS section 16.
[147] Ibid.

North Vietnam shifted partners from the militant Chinese to the negotiation, war ending-minded Soviets, but how would all this play in Paris?

ROSTOW'S PICTURE CHANGES

Up through June of 1968, the so-called peace talks actually were pre-talks. In other words, the parties were discussing conditions that must be met before substantive talks concerning an end to the war could arise. At this point, nobody was seriously discussing peace. On June 4, 1968, Soviet Ambassador Kosygin sent Johnson a note, which not only changed the game, but also dramatically increased the stakes. There is "a real possibility to find a way out of the situation, which has developed in Vietnam with the aim of halting the many years old and bloody war being conducted there," proclaimed Kosygin. He then offered: "That a full cessation by the United States of bombardments and other acts of war in relation to the DRV could promote a breakthrough in the situation and would open perspectives for peaceful settlement." He then assured Washington that stopping the bombing would result in no adverse circumstances or loss of prestige of the United States.[148] The note ended encouraging the continued contacts between United States and the Soviets. "Harriman and Vance were excited" by the Kosygin letter, exclaimed Clifford. They were "certain that the Soviet Union, which was giving Hanoi vast amounts of aid, could help settle the war."[149] Unbeknownst to Clifford and the suddenly optimistic members of the Johnson negotiating team, there were events playing out elsewhere that could very well derail their plans.

MR. CLIFFORD GOES TO WASHINGTON, OFFICIALLY

Although, the June 4, 1968 letter from Kosygin stimulated great optimism among diplomats Vance and Harriman, it created great conflict in an already deeply split Johnson administration. Dean Rusk and Walt Rostow, known "hawks," pronounced it meaningless. Clark Clifford, on the other hand, saw opportunity. Their division reached the level of intensity where Clifford accused, Rostow, who monitored the administration's flow of documents, of intentionally withholding the Kosygin letter from him for twenty-four hours. Clifford alleged that this delay afforded Rostow time to establish an opposition.[150] Due to this deep dissension within in his administration, it was obvious that Johnson would have to decide the

---

[148] Ibid.
[149] Clifford, 546.
[150] Clifford, 546.

path. When the President eventually decided to move, Clifford played a significant role in getting him there. How Clifford, the Secretary of Defense, became the leading proponent of peace in the Johnson administration is a tale of personal growth, hypocrisy, guilt and attempted redemption.

A powerful and skilled lawyer, Clifford became the ultimate Washington advisor. Working unofficially, outside of any significant administrative office, Clifford counseled Presidents Truman, Kennedy and Johnson. One example of his great influence over US presidents occurred on May 12, 1948. With two days remaining of British control of Palestine, President Truman had to decide whether to recognize the independent State of Israel. Secretary of State and former World War II hero George Marshall, and almost all administrative officials, opposed such recognition. Clark Clifford, holding only a low-level advisory position, argued the opposite.[151] On May 15, 1948, the United States officially recognized the State of Israel. Many, including Israel's initial President, Chaim Wiezmann, submit that Clifford's debating skill convinced Truman in favor of recognition.[152]

In 1991, despite his long and illustrious carrier, at age 85, then retired from public life, Clifford began his autobiography's chapter on Vietnam with the lament, "I come now with a sense of almost infinite sadness, to the most painful, tormenting event in my years in public service."[153] As we will discover, his pain was a product of Clifford's assumption of personal responsibility for the war's escalation from 1965-1968. When redemption through an early peace in November 1968 dissolved, he angrily blamed the Nixon-Chennault conspiracy as its cause. In what follows, we will examine the history of the Vietnam War according to Clifford. We take this trip inside Clifford's mind because he is our star witness concerning the administration's perception of just how sincere all parties were in the peace process in the fall of 1968. As discussed in later chapters, in Section II herein, we will also learn his views on the conspiracy, its effects initially and ultimately. For the purposes of keeping an early score, Clifford truly believed; 1) the North Vietnamese were sincerely interested in the peace process; 2) The South Vietnamese **were** sincerely interested in the peace process 3) The South Vietnamese **were not** sincerely interested in the peace process 4) Nixon orchestrated the conspiracy with Anna Chennault as his tool; 5) the conspiracy **did** influence the South Vietnamese no-show at the Paris talks; 6)

[151] Ibid., 3.
152 "Weizmann Thanks Clark Clifford for His "Magnificent" Help in Getting Truman to Support Partition and Recognize Israel," http://www.shapell.org/btl.aspx?weizmann-thanks-clark-clifford-for-his-magnificent-help-in-getting-truman-to-support-partition-and-recognize-israel. (accessed December 8, 2014)
[153] Clifford, 403.

the conspiracy **did not** influence the South Vietnamese no-show at the Paris talks, and; 7) a realistic chance of peace was lost.[154]

To understand Clifford's actions and beliefs in 1968, it is necessary to travel back to the spring of 1965 when the United States stood at a cross roads concerning the war in Vietnam. The key issue centered upon whether the US should continue with what had been primarily an air war or initiate a significant influx of ground troops. According to Clifford, the United States first commenced bombing North Vietnam as a carefully calibrated retaliatory reaction only. Shortly thereafter, this plan "was replaced by a program of sustained bombing long sought by the American military, code name 'Rolling Thunder.'"[155] As Clifford described it, the military strategy consisted of deception, not of the enemy, but of the American public and president. This deception's complexity, intelligence and deviousness almost render it beautiful. Understanding a politician's natural resistance to a ground attack that risked a great loss of life, the military recommended an air war primarily waged by bombing. The insidious connection between bombing and ground troops did not reveal itself until later. Clifford points out that "once bombing of the North began, the military would require, and demand, American combat troops, first to protect American air bases from where the bombing was launched and then inevitably to begin offensive operations against the enemy."[156] Therefore, his argument was simple; air wars required airplanes, airplanes required bases, bases required troops to protect them. If the troops protecting the airplanes were attacked, they must fight back and if they fought back, they needed a sufficient number of troops to support them and so on and so on. Clifford claimed that senior military planners, well aware of this eventual tie-in to troops, "already believed that only American ground troops could avert Saigon's defeat; but fearing the President would be more hesitant to start sustained bombing of the North if he knew that American ground troops would also be required, they did not inform them of this essential fact."[157] Continuing with this strategy, in March 1965, CIA Director John McCone wrote a letter to the president stating his assessment was that victory in Vietnam required substantial increases in the number of troops.[158] Johnson asked Clifford, then working as a high powered lawyer in the private sphere, to act as an outside adviser with the purpose of reviewing and commenting on the McCone letter and then to appear later at a meeting of all major administration officials on the topic.

---

[154] Yes he had both beliefs, the bolding was not a typographical error
[155] Clifford, 406.
[156] Ibid., 405.
[157] Ibid., 406.
[158] Ibid., 409.

In his reply of May 17, 1965, Clifford opined, "I believe our ground forces in South Vietnam should be kept to a minimum... my concern is a substantial buildup of US ground troops would be construed by the communists ... as a determination on our part to win the war on the ground... this could be a quagmire."[159]

On July 21, 1965, Johnson called his advisers, major staff, and his cabinet to Camp David to seek a consensus decision on how to prosecute the war. Undersecretary of State George Ball represented those against the war, arguing for de-escalation versus Secretary of Defense Robert McNamara, who urged massive troop escalation. Everyone, in the room related Clifford, "seemed deeply aware that we're facing belatedly in my opinion -- a momentous decision."[160] Ball emphatically argued "We can't win ...the war will be long and protracted with heavy casualties. The most we can hope for is a messy conclusion. We must measure this long-term price against the short-term loss that will result from withdrawal." Ball feared that once escalation began, it would be difficult to control. He compared it to riding a tiger's back. Once on top, "we cannot be sure of picking the place to dismount."[161] During this debate, Clifford chose to remain silent. He explained, "As the sole private citizen in the room, present only as a personal friend and adviser to the president, I felt I should express my opinions privately to him."[162] Still, he did ask a General, "if the military plan that you propose is carried out, what is its ultimate result if it is successful?" The General answered: "in all likelihood, we would be able to withdraw most of our forces. But there was a chance that we would stay for a long time."[163] Obviously, that answer did little to erase Clifford's reluctance.

After they left the room, Clifford and Ball conferred. Ball assumed that Clifford had deep doubts about the war and McNamara's proposals. Clifford told him "not only did I have such doubts, but I sent the President a letter stating my concerns in May."[164] Ball implored Clifford, to influence the President, and gave him a series of memoranda he prepared against the war.[165] Armed with Ball's

---

[159] Ibid., 410.

[160] Ibid., 411.

[161] George W. Ball. "Top Secret: The Prophecy the President Rejected, *The Atlantic*, 230 (July 1972): 35-49.

[162] Clifford, 414.

[163] Ibid., 414.

[164] Ibid., 416.

[165] Ball continued to work in the Johnson administration until he was appointed Ambassador to the UN on June 26 1968. He resigned on September 25, 1968 to work full-time on the Humphrey presidential campaign. He explained, "I cannot permit myself to remain quiet any longer about Nixon. He's a liar, dishonest, and a crook. This is my

research, and his own conclusions, Clifford advised Johnson privately that he opposed involvement in Vietnam because he did not believe that the containment policy, which he helped write in 1947, still applied.[166] He foresaw "a calamity for the troops and the nation if ground troops were sent to Vietnam."[167] He argued, "American troops should not be committed to combat except when the national security is clearly at stake."[168]

On July 25, 1965, Johnson and his advisers and administrators returned to Camp David for another meeting on the topic of Vietnam. This time Clifford was not quiet. When it was his turn to argue, he remembered, I "put more passion into what I was saying than any presentation I had ever made to a President." He said, "I hate this war. I do not believe we can win... it will be a huge catastrophe... it will ruin us. Five years, 50,000 men killed, hundreds of billions of dollars -- it's just not for us."[169] He forcefully made his case against the massive escalation proposed by Secretary of Defense Robert McNamara and the military, when "under discussion was a decision that would change American history."[170] Unquestionably, he argued the minority position, but Clifford triumphed in the past against odds just as long. Once he convinced Truman to support the creation of Israel when his entire administration was against it. Here, leaving no question as to his valiant and personal efforts in an attempt to save America from sure disaster, he reinforced the credibility of his memories of the meetings by providing his reader with the finest details. "Two Filipinos would serve drinks. The President drank Fresca, I sipped club soda," he remembered.[171] His protestations came to no avail. Clifford succinctly summed up the Camp David debates: "I had argued my case and lost, in a face-to-face debate with McNamara, in the unlikely tranquility of the summer weekend at Camp David."[172] What had been primarily an air war with advisers on the ground now became a massive air and ground war. Johnson chose to mount the tiger. The United States soon began

---

country. We would get poor leadership." He also declared that he couldn't live with himself if he didn't work to defeat Nixon. DOS, section 36.

[166] Clifford, 403. The containment policy was popularly known as the "Domino Theory." Essentially, this belief held that the fall of Indochina to communism would bring about, in rapid succession, a similar collapse of the other nations of South East Asia. See Herring, 12.

[167] Clifford, 404.

[168] Ibid.

[169] Ibid., 419. Remarkably Clifford statements were prescient

[170] Ibid., 418.

[171] Ibid.

[172] Ibid., 404.

its substantial escalation of troops in Vietnam, reaching a zenith of over 500,000 troops in 1968.[173]

With the benefit of hindsight, there remains little question that Clark Clifford's arguments in the summer of 1965 proved true. Despite his loss to McNamara, surely, Clifford would remain the voice of peace and reason, continuing in his efforts to convince the president as to the righteousness of his position. Not so fast, the exact opposite became true. Clark Clifford, who believed that the war served no national interest and would bring nothing but calamity and failure for America, morphed into one of America's strongest proponents of the war, consistently supporting Johnson's further escalations of the war. To understand this dramatic turnabout, we must examine Clifford's insider/outsider situation and his later peace-through-war justification, in addition to some very puzzling remarks he made during a 1969 oral history.

Clifford served as an outside adviser to the Johnson administration from 1964 through 1967. He enjoyed this role, commenting: "I like the freedom of practicing on my own, in addition, I do not wish to give up the ability to speak frankly to the president, something I can do more effectively as an outside adviser than as a member of the Cabinet." [174] Clifford believed that "even if he ignores the advice, every president should ensure that he gets a third opinion from selected and seasoned private citizens he trusts... they can give the president a different perspective on his own situation; they can be frank with him when White House aides are not."[175]

Clifford's argument that, unfettered by the necessities of politics and position, an outside adviser can maintain the uniquely independent ability to present unfiltered necessary opinions makes sense. What challenges reason was his explanation of why he abandoned his own definition of an outside adviser. In an attempt to justify his actions in becoming a very vocal proponent of increased escalation of the war, Clifford defends:

> A final reason for my position from 1965 to 1967 resulted from my relationship with President Johnson. Once the President has set the basic course, I felt that what was needed was support, not more criticism I had opposed the buildup of 1965, and lost, but once the course had been set,

---

[173] "Years of Escalation: 1965-68," http://www.ushistory.org/us/55b.asp. (accessed December 8, 2014)
[174] Ibid., 439.
[175] Ibid., 423.

I looked for ways to make it succeed, instead of continuing to argue an issue, which had been decided.[176]

Whoa, what a fast spin! What happened to the different perspective, what happened to the necessity for frank talk and advice? Why did he support a war that served no purpose other than destruction? Perhaps the answer lies in the phrase coined by George Ball "nothing propinks like propinquity." Later dubbed the "Ball Rule of Power," the phrase simply "means that the more direct access you have to the president, the greater your power, no matter what your title."[177] Clifford had the ear of the president, thus he had power. If he continued to inform the president of ideas that the he did not want to hear, he risked losing his access and thus his power, or in Ball's terms, he would no longer *propink!*

Clifford provided a different answer in his autobiography; do pay attention, because it gets a little tricky. Clifford remained opposed to the war, but he strategized that only strong prosecution would facilitate peace. Clifford believed the only way to get out of Vietnam was to persuade Hanoi that "we are too strong to be beaten and too determined to be frightened."[178] He wanted to make the war more costly for Hanoi. Breaking it down to its smallest elements, Clifford believed that to have peace in an unjustified war, which did not threaten American security or further its best interests, instead of de-escalation or pulling out, the best plan was to kill as many of the enemy as possible while, at the same time, risking large numbers of American lives. Clifford believed that the peace-through-war strategy was working. He trusted the optimistic reports from General Westmoreland, Ambassador to South Vietnam Ellsworth Bunker, and Secretary of Defense Robert McNamara, that the United States military was making headway and that victory was not far distant.[179]

In summer 1967, Clifford visited Vietnam, what he found devastated him. He soon realized the progress reports sent to the White House, touting the success of the military campaign, amounted to nothing more than propaganda. Clifford's reaction to his discovery perhaps best represents his then strategic philosophy. "The trip had buried for me, once and for all, Washington's treasured domino theory; on the other hand, I continued to support the policy, because it seemed to provide the best way out of the war... if we are to have a chance to get this war

---

[176] Ibid.
[177] Hugh Sidey "Learning How to Build a Barn" *Time Magazine* (October 17, 1983) http://www.time.com/time/printout/0,8816,952191,00.html (accessed November 26, 2007)
[178] Clifford, 437.
[179] Ibid., 447.

over with, we must hit them harder." [180] Therefore, although the war had no
underlying justification, and was not progressing satisfactorily, instead of pulling
out, Clifford believed the United States should escalate. Despite his epiphany in
summer 1967, it appears that he forgot it three months later. When asked his
opinion on the war during another policy conference, Clifford stated, "This will
never be a popular war... [yet] we must go on, because what we are doing is
right." [181] If Clifford were alive today for cross-examination, the question of what
was "right" about what the US was doing begs an answer.

What was Clifford, a private dove, a hawk-dove, or was that a dove-hawk?
His status is more than a rhetorical question. Thomas Hughes, Director of the
Bureau of Intelligence and Research (INR) from 1963 to 1969, in introducing a
recently declassified study of the Vietnam War, commented brilliantly as to
Clifford's private dove/public hawk status,

> [T]here is a twofold problem with... the private doves. First their public
> hawkishness misleadingly conveyed the image of a unified
> administration, instead of one marked by widespread skepticism and
> doubt. Second since their private convictions remained largely unshared
> ... [and] their communications with the President remained confidential,
> they were largely unaware of the strength and persistence of one
> another's opposition to the war. [182]

Whatever his designation, or his alleged motivation, from late 1965 until the end
of 1967, Clifford, after vigorously opposing him at the onset, supported
McNamara's policies of escalation "as a private citizen and personal adviser to
the president." [183]

In January 1968, although the President remembered his initial opposition to
the buildup in 1965, because Clifford supported his policies in Vietnam
consistently thereafter, LBJ nominated Clifford to replace outgoing Secretary of
Defense Robert McNamara. Indeed, Clifford did *propink*. Unknown to Johnson,
Clifford was ready for another metamorphosis. "If at the time of my appointment,
I held the views I was to develop only a few weeks later, I would've had an

---

[180] Ibid., 449.
[181] Clifford, 455. As you will discover herein, Clifford met another epiphany in 7/68 but he
seemed to demonstrate a pattern of failing to have them sink in.
[182] Thomas L. Hughes, "The National Security Archive, INR's Vietnam Study in Context:
A Retrospective Preface 35 Years Later,"
http://www.gwu.edu/~nsarchiv/NSAEBB/NSAEBB121/hughes.htm. (accessed November
26, 2007)
[183] Clifford, 460.

obligation to inform President Johnson, who might then have chosen someone else for the position," claimed the new Secretary. [184] Clifford became ready to take on the wings of the "dove" full time. This change of part can be primarily linked to three factors; his fall trip to South Vietnam, Chief of Staff General Earl Wheeler's February 1968 military assessment and the corresponding conclusions of the CIA, the Pentagon, the "Wise Men" and McNamara's role reversal.

Clifford traced his disenchantment with the war to his summer 1967 Vietnam visit. Putting aside the progress reports he received, he realized firsthand that the foundation for his peace-through-war doctrine was crumbling. Instead of progress towards victory, he saw quagmire; instead of withdrawal, he feared endless involvement. The curious element here is that Clifford chose to trust the military at all. In 1965, when he voiced his initial opposition to the war, he steadfastly believed that the general's argument in support of the war "was ridiculous and disturbing." He did not believe the military was being straight with the Johnson administration. [185] Why Clifford chose to place his trust in a military organization that he knew previously lied to the administration on its purpose (air war versus ground war) and progress remains a mystifying question.

In February 1968, General Wheeler provided a very pessimistic assessment of the situation on the ground. In a memo to the president, he advised that the United States and South Vietnam barely succeeded in fighting off the Tet Offensive and he visualized "much heavy fighting ahead. Casualties would probably remain high." [186] He concluded that the situation demanded 205,000 additional troops and even then, the prospects for victory were not assured. [187] General Westmoreland agreed with the troop increase but his prognosis was far more optimistic. Clifford, who was waiting to be officially confirmed as the next Secretary of State, was assigned by Johnson the task of studying this request and analyze the situation in general. Clifford turned to three sources of information to help him, the CIA the Pentagon and the "Wise Men."

The CIA concluded that the military situation in Vietnam was at a hopeless stalemate because neither side had the power nor ability to drive either one out of South Vietnam, therefore, a troop increase would bring further fighting, but little

---

[184] Ibid., 465.

[185] Ibid., 414.

[186] Ibid., 543.

[187]This request was complicated by the fact that on 10, March, the New York Times published a leak from inside the Pentagon to the effect that General William Westmoreland was asking for 206,000 more troops. Neil Sheehan and Hedrick Smith reported this leak. Chalmers Johnson, "The Disquieted American," http://books.guardian.co.uk/lrb/articles/0,,890302,00.html (accessed November 29, 2007)

positive results.[188] The Pentagon Office of System Analysis headed by Alain Enthoven, issued a report that found "a bleak picture of failure" in Vietnam concluding that despite the enemy's depth of losses they possessed, "no lack of capability or will to match each new United States escalation."[189]

Responding to this new crisis Clifford called another meeting of the "Wise Men." These men were a group of great Americans comprised of: Dean Acheson, George Ball, General Bradley, McGeorge Bundy, Clark Clifford, Arthur Dean, Douglas Dillon, Justice Abe Fortas, Averill Harriman, Henry Cabot Lodge Jr., Robert Murphy and General Maxwell Taylor. In November 1967, they previously met and gave advice that Johnson should stay the course in Vietnam. They were called together again in March 1968 to consider General Wheeler's request for further escalation. General Matthew Ridgway and Cyrus Vance joined their ranks replacing Robert Murphy, General Taylor and Abe Fortas. This time, after careful debate, seeing no reasonable prospect for victory, they reversed course and recommended disengagement from Vietnam as opposed to further escalation.[190]

Clifford's old Camp David debating partner, Robert McNamara, remained, until the end of 1968, at least publicly, a powerful force behind increased escalation of the war. Behind the scenes however, he voiced a dramatic policy reversal during an episode of severe emotional distress.[191] In a February 1968 meeting of presidential advisers, McNamara, to the surprise of all present, declared that the "continuation of our present course of action in southeast Asia would be dangerous, costly in lives, and unsatisfactory to the American people." Further, he said "continuing our present course will not bring us by the end of 1968 enough closer to success in the eyes of the American public to prevent the continued erosion of popular support for involvement in Vietnam." [192] He recommended no new troops, no expansion of the war and instead urged a halt in

---

[188] Pentagon Papers, 612-13.

[189] Ibid., 615.

[190] Clifford, 511-18.

[191] During a meeting of presidential advisers on February 27, 1968, Walter Rostow opened a conversation on whether to intensify the bombing. In response, McNamara, who was ending his term as Secretary of Defense, a man known for his strength and determination if not arrogance and self-righteousness, stated emphatically: "The god damn Air Force, they're dropping more on Vietnam than we dropped on Germany in the last year of World War II, and it's not doing anything!" According to Clifford, his voice faltered and for a moment, he had difficulty speaking between suppressed sobs. He stated to Clifford, "We simply have to end this thing. I just hope you can get hold of it. It's out of control." That was the last full day of office McNamara served in the President's Cabinet. Clifford, 485.

[192] Ibid., 457.

the bombing and "making an all-out effort to negotiate with Hanoi."[193] With the voice of the "hawks" quieted, it was now time for the "doves" to swoop in.

Clifford, based upon his personal findings, and the conclusions of the CIA, Pentagon and the "Wise Men" reached a decision. Convinced that the peace-through-war strategy failed, and that the war did not serve America's strategic interests, he argued that the United States must end this war through negotiation. Nevertheless, he did recommend an increase of 20,000 troops but this was only a means to buy time for the South Vietnamese army to develop greater capability. [194] There is no zealot like a convert, and having lost his argument in 1965, Clifford did not want to lose again.[195]

We cannot leave this section without presenting an extremely troubling contrary version of the above version of events, put forth by no one other than, Clark Clifford. In his autobiography, he left no doubt that, in July of 1965, he held the banner for those opposing an escalation of the war. He made clear the agony and frustration he suffered by losing a historically significant debate to McNamara. However, in March 1969, during an oral interview, Clifford introduced into the mix quite a different version of reality. When questioned on his role in formulating American military policy for the Vietnam War 1965-1966, Clifford replied:

> I played no real part in the Vietnamese question in '65 and '66. I think, again, the reason for it was there was no particular issue involved. The policy was quite clear and the only issues involved were those taken up with the Secretaries of State and Defense about when was the time to send men and which men ought to be sent and how did you build up your logistic force and then the decision to put airfields in, different procedures of that kind on which I would have no expertise. I wouldn't be of any help to the President (emphasis added). [196]

"No particular issue," "no real part" played; the contradictions are staggering! We are now left with two fundamental questions; what really happened in 1965 and what role, if any, did Clifford play? Jack Valenti, the President's chief assistant at

---

[193] Ibid., 458.
[194] Pentagon Papers, 616.
[195] The saying "there is no zealot like to convert," although not originated by Philip Scranton P.H.D. of Rutgers University, was used by him at a recent history conference, therefore I borrow it from him giving him, of course, proper credit.
[196] Transcript, Clark Clifford Oral History Interview I, 3/16/69, by Joe B. Frantz, LBJ Library. Online; Note emphasis added

that time, may provide a solution.[197] According to Clifford, Valenti, acting as a secretary, permanently recorded Clifford's remarks during the July of 1965 Camp David conferences. Clifford claimed that his note, stored in the Johnson Library, clearly documented Clifford's strong opposition to the war, and his predictions that United States would lose 50,000 men and that the war would ruin the United States. [198] Still puzzling is the question of why Clifford later denied his involvement in 1965 during the 1969 oral interview. Shortly out of office, was he trying to distance himself from what he thought was a disaster? Did he feel guilt about losing the 1965 debate and his subsequent "hawk" role thereafter? These questions, unfortunately, must remain unanswered. What we do know, however, is that Clifford felt personally responsible for the escalation of this war and he sought redemption through his work to end it.

JOHNSON FLIES WITH THE HAWKS

Retuning to Kosygin's optimistic letter of June 1968 that predicted a "peaceful settlement" with full cessation of US bombing, LBJ was not as optimistic. Faced with a deeply divided staff, Johnson could not get past Moscow's failed promise of 1965, holding that if the United States stopped the bombing, "something good will happen." Based on that statement, LBJ stopped the bombing for 37 days, but nothing good happened.[199] Still wary of Soviet assurances, Johnson decided to adopt the "hawk" view. Now unwilling to trust Moscow's general statements, he demanded specific explanations and explicit assurances that there would be no adverse military consequences before he would halt the bombing.[200] The Soviets, noticeably disappointed, expressed through Ambassador Dobrynin, their sense that "the United States had missed an opportunity." [201] Nevertheless, despite their disenchantment, the Soviets decided to become more invested in the process.

On July 13, 1968, Soviet leaders, in a letter to Hanoi, tested the idea that the United States be given security assurances before a bombing halt and that the Saigon government become part of the negotiations. One month later, Hanoi rejected the Soviet recommendations, leading them to conclude that their

---

[197] Yes, that guy with the white hair from the Academy Awards

[198] Clifford presents the Valenti note verbatim, on page 420 of his autobiography. However, he does not cite to its location the Johnson Library. Ordinarily a verbatim quote by man of Clifford's reputation would be enough in a search for credibility, yet without its location in a footnote, a word of warning is put forward that this author has not confirmed its existence.

[199] Gaiduk, 165.

[200] Clifford, 547.

[201] Gaiduk, 166.

Vietnamese comrades "do not offer a constructive thesis aimed at peaceful settlement of the Vietnam question in accordance with the present favorable situation."[202] The problem according to Soviet analysis was the still-present China factor. The Chinese wanted to continue the war in Vietnam because, according to the Soviet embassy in Beijing, "a settlement in Vietnam would strike a blow at Mao's military strategy in the protracted war and would lead to the debunking of other ideas of the 'great leader.'" [203] Once again, an impasse surfaces, but, changes in the world at large and innovations in language, might still pave the road to resolution.

CHANGES IN THE WORLD: THE SOVIETS GAIN CACHE WHILE BOUNCING CZECHS

Starting in January 1968, Czechoslovakia, a member of the Warsaw Pact while under the leadership of Alexander Dubcek, initiated counterrevolutionary actions, which troubled the Soviets. On August 20, 1968, forces of approximately 500,000 troops, chiefly from the Soviet Union, "in a blitzkrieg-like advance" invaded the sovereign state of Czechoslovakia. [204] The counter-revolution was easily crushed, which should be of no surprise. Yet, why show such massive show of force for such a tiny weak country and who was the audience? Similar to a dog marking its property, the Soviet action made it clear to Beijing and Hanoi that the USSR was "the" communist power. In reaction, the Chinese, demonstrating their great displeasure with the Soviets, indicted them with the charge of "social imperialism" of a criminal nature "which was portrayed as being equal in gravity to the imperialism of the United States." [205] In July 1968, one month before the Czechoslovakian invasion, Soviet Prime Minister Brezhnev announced a doctrine known as "Limited Sovereignty," which arrogated to the USSR "the right to intervene in any socialist country where socialism was deemed in danger."[206] Because of the invasion and the new doctrine, it is not unreasonable to postulate that China reached an epiphany, the United States did not pose their greatest

---

[202] Political Letter of the Soviet Embassy in Hanoi, "Soviet Vietnamese Relations After the April Talks Of 1968," (September 1, 1968). Quoted in Gaiduk, 168.
[203] Gaiduk, 169.
[204] "Soviet Invasion of Czechoslovakia,"
http://www.globalsecurity.org/military/world/war/czechoslovakia2.htm. (accessed November 27, 2007)
[205] Rand Corporation, "Chinese "Deterrence: Attempts: Failures and Successes,"
http://www.rand.org/pubs/monograph_reports/MR1161/MR1161.app.pdf. (accessed November 27, 2007)
[206] Zhai, 174.

security threat, rather it was the Soviet Union, dangerous, ready, and willing to act who posed the greater risk. The dance changed and the partners changed. Instead of the Soviets and the Chinese courting the North Vietnamese, it was the United States playing the role of the prettiest girl at the dance. According to historian Eugene Lawson,

> While Soviet pressure on China was growing, American actions indicated a reduced threat to Beijing. The suspension of US bombing and the pullback of American troops in Vietnam revealed Washington's intention to disengage from Indochina. If the Soviet Union now posed a greater threat to China's security, it was in Beijing's interest to seek an accommodation with the United States and to encourage progress in the Paris talks to his give Washington a way out. [207]

After the Czechoslovakian invasion, there indeed was a profound change in Chinese policy. Beijing stopped censoring news about the Paris peace talks, but more important, after four years of strong criticism of any act or policy by Hanoi that would lead to a peaceful settlement to the conflict, China refrained from intervening in the negotiations. The powerful consistent Chinese impediment to the peace process suddenly lessened.

The Soviet invasion of Czechoslovakia also effected the North Vietnamese, but one quite opposite to the Chinese. The DRV's strong and public approval of the Soviet's actions served as another positive outgrowth of the USSR's invasion. This endorsement did not sit well with the communist Chinese. During an October 1 celebration in China, the North Vietnamese delegation officially ranked in importance behind the essentially irrelevant Australian communist party.[208] Moscow interpreted North Vietnam's endorsement of their aggressive actions as a turn towards them and away from Beijing, "particularly in the question of negotiations." Accordingly, by the end of September, "Moscow hurried to use this new display of Hanoi's loyalty by more actively promoting the success of the Paris talks as soon as the dust over Czechoslovakia settled." [209]

Finally, the invasion served as a test of the Soviet's new relationship with the United States. Citing the lack of an agreement with Czechoslovakia, and of course, secretly not wanting to lose the Soviets as their negotiating partner/broker in the peace process, the Johnson administration did little if anything, to protest

---

[207] Eugene K. Lawson, *The Sino-Vietnamese Conflict* (New York, NY: Praeger, 1984), 217.
[208] Ibid., 216.
[209] Gaiduk, 177.

the Czechoslovakian invasion.[210] At first glance, this lack of response may appear baffling especially in light of Congress and the public's outrage to the Soviet aggression. However, Johnson's eyes were on settling the Vietnam War and alienating the USSR, which he perceived to be an essential partner in the peace process, was not a desirable alternative.[211]

Due to a myriad of events, power politics and world conditions, China and the USSR, the principal suppliers of the North Vietnam's ability to wage war now both encouraged negotiation. This unprecedented alignment of the stars could have led to momentous results.

CHANGES IN LINGUISTICS

Despite the above changes, peace was still not at hand; instead, the fall of 1968 presented a conundrum. The DRV would not agree to begin negotiations concerning substantive issues unless the United States would order an **unconditional** bombing halt. On the other hand, the United States would not halt the bombing unless three conditions were met. First, the DRV must respect the DMZ by stopping the flow of troops and armaments into the South. Second, the DRV must agree not to attack South Vietnamese cities. Third, and a most troubling condition, the DRV must agree to include the Saigon government in the subsequent substantive negotiations.[212] How could there be forward movement when both sides' conditions were contrary? Sometimes the interpretation, or spin on a word, is mightier than the sword. The following analysis will reveal how conundrum became compromise through the clever art of word-wise diplomacy.

FACTS OF LIFE-PART II- IT LIVES IT LIVES

On September 3, 1969, Chief Paris negotiator Averill Harriman noticed a change in Soviet Ambassador Zorin's attitude. He noticed that he was "more forthcoming and unargumentative than in any of our previous conversations." [213] During their meeting, Harriman argued that Hanoi's continued refusal to give an indication of what would happen once the bombing stopped was unreasonable, and he requested that the Soviet Union use its influence or ingenuity to find a way

---

[210] Ibid., 176.
[211] David Roth, "The American Reaction to the 1968 Warsaw Pact Invasion of Czechoslovakia,"
http://kb.osu.edu/dspace/bitstream/handle/1811/45699/david_roth_thesis.pdf?sequence=1. (accessed December 17, 2014)
[212] Gaiduk., 178.
[213] DOS, section 2.

forward. As a sign of good will, Harriman informed his counterpart that the United States would agree to the presence of the NLF at the negotiations, but Saigon must also attend. When pressed on the South Vietnamese issue, the ambassador commented that he "did not believe that it constituted an insurmountable obstacle."[214] The question remained, what innovation could solve this puzzle of conflicting conditions?

On September 21, 1968, the innovation Harriman and Zorin discovered regarding the two security conditions requested by the United States turned out to be simply not to call them conditions. In regards to the bombing halt, the US condition that it not be exploited morphed into the "Facts of Life." The negotiators made it clear that when talking about the cessation of bombing or the sanctity of the DMZ, it was unwise to use words such as conditions or reciprocities because these terms run into considerations of face or prestige. "It is a simple fact of life that a bombing halt could not continue if the DMZ were not respected, (or) if there were significant attacks on major population centers in South Vietnam." [215] Therefore, due to the magic of words, Johnson's requirements of a bombing halt ceased being "conditions" and instead became understandings. Through this device, both sides could walk away from the table and legitimately argue to their constituency that got what they wanted.

The Soviets understood the "Facts of Life," but did Hanoi? Despite Secretary Vance's claims that he explained the "Facts of Life" to the DRV on eight occasions, Johnson still wanted direct assurances from Hanoi and the Soviets as to their understanding. On October 25, 1968, Presidential Advisor Walt Rostow met with Soviet Ambassador Dobrynin and asked him, "are you... prepared to tell me that they (DRV) understand the "Facts of Life?" He replied, "I can only say that from the reports to me, as well as your reports to our people in Paris, you have expressed yourselves very clearly."[216] Johnson remained uncomfortable and continued to press. Due to the President's reluctance on the "Facts of Life" issue, Harriman prepared a memorandum stating that during at least 12 meetings with the DRV he had raised the issue. He declared throughout these meetings,

> When these subjects have been discussed, at no point has the other side given us any basis for believing they did not understand precisely what we are talking about and what is expected of them ... we do not look on them as a conditions for stopping the bombing but as a description of the

---

[214] Ibid.,
[215] Ibid., section 29.
[216] Ibid., section 122.

situation which would permit serious negotiations and thus the cessation to continue. [217]

Harriman later stated that our judgment was that "the DRV will carry out what we have demanded of them with respect to the DMZ and indiscriminate attacks against the major cities... as we've previously stated on several occasions, the bombing should be resumed if our demands with respect to either the DMZ of the cities are violated."[218]

Even with strong assurances from his staff, Johnson wanted one more guarantee; he wanted the Soviets to commit their integrity to the proposition in writing. On October 28, 1968, Johnson achieved his goal. The Soviets responded to his demands by stating that it is their belief that the Vietnamese leaders are serious in their intentions and doing everything possible to put an end to the war in Vietnam and to reach a peaceful settlement. It was Rostow's opinion that, "It seems to us that doubts, with regard to the position of the Vietnamese side, are without foundation (groundless)." Further, he asserted, for the first time, "Moscow is responsive to our request that they commit themselves about the intent and integrity of Hanoi." [219]

Although unquestionably a positive development, an agreement on the "Facts of Life" did not close the deal. Left open was the conflict regarding Saigon's participation in negotiations. The agreement to the "Fact of Life," once understood and confirmed by all parties, represented the acceptance of the simple idea, civilized countries understand how other nations will act or react based upon their own actions. Agreeing to allow Saigon to participate at the negotiation table was something more. Hanoi now was asked to give up a strongly held principle. In exchange for a bombing halt, the North Vietnamese had to acknowledge the political viability of a government, which they consistently and angrily deemed as nothing more than a corrupt puppet of the United States. Their reaction to this request provided a far stronger test of North Vietnam's sincerity than the "Facts of Life" agreement.

On September 21, 1968, Soviet Ambassador Oberemko, during the discussions with Secretary Vance, questioned whether the "inclusion of Saigon representatives was the major roadblock to serious discussions?" Vance replied "yes." To underscore the importance of the issue, after conferring with Harriman, he sent a letter to Oberemko, emphasizing that it was "unthinkable for the United

---

[217] Ibid., section 132.
[218] Ibid.
[219] Ibid., section 138.

States to stop bombing without the inclusion of South Vietnamese representatives in [the] Paris negotiations."[220] Vance, putting pressure on the Soviets implored, "[the] time has come for the Soviet government to weigh in on this subject."[221] In addition to his appeals, Vance, understanding the power of interpretation and the absolute necessity to avoid the term "conditions," cleverly introduced the concept of "definition." Essentially, he informed the Soviets that the inclusion of the GVN was necessary to permit serious conversations to take place and therefore their presence did not constitute a condition, but rather it comprised the "definition" of serious discussions.[222]

In early October 1968, Soviet Minister for Foreign Affairs, Andrei Andreyevich Gromyko, visited the United States seeking a solution on the question of including Saigon. He candidly admitted his difficulty in convincing the North Vietnamese to accept Saigon at the conference and asked Secretary Rusk to consider whether the United States could replace President Thiệu with somebody more acceptable to Hanoi. He added, "Authorities in Hanoi took very strong views towards these individuals, and that the character of the regime in the South was a major obstacle."[223] This request was refused and it was reiterated that Saigon must be involved in the negotiating process.[224]

THE ICE BREAKS

On October 9, "finally, not without great Soviet efforts, the North Vietnamese budged."[225] During a tea break, a dramatic breakthrough appeared. Once again, Secretary Vance declared that the inclusion of representatives of the South Vietnamese government was utterly indispensable. Le Duc Tho then said, "If you want to discuss this matter further we are prepared to do so." Noting that the North "Vietnamese were prepared to discuss this subject in a private meeting."[226] On October 11, 1968, United States and DRV representatives met specifically to discuss the issue of Saigon's inclusion. At this meeting, DRV delegates asked, "If North Vietnam accepted the participation of the Saigon government would the president immediately stop the bombing?" Harriman at that point said he would consult with Washington.[227] At the conclusion of their formal talks, "over tea, Le

---

[220] Gaiduk, 178. See also DOS, section 26.
[221] DOS, section 34.
[222] Ibid., sections 24 and 26.
[223] Ibid., section 47.
[224] Gaiduk, 179. See also DOS section 47.
[225] Ibid.
[226] DOS, section 54.
[227] Ibid., section 58.

Duc Tho and Xuan Thuy (the chief North Vietnamese negotiators) both said that they believed that rapid progress could be made if we were really determined to move toward peace."[228]

On October 12, 1968, Oberemko, during a discussion with Harriman, began by stating that unofficially, "I have good reason to believe that if the US stops unconditionally and completely the bombardments and other acts of war against the DRV, the delegation of North Vietnam will agree to the participation of the representatives of the Saigon government in the talks on the problem of political settlement in Vietnam." He hoped that what he just said "would help move the talks off dead center and that this view was shared by the North Vietnamese." He added, "we consider now is the right time to act. The situation is most favorable right now and this opportunity should not be lost" and "that if positive action was not taken now it would be a major setback for those who want peace and that it would be a very long time before peace can be reached."[229] Oberemko then warned against any new conditions. Finally, he stated, I can tell you "on good authority that if the question of the unconditional and complete cessation of bombardments and all acts of war against North Vietnam is resolved positively and promptly, the delegation of the DRV is ready to discuss seriously and in good faith other questions relating to the political settlement in Vietnam." [230]

Oberemko's statements on good authority were insufficient for Johnson. Instead, he wanted the Soviet official position with direct assurance from Moscow that Oberemko was not simply repeating a message, but rather acting upon instructions. On October 13, 1968, Dobrynin removed all doubt when he confirmed "our charge d'affairs (Oberemko) acted in accordance with the Soviet government's instructions." Indeed, he added, "the new display of goodwill on part of the DRV, of which we are speaking now, is creating, in a profound conviction, a real possibility of speedy progress in this direction."[231]

Finally, the intransigent North Vietnamese relented on an issue of significance. Recognizing the momentous nature of Hanoi's concession, President Johnson proclaimed, "It is the universal judgment of our diplomatic and military authorities that North Vietnam's acceptance of GVN participation is a major event--potentially setting the stage for an honorable settlement of the war."[232] The NVN's agreement to meet with Saigon did not come without cost or criticism. On October 17, 1968, Chen Yi, Vice Premier of the People's Republic of China,

---

[228] Ibid.

[229] Ibid., 60.

[230] Ibid.

[231] Gaiduk, 180.

[232] DOS, section 140.

strongly chastised Le Duc Tho, accusing him of having lost the initiative in the negotiations and concluding, "You lost to them once more." Yi declared, "with your acceptance of the quadripartite negotiations, you've handed a puppet government legal recognition, thus eliminating the National Liberation Front's status as the unique legal representative of the people in the South." [233]

A QUESTION OF TIMING

Although the sides reached understandings on major factors, through a combination of "Facts of Life" appreciation and the application of definitions, an agreement had not yet been reached. For the next two weeks, the United States and North Vietnam would engage in intense, if not acrimonious, debate on the issues of timing and composition. It was the United States' understanding that once it halted the bombing, this would trigger an immediate meeting between the US, Hanoi, the NLF and Saigon. Hanoi, however, either through misinterpretation or deliberately obstinate behavior, indicated that it was their understanding that the talks would take place one week after the halt. This delay simply would not do because Johnson could not explain for one week why he had halted the bombing because the North Vietnamese part of the bargain would only become evident through their actions or inactions and the presence of Saigon at the table. Johnson believed that one week was too long a period to wait for these revelations and during that delay, he risked losing the support of the American public. One should note that, a delay of one week would take the initiation of negotiations past the presidential election date.

The North Vietnamese finally agreed to a three-day period between stoppage and negotiations. On October 27, 1968, LBJ called a meeting of his advisors. Everyone in the room agreed that the United States achieved its objectives. Still unsure that the security of US forces was not endangered by a bombing halt, Johnson declared, "Before he would agree to anything he needed another discussion with General Abrams." The Abrams conference provided Johnson with the assurance he needed when the General opined, if he were president, he would have "no reservations about doing it, even though I know it is stepping into

---

[233] Cold War, International History Project, Virtual Archive, "Discussion Between Zhou Enlai and Chen Yi, October 17 1968,"
http://www.wilsoncenter.org/index.cfm?topic_id=1409&fuseaction=va2.document&identifier=5034CD21-96B6-175C-9DAF353B89FA26B2&sort=Collection&item=The%20Vietnam%20(Indochina)%20War(s). (accessed November 27, 2007)

a cesspool of comments. It is the proper thing to do."[234] Analyzing why the president did not share the optimism of the group, Clifford concluded that Johnson was still concerned that there would be criticism that he was acting to help Humphrey. To lessen the president's concern, Clifford argued to him "it would be irresponsible to miss an opportunity for negotiations that might be lost after the election."[235]

HOW DO WE PLAY SO EVERYONE CAN GET ALONG

Another issue remaining concerned the status of the parties appearing at this quadripartite meeting. Would they be independent political entities recognized by the others or have some other status? Eventually, again with the help of the Soviet Union, the United States and Hanoi agreed to a "your side our side" formula. Under this plan, the NLF would be on Hanoi's side and Saigon would be on the United States side of the table. How each side viewed the political sovereignty of its partner was then up to them, but all would sit and have voice at the table.[236] The United States negotiators hoped that this formula would shake out into a workable dynamic once the process began. However, in an environment where the definition of a word was paramount, this open definitional strategy was rife with problems. Saigon, always fearful of losing status as the "true" representative of the South Vietnamese people would be very sensitive to any status either implied or expressly granted to the NLF.

On October 29, at 2:00 a.m., President Johnson called a meeting of all the important representatives of the administration. It was now decision time. The President first provided a comprehensive summary of events taking place to date. He summarized the understanding on the parties and the fact that "the Soviet Union, which is played part in this negotiation, knows the circumstances intimately." He then concluded:

> It is the universal judgment of our diplomatic and military authorities that North Vietnam's acceptance of GVN participation is a major event - - potentially setting the stage for honorable settlement of the war. Many experts felt Hanoi would never do this. Until now Hanoi and also repeated they would never talk to the Thiệu government... the agreement at which we have arrived is, then, precisely the one which ... we've been

---

[234] Clifford, 585-86.
[235] Clifford, 579.
[236] DOS, section 21.

seeking in recent months. We've given away nothing to reach this agreement. It is wholly consistent with my public statements.[237]

The president, despite all his suspicions, his constant need for reassurances and wariness due to past disappointments, was ready to announce to the citizens of the United States, that on October 31, 1968 he would halt the bombing and on November 2, 1968, negotiators from Hanoi, the NLF, the US and Saigon would meet to discuss substantive issues aimed at ending the war. Yet, there were still dark clouds on the horizon. Agreements were in place between United States, Hanoi and the Soviets, but less certain was Saigon's stand. Did they share the US's interest in peace and exactly how would they react to the presence of the NLF at the table? This cloud, although in the forecast at least at that point, was judged reasonably stable. However, there were other clouds, unknown and unsuspected, organizing a storm designed to rain on Johnson's peace parade.

CLOSING ARGUMENT

We now approach the first hurdle and we initiate our leap in an attempt to clear it, but first we must employ the stop action camera before we calculate the possibilities of success. Let us review the evidence. There can be no question that there was a shift of influence upon North Vietnam from China to the Soviet Union. There is also no question that the Chinese, at least until October 1968, strongly advocated a no negotiations and protracted war stance. The Soviets, however, evolved from initial indifference to assuming an active role as broker in the peace process. However, the philosophy of the supply partner did not guarantee the position of the always-independent nationalist North Vietnamese. We discovered that Hanoi suffered significant military losses during Tet and that the bombing campaign effectively destroyed their economy. According to General Abrams:

> There has been a steady deterioration in Hanoi's position in South Vietnam ever since the military defeats which overtook their general offensive at Tet and again in May/June. The August/Sept offensive did not even get off the ground and was the weakest of all three attacks. After ten months of enormous effort, Hanoi and the NLF have nothing to show for the loss of over 150,000 killed, plus the thousand killed by B-

---

[237] Ibid., section 140.

52 and other air attacks, or who died of wounds or disease, or were captured, or defected, or were eliminated by arrest.[238]

Finally, to the surprise of the DRV, Saigon's government and its army were operating far more efficiently than expected. We also know, that despite serious losses, the DRV maintained the ability to continue to wage war due to the fact they received significant supplies from the Soviets and the Chinese. However, that supply source was not endless and did not come without conditions, which became more relevant as Hanoi's prosecution of the war rendered it less self-sufficient and more dependent.

Shifting from the military to the political, there is no question that Hanoi's position changed from initial intransigence to a position of bargaining and compromise in regards to significant factors. Still, that in and of itself does not prove sincerity. It would be helpful at this stage, before we unfreeze the camera's lens pointed at the race, that we turn to examine the role of the United States presidential election. Was peace the factor that motivated the Soviets and the North Vietnamese towards the bargaining table or were their actions nothing more than a calculated attempt to influence the outcome of the American election?

The Soviets wanted to complete peace efforts before the election, claims Gaiduk, because they were apprehensive regarding Nixon. "In Moscow's view, Nixon was too unpredictable and reactionary to be a reliable partner in settling the conflict in South East Asia." He further explained, "The Soviets preferred to reach an agreement between Washington and Hanoi before the presidential elections as a result, Moscow was involved at every stage of resolving the problems that threaten to delay and even to disrupt a settlement."[239] At the same time, UN Soviet diplomat, Mikhail Kosharyan expressed fear that Nixon "would expand the influence of the military industrial complex in America and heighten international tensions. By contrast, he said the Soviets believed that Johnson wanted rapprochement and peace."[240] Leaving no question as to their preference, Moscow's Ambassador Dobrynin later wrote that he received instructions to help Humphrey win the 1968 election, "Moscow believed that as far as its relations with Washington were concerned, Humphrey would make the best president at

[238]DOS, "paragraph 61. Telegram From the Embassy in Vietnam to the Department of State," http://2001-2009.state.gov/r/pa/ho/frus/johnsonlb/vii/21592.htm. (accessed December 22, 2014)
[239] Gaiduk, 180.
[240] Dallek, *Nixon and Kissinger: Partners in Power*, 582.

that time."[241] Historian Larry Berman alleged that the Soviets attempted to back "their" candidate by attempting to give financial aid to the Humphrey campaign; however, Humphrey declined their help.[242]

The North Vietnamese view of the American presidential election offered greater complexity. After analyzing both the Republican and Democratic platforms, "under a microscope," Hanoi concluded that the Republican plank was general and did not contain any concrete suggestions on ending the war, but they remarked "the North Vietnamese know who (Republicans) are and how they are, obviously implying disapproval." When attention turned to the Democratic platform, Hanoi believed that two elements were dangerous. The first was "the principle of reciprocity," and the second was the US continued support of the South Vietnam regime.[243] It was the generally accepted principle of the Johnson administration that Hanoi had "fear of the Nixon victory and what that may portend." [244] According to David Danielson, Hanoi understood Nixon's character. During a tea break, one of the North Vietnamese negotiators, when referring to Nixon, candidly informed Danielson "he would not want to buy a used car from that man."[245] With the possibility of an anti-Communist, untrustworthy, erratic president, would the North Vietnamese manufacture false peace proposals designed to manipulate the election in Humphrey's favor, understanding that any progress towards peace during the Johnson administration would benefit his campaign?

It is obvious that the possibility of the Nixon presidency did not enamor the Soviets or the North Vietnamese, but does their preference provide the motivation to create a false peace scenario? Regarding the Soviets, despite their concerns in the American election, their motivation for the peace arose from a combination of apprehension with China and a quest for their own power. Turning towards the North Vietnamese, upon initial examination, it might appear that manipulating the election may have been the source of their new flexibility. When one examines the situation closely, this rationale weakens. If the North Vietnamese wanted to

---

[241] Larry Berman, *No Peace, No Honor: Nixon, Kissinger, and Betrayal In Vietnam* (New York, NY: Touchstone Books, 2001), 28
[242] Ibid.
[243] DOS, section 28.
[244] Ibid., section 68.
[245]Davidson, interview. Further, "Would you buy a used car from this man?" was the tagline of a poster that featured a scowling Richard Nixon which was distributed by the Democratic Party before the 1960 US presidential elections. The implication was that Nixon was as trustworthy as a used car salesman, in other words, not at all. See Gary North, "Would You Buy a Used Deficit From This Man," http://www.lewrockwell.com/north/north348.html (accessed November 27, 2007)

forestall a Nixon presidency, earlier agreements in the peace process would have certainly had greater efficacy in strengthening the Humphrey campaign. Even after agreeing to the major factors, the deal almost fell apart on the issues of time and composition. If the North Vietnamese were only showboating for the American election, those disagreements, and the resulting delays, would not have transpired. Logically, to prevent a Nixon election, they would have to strengthen Humphrey, and to strengthen Humphrey, agreements with the Johnson administration needed to be made in sufficient time to benefit "their" candidate. The fact that Hanoi needed to be strong-armed by the Soviets to come to the table before the election weighs heavily against the claim of election manipulation as a primary motivation.

Johnson had his own take on the matter. He thought the North Vietnamese would stall because they believed they would get a better deal with a Humphrey-led administration pursuant to the stance articulated in his Salt Lake speech.[246] This position makes little sense because if Hanoi did not cooperate with Johnson, Humphrey (who was trailing in the polls) could not benefit by momentum generated by the peace overtures and would end up losing the election. Simple logic demands that to help Humphrey, the North Vietnamese would have to have cooperated with Johnson earlier. In summary, although the North Vietnamese might have preferred a Humphrey presidency, it is reasonable to conclude that this preference did not significantly influence the question of whether their efforts in the peace process were sincere.

DOES HE MAKE IT?!

Return to live-action, our runner raises his lead foot, it approaches the hurdle, does he clear? In civil law, the attorney bringing the case on behalf of the plaintiff has the burden of proving their case beyond a "preponderance of the evidence." The judge, in an attempt to explain the burden, often employs the following example to aid the jury in making that determination. He instructs the jurors to assume a two-sided scale, on each side, there is the exact same weight of sand and the scale is in equipoise. If only one grain of sand is added to the plaintiff's side of the scale and that is sufficient to tilt the balance, ever so slightly, then the plaintiff has met its burden and wins its case. Like any juror in any civil case, you must respond by way of a jury verdict sheet, which is provided in Appendix V. A judge will also point out that it is not the amount of evidence that creates its weight, rather it is the quality. If you determine the argument for the sincerity of

---

[246] DOS, section 51.

the parties towards the peace process in October and November of 1968, weighs more, even if ever so slightly than the evidence in favor of insincerity, you vote YES to question #1 on the verdict sheet and the race moves on. If not, read ahead anyway, you may change your mind.

CHAPTER 2

The Conspiracy

As we approach the second hurdle in our analysis, (was there a conspiracy and if so what was its nature?), I am reminded of the movie "Clue." In 1985, Director Jon Landis, of *Animal House* fame, released a film based on the board game. It received less than glowing reviews, but it possessed an interesting twist. The conceit of the film consisted of presenting identical evidence supporting three separate endings. Was it Colonel Mustard, the Butler or Miss Scarlet who murdered the other guests? The evidence in the present matter, like "Clue," can also support multiple deductions, but as in every good detective story, it is up to the reader, based upon that evidence to derive the most logical and reasonable conclusion. To prevent confusion, I will spoil some of the plot and divulge four possibilities. 1) Anna Chennault, motivated by her strong anticommunist beliefs, her fear of tumbling dominos and haunted by the fall of China and personal demons, acted on her own to convince South Vietnamese President Thiệu to avoid the peace conference. 2) Using Chennault as his main conduit, Nixon convinced Thiệu to change his mind and not attend the conferences. This alteration in course was due to Nixon's assurances that his Presidency, as opposed to a Humphrey victory, would be in Saigon's greater interests. The *quid pro quo* for these promises was the South Vietnamese not attending the Paris peace conferences.[1] 3) Thiệu never intended to attend the conference and Nixon's alleged acts were irrelevant. 4) Nixon directly conspired with Thiệu to create, from the beginning, a charade of cooperation with the purpose of ultimately humiliating and defeating Humphrey. With these scenarios in mind, we turn to the evidence.

---

[1] This is a legal term of art that represents an equal exchange or substitution. See Yahoo Dictionary, http://education.yahoo.com/reference/dictionary/entry/quid%20pro%20quo (accessed November 27, 2007)

NIXON, OR THOSE WHO REPEAT THE ACTS OF THEIR PAST ARE DOOMED TO CREATE HISTORY

The credibility of the major players of any alleged conspiracy is paramount and, of course, our analysis must start with the alleged chief conspirator, Richard Nixon. His reputation for truth, how he acted in the past, and the nature of his character are essential elements for study. Who indeed was Richard Millhouse Nixon? The journey of discovery begins in 1946, when Nixon, then a rookie Republican politician, was engaged in a battle to defeat Democratic incumbent Jerry Voorhis for California's 12th Congressional District seat. The Congressman, anxious to show up this newcomer, agreed to Nixon's request for a debate. He soon learned that he made a very serious mistake. On the night of the debate, Nixon placed "ringers" in the audience who circulated numerous flyers claiming that Voorhis was a socialist who readily accepted the endorsement of a Communist organization. The fact that Nixon knew that this flyer deliberately misrepresented the truth, or in less delicate words presented lies, did not seem to trouble the candidate During the debate, when Voorhis was asked about this so-called endorsement, a well-rehearsed Nixon dramatically produced the bogus document aggressively waving it at the visibly shaken Voorhis. Nixon's carefully placed spectators took this opportunity to rain jeers upon the Democratic candidate, loudly branding him a communist. It was obvious to all present that Nixon won the debate. When an old friend, wise to the subterfuge, asked Nixon afterwards why he resorted to such questionable tactics, he replied both casually and ebulliently, "sometimes you have to do this to be a candidate. I'm going to win."[2] Nixon's tactics were not the only suspect part of his campaign. Despite his pretension of recording every contribution to his war chest, most of his lavish 1946 financing was never officially acknowledged. "Richard Nixon's, furtive, mincing attitude toward political money, the gradual atrophy of ethics that ended so painfully 30 years later, began in the first campaign."[3] Nixon won that election.

In 1950, after only four years of congressional office, Nixon turned his eye towards the California Senatorial race. His democratic opposition was Helen Gahagan Douglas. Douglas, the wife of famous movie star Melvin Douglas and a star in her own right, was in for the campaign of her life. Having successfully played the communist card against Voorhis, Nixon was sure to use it again against Douglas. Deliberately misrepresenting her voting record, Nixon printed up 500,000 flyers, printed on pink paper claiming that Douglas supported

---

[2] Roger Morris, *Richard Milhous Nixon: the Rise of an American Politician* (New York, NY: Henry Holt & Co. 1990), 320.
[3] Ibid., 309.

communist causes. The choice of pink paper was a clever connection to his smear that Douglas was a communist or "pinko" or the "Pink Lady."[4] Hedging his bets, Nixon looked the other way when his campaign supporters fanned the flame of anti-Semitism by seizing on the fact that Douglas's husband was Jewish. Nixon supporter Gerald Smith opened a Republican rally by exclaiming: "Help Richard Nixon get rid of the Jew Communists!"[5] At another rally, Smith decried, "Do not send to the Senate the wife of a Jew!" [6] When called upon the carpet for these vile remarks, Nixon of course, distanced himself from them. After all, how could he be responsible for controlling the remarks of others? At first blush, this would make sense, however, one must understand the Nixon technique. Nixon was a master of having others float ideas that would appear contemptible or calculated if coming from his lips. When confronted with these statements, he would make sure to repeat them in full, just in case anyone missed them the first time, and then deny responsibility for them thereby getting across his view and appearing to have clean hands.

Stephen Ambrose provided an excellent example of the "Nixon technique" applicable to the matter at hand. Close to the 1968 election, one of Nixon's closest aides, Governor Robert Finch, declared to the press "President Johnson timed the Vietnam bombing pause to help Vice President Humphrey in Tuesday's election." When Nixon was confronted with this remark on NBC's "Meet the Press," he responded "I know, for example one of my aides who -- so-called aide [he even denies the obvious connection!]--who made this statement is Lt. Governor Robert Finch. He completely disagrees with my appraisal of this. His appraisal of the situation around the country is that many people believe that the bombing pause was politically motivated and timed to affect the election. I don't agree with him, but he is a man in his own right and he has made the statement."[7] One cannot avoid standing back and being amazed at the utter chutzpah of Nixon's remarks.[8] He first pushed himself away from Finch calling him a "so-called aide" then he

---

[4] Morris, 582. Note, the word pinko was coined in 1926 by *Time* magazine as a variant on the noun and adjective pink, which had been used along with *parlor pink* since the beginning of the 20th century to refer to those of leftish sympathies, usually with an implication of effeteness. See Joseph J. Firebaugh, "The Vocabulary of 'Time' Magazine," *American Speech*, 15, 3, (October, 1940)

[5] Morris, 550.

[6] Morris, 599.

[7] Ambrose, *Nixon: The Triumph of Politician 1962 – 1972*, 213.

[8] Chutzpah is a Yiddish word commonly defined as follows a man who murders his parents and throws himself upon the mercy of the court because he is now an orphan has chutzpah. See Urban Dictionary, http://www.urbandictionary.com/define.php?term=chutzpah (accessed November 26, 2007)

repeated the political allegation, just in case anybody missed it, then underscored it by claiming it's going around the country and then disagreed with it keeping his dirty hands clean. Similarly, Smith's anti-Semitic tirades have the stain of the "Nixon technique" all over them.

Another example of the Nixon "technique" occurred during the race for California Senate at a Democratic campaign rally at the University of Southern California, when the audience physically assaulted Douglas by spraying her with beverages and pelting her with ice. Embarrassed, the University publicly apologized to her. Nixon, of course, denied responsibility for the actions of his supporters and rejected the notion that he somehow had control over that event. Meanwhile, his campaign headquarters "seemed to know of the event... almost instantly."[9] In the days before cell phones, social media and the internet, it is rather shocking that headquarters would have such immediate information unless of course they knew about it beforehand. Murray Chotimer, Nixon's campaign manager, described Nixon as "a perfectionist general who demanded absolute precision and carefully planned coordination of every move... Nixon wanted to do everything himself." Tom Dixon, a radio announcer hired by the Nixon campaign to do campaign commercials, commented, "if someone threw paint on Helen Douglas, he knew about it." [10] Nixon again had others do his dirty work for him while denying his involvement thereafter. We will see herein how the "technique" possibly played a major role in the Chennault-Nixon conspiracy when Nixon denied involvement and instead blamed the affair on another, Anna Chennault. In any event, in a campaign described by the Los Angeles Daily News as the "dirtiest in state history," Nixon was elected senator of California.[11]

Although occurring subsequent to the events subject to this analysis, the criminal conspiracies, litany of dirty tricks, lies, law breaking and immoral acts conducted by the Committee to Reelect the President (CREEP) during Nixon's 1972 re-election bid pursuant to his instructions are further proof of his character or actual lack thereof. These acts are well chronicled by authors Bob Woodward and Carl Bernstein in their works *All the President's Men* and *The Final Days* and need no repeating here, but must be part of the equation when evaluating Nixon's credibility [12] Author Joan Hoff well described the Nixon's character during his election campaigns,

---

[9] Morris, 562.
[10] Ibid.
[11] Morris, 615.
[12] Bob Woodward and Carl Bernstein, *All the Presidents Men* (New York, NY: Simon & Schuster, 1974) and Bob Woodward and Carl Bernstein, *The Final Days* (New York, NY: Simon & Schuster, 1994

> I am not saying, as many others have that Richard Nixon was unprincipled. Assorted presidents have been unprincipled, that is, lacking positive moral scruples as defined by society at the time. The difference with Nixon... is that he was aprincipled. An unprincipled person is one who consciously lacks moral scruples and is presumably aware that standards are being violated. In contrast, the aprincipled person seldom reforms his behavior or expresses remorse for transgressions against societal norms because there is no conscious admission of wrongdoing.[13]

This aprincipled man, willing to do almost anything to win election, this man who eventually, upon the brink of an unprecedented impeachment, would resign in disgrace from the office of the presidency, was the person who would meet with Anna Chennault in 1968 and allegedly hatch a conspiracy. Who, however, was Anna Chennault?

ANNA CHENNAULT, THE CHINESE WILLIE LOMAN: ATTENTION MUST BE PAID!

On July 26, 2007, Chennault agreed to meet with my daughter Jessica, serving as note taker, and myself at her Georgetown office in Washington D.C. The meeting was surprisingly easy to set up and her staff was extremely accommodating. When we arrived at her beautiful brick townhouse with its golden plaque designating it as the "Chennault Foundation," we were immediately ushered into a conference room to await the appearance of the lady. Sweet incense filled the air. Ornate pieces of Asian art decorated the shelves lining the walls of the reception area. The conference room, dominated by a huge portrait of Mrs. Chennault, also featured, in the corner, a bronze statue of the Madame. Numerous pictures of Chennault either holding hands with or being hugged by some of history's greatest leaders filled the room. Framed letters from Presidents Reagan, Ford, and Nixon either congratulating or thanking her for various deeds, adorned the walls. Exotic gifts, encased in glass displays, housed tributes given to her by world leaders. There was no question that this conference room portrayed a message to all of its visitors; this was a substantial woman and she damn well wanted you to know that.

Anna Chennault, child of Chen Ying-Yung and Isabelle Liao, was born on June 23, 1925 in Beijing, China, into a family of upper middle-class merchants,

---

[13] Joan Hoff, *Nixon Reconsidered*, (New York, NY: Basic Books 1994), 3.

scholars and diplomats. [14] She began her autobiography by immediately confessing that because she was born female, she disappointed her family "who were counting heavily on a boy." [15] Anna, even at a young age, was aware of a mistreatment and the powerlessness of Chinese women. She admired Li Ma, her wet nurse, because as a statement against the suppression of her sex, she had discarded the grotesque symbol and practice of feet binding. [16] Anna describes, "but the humiliation of centuries dies hard, and Li Ma's feet may as well have been bound for the shame instilled in her." [17] Her sense of female worthlessness in her birth country was also illustrated by a story she tells about a situation at a train depot when Chennault and her family, displaced due to the war between China and Japan, traveled across China to seek refuge. Suddenly, panic ensued as everybody, at the same time, attempted get onboard a train to escape an impending conflict. Japanese guards, on the train, responded to the melee by knocking down bodies. In the middle of this chaos, a middle-aged man succeeded in getting on the train with only his eight-year-old son. When asked if others came with him, the father answered, "eleven, but it does not matter, this is my eldest son, and today our family has been blessed." Anna commented to herself: "never a thought of the mother or wife or daughter if a man is in danger. What are women, still animals?" [18]

Chennault drove home her point about the second-class nature of being a woman in China by relating another anecdote from the same journey. Here, a young woman fell out of the train and her mother frantically yelled for the train to stop. "Don't cry, her husband consoled her, if she's alive, someone will find her and take her for slave girl. At least it was not one of our sons." [19] Chennault, derided for her lack of value by her family and her culture, left no question in her autobiography that this second-class gender status deeply affected her. Chennault

---

[14] Forslund, 1.

[15] Chennault, 3.

[16] "Great pain has been suffered for centuries for women to achieve perceived beauty. Probably the most detrimental act was one that approximately one billion women in China have performed for nearly one thousand years. This act, foot binding, was an attempt to stop the growth of the feet... Foot binding kept women weak, out of power, and dominated by her husband. When women bound their feet, men could dominate more easily and not worry about women taking their power. The process took place so early, the young girl had no choice but to follow her family's order and have her feet bound." Candace Hutchins. "Chinese Foot Binding," http://www.ccds.charlotte.nc.us/History/China/04/hutchins/hutchins.htm (accessed November 30, 2007)

[17] Ibid., 14.

[18] Ibid., 80.

[19] Ibid.

dedicated herself to the proposition "that she would defy the female traditions of the country's past" and would "not allow gender to stand in her way."[20]

It was also abundantly plain that, throughout her life, Chennault suffered from "daddy" issues, which significantly influenced her choices. While still a schoolchild, her mother became very ill requiring a lengthy hospitalization. Anna visited her every afternoon, staying with her until dusk. Because her father was out of the country on business, the burden of keeping her family together and caring for her mother fell on her. She bitterly lamented, "Why was he off in some remote country instead of at mother's bedside?" [21] Despite her mother's continued painful deterioration, her father remained absent. As her mother lay dying, she asked her child to take her place in the family. When her mother died, a very young Anna was left as head of the household with a monthly budget of $300, requiring her to cut corners and learn to do without. By the following year, the financial strains were so great that she could not manage the household and go to school. Yet, her father remained overseas. [22] After the war, by letter, he instructed his daughters to leave China and join him in the America. Although her departure was arranged, Anna decided not to go:

> I was not about to leave China. I still remembered father abandoning us during the war and leaving mother to die alone. And I did not like the threat that had accompanied the message. If I didn't leave for the United States, he would stop sending me money and I would have to fend for myself. It was a kind of challenge I felt compelled to take on. I had been through devastating times and was proud of having survived. I felt confident that I could make it on my own.[23]

Her father's rejection was not without ramifications. As a young teenager, Anna attended Lingnan University in China. Her favorite teacher was Professor Wu. He was 40 years old, almost 25 years older. Chennault enjoyed the fact that her fellow students believed that the professor favored her. "It pleased me secretly to think this might be true, that this scholarly man…, that this awesome man might secretly be in love with me, a girl in her teens. To please him, I worked hard," confided Chennault.[24] This was not an isolated incident. In 1947, 22-year-old Anna Chen agreed to marry 52-year-old General Claire Chennault. Again, she

---

[20] Forslund, 17.
[21] Chennault, 36.
[22] Ibid., 38.
[23] Ibid., 85.
[24] Ibid., 72.

was attracted to an older powerful man. The attraction between Chennault and the General, finds Forslund, "is not hard to understand when one considers their personalities, needs, and goals. Possibly she saw him as a strong protective father figure."[25] Although Chennault initially disliked Richard Nixon, another powerful older man, she eventually found him "compelling" and was "drawn" to working for him. It is reasonable to conclude that her desire to impress Nixon, to achieve goals, which she perceived as in his best interest, may be a factor that would argue on the side of her acting on her own when she spoke to President Thiệu.

In addition to motivations stemming from her childhood, Chennault, driven by her personal and political revulsion to communism, perceived the United States' failure to support Chiang Kai-shek as the major factor contributing to the communist triumph in China.[26] Her anti-communist orientation rooted in her childhood. Throughout her autobiography, she associated a disliked family matriarch with her politics. She described her grand aunt as an eccentric old woman who lacked humanity, forcing others to kowtow to her. This aunt did "her best to look ugly and frumpish and had a face of ice and iron." Referring to her Aunt's politics, Anna commented: "Everything that detracted from the cold harsh purpose of communism, as she saw it, was a felony."[27] In a sarcastic tone, she portrayed her grand aunt as someone who, supposedly dedicated to equality and injustice, was not above arranging her own son's marriage, handpicking the woman he should marry, and then "mistreating her daughter-in-law to such a degree that the girl kept trying to run away from home."[28] Here Chennault links her personal dislike of her great aunt with communism, describing how the Aunt denounced the custom of gift giving as a useless form of capitalism. "We never could figure out what capitalism was; only that it provided an excuse for grandaunt Liao to withhold the presents to which we felt entitled."[29]

Chennault's quest to fight communism was also a product of the relationship with her husband, her hero, and China's hero, General Claire Chennault. In 1941, Claire L. Chennault, was a retired captain from United States Army Air Corps.

---

[25] Forslund, 22.

[26] Post WWII, the US supported Chinese Nationalist Party Leader Chiang Kai-shek against Mao ZeDong's communist forces who fought a civil war for the control of China, which ended in victory for the communists. Chiang Kai-shek forces were driven to exile in Taiwan. See Jay Taylor, *The Generalissimo: Chiang Kai-shek and the Struggle for Modern China* (New York, NY: Belknap Press, 2011) for an in-depth analysis.

[27] Chennault, 34.

[28] Ibid.

[29] Ibid.

Upon the urging of Chiang Kai-shek, he organized he led a secret Air Force, which fought against the Japanese invasion of China before World War II. Formed in 1941, this Air Force, formally known as the American Volunteer Group (AVG), was later nicknamed the "Flying Tigers" due to the famous signature emblem on their planes. The Flying Tigers consisted of United States Army Air Forces (USAAF), United States Navy (USN), and United States Marine Corps (USMC) pilots and crew, recruited under a secret sanction, authorized by President Roosevelt prior to World War II.[30] At a time of very serious suffering, the Chinese greatly appreciated the General's efforts and he quickly became a national hero. After World War II, Chennault continued his association with Chiang Kai-shek, then leader of the faction known as the Nationalists, arguing that the United States should offer support sufficient to facilitate a total Nationalist victory against the Mao-led Communists. The United States, despite providing some assistance for the Nationalist movement, did not fully accept the Chennault position. In Washington, according to Anna, "The popular concept of Chinese communism was that it was not 'real' communism but a synthetic product considerably less harmful than the original."[31] When General George Marshall was sent to Chung King with the mission to work out a coalition between the communists and nationalists, General Chennault responded: "Crazy, just crazy, they must be crazy in Washington to think it can work."[32] Chennault contends he could not understand America's official blind spot over the futility of a coalition between communists and nationalists. He believed that "the communists' ploy is really very simple. Under strength they back down; sensing weakness they take advantage."[33] Despite their certainty in their position's righteousness, the Chennault mission to save China from communism failed.

In May, of 1949 the General Chennault, in a last-ditch effort to get more support, warned the Congress of a potential domino effect resulting from the fall of China to the Chinese Communist Party (CCP). He cautioned, "If we do not act soon, all China will be lost. The Chinese Communist government will be on the

---

[30] Daniel Ford , *Flying Tigers: Claire Chennault and His American Volunteers, 1941-1942* (Washington, D.C.: Smithsonian Books, 2007). See also "The Flying Tigers-American Volunteer Group - Chinese Air Force: A Brief History with Recollections and Comments by General Claire Lee Chennault," http://www.flyingtigersavg.com/tiger1.htm. (accessed November 26, 2007)
[31] Chennault, 132.
[32] Ibid., 133.
[33] Ibid., 134.

borders of Indochina, Siam, and Burma."[34] Initially assuming the role as the dutiful wife, Anna "watched her husband's tireless quest to rouse the American public from its seemingly calm acceptance of China coming under Communist control." Upon the death of her husband in 1958, she soon would lead the cause.[35] Having lost the battle over China, Anna Chennault and similar believers formed what came to be known as the "China Lobby" which was dedicated to the goal that other Asian countries would not fall under the specter of communism. Soon Anna became more active in her husband's public anti-Communist campaign. At a Dallas public affairs luncheon club in May of 1955, she stated "We have lost enough territory [to communism] already in Asia and the Far East, and I do not think that we can afford [to lose] anymore territory, if we want to remain free."[36] Chennault was particularly adamant against establishing any coalition with the communists. Based upon her personal experience in China, "Chennault was undoubtedly sincere in opposing serious peace negotiations with Hanoi, fearing that, whatever their original intentions, the Americans would end up abandoning the Thiệu regime, as she believed they had done shamefully in China."[37]

Mostly owing to her being a widow of the great General Chennault and her prior relationship with Chiang Kai-shek, Anna Chennault established powerful political contacts in Southeast Asia. It was obvious she relished her new position in Washington. It was well known in the capitol that "she love[ed] being the mystery woman, and the 'Dragon Lady.'"[38] Her apartment in Washington, DC became, according to Chennault, "a popular watering hole for ranking Republicans," where Anna claimed major policies and strategies of the American government were hatched.[39] In a comprehensive, if not exactly complementary analysis, the *Washingtonian* magazine featured Anna Chennault in a 1969

---

[34] Forslund, 32. See also statement of Major General Claire Chennault, United States Army (retired), Congressional record, 81st Congress, first session, volume 95. Part 4, May 3, 1949, 5480 -82.

[35] Ibid., 34.

[36] Forslund, 35.

[37] Bundy, 37.

[38] "The Three Faces of Anna Chennault" (*The Washingtonian,* September 1969). Article is archived within Lyndon Baines Johnson Library and Museum, Folder: "Anna Chennault: South Vietnam and U.S. Policies"- Reference Files (the X-envelope), paragraph 53. The term "Dragon Lady" is a slang reference to Madame Ngô Đình Nhu, sister in- law to Ngo Diem the first President of South Vietnam from 1955–1963, who was a bachelor. She was known to control her brother in law, and hence, control Vietnam. The term thereafter was used to describe Asian women who are in position of power over men. "Dragon Ladies" are aggressive, intimidating, calculating, and high achieving. Nevertheless, generally, they are also intelligent and beautiful. See Robert Trumbull, "First Lady of Vietnam" *The New York Times,* November 18, 1962.

[39] Chennault, 167.

personality profile. The following quotes are instructive: "She has money, charm, good looks, and friends in high places. But, like her beauty, which is a combination of natural resources and skillful development, Anna's assets have been enhanced by Anna."[40] Commenting further on her credibility, the article singled out a book, authored by Chennault entitled "*A Thousand Springs*." Within she described her relationship with the General as a lush love story but "(t)here are, however, variations on the story which rather dim the luster of the love theme. In one, Anna is featured not as an innocent young reporter, but as an employee of Chinese intelligence in charge of keeping an eye on the general. In another, Anna's attraction to Chennault is attributed less to passion than to the appeal of his exalted status in Asia."[41] When referencing the romantic dialogue attributed to the General in love scenes with his young wife, the magazine quoted an old friend of the Chennault's who exclaimed: "he [the General] would never have talked that way... after I finished the book I went upstairs and threw up."[42] The article sums up, "Skeptics around town, however, insist that Anna sometimes allows people to carry away the impression that she is far more of an international operator than, in truth, she is." [43]

ANNA CHENNAULT: DRIVEN PATRIOT, CONSPIRATOR, DRAGON LADY?

On July 12, 1968, Anna Chennault, widow of famous World War II General Claire Chennault, renowned Washington lobbyist in her own right and chairperson of The Women for Nixon National Advisory committee, arrived for a meeting with Republican presidential candidate at his apartment in New York City.[44] The woman Richard Nixon met at his apartment that day, as described above had been told since birth that she was worthless and had as a result, an overwhelming desire to prove that assumption wrong. Rejected by her father, she

---

[40] Lyndon Baines Johnson Library, "the X-Envelope" paragraph 53.
[41] Ibid.
[42] Ibid.
[43] Ibid.
[44] There is some dispute as to who contacted whom to arrange the meeting. According to William Safire, Chennault wrote to Nixon on Flying Tiger Airline stationary about her friendship with Ambassador Bui Diem. She called him her close friend and revealed that he travels between Saigon, Washington and Paris every month. She told Nixon "I'd like very much to suggest you meet him and talk with him if arrangements can be made, I myself, will be leaving for South East Asia around July 15 and I can bring him to you either before July 15 or after the convention" William Safire, *Before the Fall: An Inside View of the Pre-Watergate White House* (Garden City, NY: Doubleday and Company, Inc., 1975), 88.

craved the acceptance and approval of older powerful men. She was a woman with a righteous cause, inflated importance and perhaps questionable credibility. As a substantial woman with motivation, means, opportunity, and ability, Anna Chennault was dangerous. Present at this meeting were John Mitchell, Nixon's Campaign Director and future Attorney General of the United States; Bui Diem, South Vietnamese Ambassador to the United States and future President of the United States, Richard M. Nixon.[45] This was not Chennault's first meeting with Nixon. Chennault met Nixon and his wife Pat thirteen years earlier in Taiwan at a banquet held in Nixon's honor by General Claire Chennault and his wife Anna. At that reception, when the General asked his wife for her impressions of their guests, she commented as to Pat, "I like her. She seemed so sweet, so willing to suffer. But the sadness shows in her cheeks..., they're so...they look as though she's been rubbing her knuckles into them for years." Her husband replied, "Oh Anna! No, really, but what about him? Don't you think there's something about him?" She answered, "I don't know what it is. I'm not comfortable with the man. Wish I knew why, bothers the hell out of me."[46]

Despite her initial chilly feelings about Nixon, she did warm up some when he sent her a sincere message of condolence upon her husband's death in 1958 and expressed a sharing of her interests by revealing "a certain fascination with Asian communism."[47] Soon thereafter, she agreed to work on Nixon's 1960 Presidential campaign being drawn there by the "compelling figure of Richard Nixon."[48]

After Nixon's unsuccessful 1960 campaign, she met him again in 1965, in Taipei, while he was on semi-official business promoting Pepsi Co. She heard that Nixon was in town staying at the Grand Hotel, and "feeling somewhat sorry for his reduced political circumstances," Chennault "decided to call him on the day he was leaving to offer him a ride to the airport."[49] The following events that occur in this seemingly innocuous encounter have great relevance because this situation presents an early example of how Nixon and Chennault could see the exact same event with completely different eyes. Chennault believed that Nixon "seemed overjoyed to hear a friendly voice and accepted my offer with celerity."

---

[45] John Mitchell has the great distinction of being the first United States Attorney General ever convicted of illegal activities and imprisoned. He was charged for his involvement in the Watergate crimes. Lawrence Meyer, "John N. Mitchell, Principal in Watergate, Dies at 75," http://www.washingtonpost.com/wp-srv/national/longterm/watergate/stories/mitchobit.htm. (accessed December 22, 2014)

[46] Anna Chennault, *The Education of Anna* (New York, NY: Times Books, 1980), 163-64.

[47] Ibid., 164.

[48] Ibid., 165.

[49] Ibid., 169.

She then related that as Nixon followed her into her car he cracked his forehead on the door. "It was a hard resounding blow that left no doubt about the pain. He bit his lip hard, not uttering a sound and turned pale. Blood was oozing out of his forehead." Nixon took Chennault's handkerchief and pressed it to his forehead. He then took it "hastily in his hands muttering I'm all right, I'm all right." According to Anna, "He seemed frantic with embarrassment ... and mumbled apologies about my dress, which was white and, by now, conspicuously splattered with drops of blood. At the airport, he thanked me repeatedly for seeing him off and promised to be in touch."[50]

Nixon's take on their Taipei meeting was just a "little" different. Although he admitted to being in Taipei, he stated in his memoir *RN,* that rather than staying at a hotel, he was a houseguest of Madame Chiang Kai-shek. Further, instead of being "overjoyed" to hear from Chennault, according to author Kathryn Forslund, "a staffer clearly described a Richard Nixon very unhappy to meet or be seen with her; Nixon said that he did not want to be indebted to Mrs. Chennault or have his stature or credibility diminished by being viewed as someone influenced by her."[51] According to Jonathan Aitken, Nixon left instructions for one of his aides to "keep her away from me, she's bad news."[52] Forslund further related that an embassy official recalled Nixon's vehement declaration that he would "be god damned if that woman is going to the airport with me."[53] In this first trial of determining credibility between the two major players of our alleged conspiracy, the verdict must be in Chennault's favor. Forslund, citing the recollections of former embassy employees in Taiwan, confirmed that Nixon did stay at the Grand Hotel and Chennault and Nixon did ride together to the airport.[54]

Despite his declaration that associating himself with Chennault would diminish his credibility and that he would be god damned if he met with her, Richard Nixon must have accepted these great risks because in 1967 he met with Chennault and requested that she serve as an adviser to his campaign on the issue of South East Asian affairs. Chennault described his request as "disarmingly conspiratorial" couched with discouraging vagueness."[55] Despite any reservation she may have had, Chennault agreed to serve in Nixon's campaign.

---

[50] Ibid., 169-70.
[51] Catherine Forslund, *Anna Chennault: Informal Diplomacy and Asian Relations* (Wilmington, DE: S. R. Books, 2002), 48.
[52] Aitkin, 365.
[53] Forslund, 48.
[54] Ibid.
[55] Chennault, 170.

A "CONSPIRACY" IS BORN?

Back to Nixon's apartment, this was no mere meeting of friends to discuss similar interests. Nobody recognized the danger posed more than South Vietnamese Ambassador Bui Diem. Diem, whom we will meet later on, had serious reservations about this little get together, which in his version, originated one night during dinner in Georgetown, when it was Chennault who suggested that they meet with Nixon. Diem admits he was enticed by the idea, but nervous. He believed "any meeting with Nixon would carry the inevitable implication I was somehow dealing behind the Democrats back." Still, he saw the meeting as presenting an excellent opportunity and decided that if Anna could arrange it, he would meet with Nixon. Nevertheless, several days before the meeting, Diem met with Johnson's Foreign Affairs Advisor, Bill Bundy, to discuss its propriety with the purpose of getting his blessing, or at the least, his permission. Diem alleged that Bundy understood his position and "accepted my assurances that I would limit myself to a general discussion with Nixon and would not go into details about the peace talks." Diem understood he received permission from Bundy and decided to go to the meeting.[56] Bundy's version was "slightly" different. Not only does he have no memory of such a meeting, but he also believed that it was hardly normal or customary for an opposition party's presidential candidate to set up "a special two way private channel with the head of state of a government with whom the incumbent president was conducting critically important secret negotiations."[57]

Bundy and Diem were not alone in their reservations concerning the possible impropriety of a foreign ambassador of a country allied in the war, meeting with any opposing presidential candidate. Upon hearing about the possible get-together, Richard Allen, Nixon's Foreign Policy Advisor, advised him "the meeting would have to be absolutely Top Secret."[58] Nixon, handwriting his response on the memo, agreed that the meeting would have to be top secret.

After the party waited a half-hour for Nixon to finish a previous appointment, the candidate arrived, proclaiming to all present:

> Anna is my good friend. She knows all about Asia. I know you (Diem)
> also consider her a friend. So please rely on her from now on as the only

---

[56] Bui Diem and David Chanoff, *In the Jaws of History* (Boston, MA: Houghton Mifflin Company, 1987), 225.

[57] William Bundy, *A Tangled Web, the Making of Foreign Policy in the Nixon Presidency* (New York, NY: Hill and Wang, 1998), 38.

[58] Safire, 88.

contact between myself and your government. If you have any message for me, please give it to Anna and she will relate it to me and I will do the same in the future. We know Anna is a good American and a dedicated Republican. We can all rely on her loyalty.[59]

At this meeting, or sometime shortly thereafter, Chennault claimed she had private conversations with Nixon during which he assured her, if elected, he would offer a better deal to the South Vietnamese than the Democrats. She never directly revealed the exact nature of this better deal, even to the present day. However, whatever the promise, she was "naïve and believed him."[60] From this point on Chennault was on a mission, but what was its nature? Did this mission consist simply of the responsibility to meet with the South Vietnamese leadership and convey to Nixon their points of view on the war, or was she an agent set out to convince President Thiệu to obstruct the peace process in exchange for a better bargain from a future President Nixon? If this mission went beyond the informational, it began a series of events, which may have destroyed an opportunity for an earlier Peace in Vietnam

LBJ's Momma Didn't Raise No Fool

We turn back to the events of fall of 1968 because how they transpire are critical items of evidence in the analysis of whether there was a conspiracy, or more succinctly, what exactly happened in Nixon's apartment back in July. Once the

---

[59] Chennault, 17.

[60] Anna Chennault, interview by author, July 26, 2007. It is interesting that none of the authors who have analyzed this topic have reached behind the words "a better deal," although its nature remains critically relevant. When I directly asked Chennault to explain the elements of the promise, she impudently said she would not tell, as if she had a secret she was not going to give away. Chennault did, whether intentionally or unintentionally, provide enough information to allow a logical interpolation. During the interview, I asked her what about Nixon's policies towards the future of Vietnam drew her to his election campaign of 1968. She deliberately evaded the question, commenting rather on Nixon's negative character and lack of credibility. I then asked her what her hopes were for Vietnam's future at the time she met with Nixon. I asked this question because I thought it might lead to the conclusion of what drew her to him was his position on Vietnam, which would logically lead to the nature of the bargain he was proposing. At that point, she very clearly and emphatically stated that she wanted a similar situation as presented in Korea. In other words, she was willing to accept two separate Vietnams, with the North controlled by the Communist Party and the South supported by the United States. Obviously, she was against any coalition or countrywide vote for the united future of Vietnam, fearing communist domination. Therefore, as I will explore somewhat later in the analysis, one can make the logical inference that Nixon's promise was of a permanent non-communist South Vietnam.

fragile peace process began in 1968, Johnson remained wary that the ambitions of others generated by the upcoming election could shatter it. His negative reaction to Humphrey's Salt Lake speech, earlier that September, was proof enough of this fear. On October 16, 1968, the president decided to inform, by conference call, candidates Humphrey, Nixon and Wallace, of the impending progress in Paris. He started by first warning that their conversation was to be held in absolute confidence. He then notified them that the United States' position on a bombing halt depended on Hanoi agreeing to several factors, which he then explained in detail. Johnson then added, "They [Hanoi] have not signed along and agreed to the proposition, which I outlined to you, nor have they indicated that this would be satisfactory situation to them in its entirety," and "despite the rumors, there is no agreement yet." He asked the candidates not to make any public speeches, as they may be counterproductive to peace. Presciently, LBJ next provided to the candidates the following analogy as an example of his concerns,

> If I have a house to sell, I put a rock-bottom price of $40,000 on it, and the prospective purchaser says, well that's a little high, but let me see. And he goes -- so as to leave to talk to his wife about it and Ladybird (LBJ's wife) whispers I would let you have it for $35, 000, and then he gets downstairs, and Ladybird says we don't like the old house anyway, you can get for $30,000. Well, he's not likely to sign up.

Nixon, agreeing with LBJ's premise, responded, "Yeah" and commented, "Well, as you know… this is consistent with what my position has been all along. I made it very clear that I will make no statement that will undercut the negotiations."[61] One has to wonder about Nixon's response, he promised no statement but mentions nothing about not taking actions. . Exactly what character did he represent in LBJ's real estate anecdote? In any event, Johnson, fully aware of what could go wrong, adopted Clifford's belief that it "would be irresponsible to miss an opportunity for negotiations" and he pushed the process forward.

OCTOBER 28 1968, NOW I'VE BEEN HAPPY LATELY, THINKING ABOUT THE GOOD THINGS TO COME. AND I BELIEVE IT COULD BE, SOMETHING GOOD HAS BEGUN

On October 28, 1968, US Ambassador to South Vietnam, Ellsworth Bunker met with the South Vietnamese President Thiệu and Vice President Ky to discuss

---

[61] DOS, section 80.

Saigon's position concerning Hanoi's acceptance of the major factors. He reported,

> We reached agreements on a somewhat changed joint announcement, but one, which I believe we can accept, and which the GVN believes will make it easier for them to cope with criticism that they have agreed to meet the NLF. It was not easy. Ky having the greatest difficulties during discussions. Their objections were to the phrase "at the next meeting." Since that phrase suggested that meetings have been taken place before their participation. They also wish to be referred to as the delegation from GVN, and they wanted the last sentence of the communiqué to make it clear that "the two presidents wish to make it clear that neither the Government of the Republic of Vietnam, nor the United States government recognizes the so-called National Liberation as an entity independent of North Vietnam. [62]

This is not the first time that Bunker reported Saigon's agreement with the US terms for peace negotiations with Hanoi. Thiệu initially agreed, without reservations, to the American negotiating position when Bunker met him on October 13, 1968. During that meeting Bunker assured the South Vietnamese president that Washington was prepared to resume the bombing if the North Vietnamese violated the demilitarized zone or attacked the main cities, Thiệu then responded: "The problem is not to stop the bombing but to stop the war, and we must try this path to see if they (Hanoi) are serious." "I thought this a statesman's view," Bunker commented in his report to Washington.[63]

Returning to October 28, notwithstanding the noted difficulty, Bunker ends his memo by declaring, "At the end it was Thanh, himself, who used the word 'agreement' to describe the outcome of today's joint meeting."[64] Despite this optimism, the Johnson administration still feared that the candidates could destroy the gathering momentum; therefore, a discussion was held on what to tell the candidates before the deal was announced. Rusk, appreciating the particular risk posed by Nixon, despite his assurances during the October 16 call, warned the president, "I think that in your talk with Nixon, you may want to say something very direct to him. For example, remind him that the Republican Party

---

[62] Ibid., 136. Further, Thiệu reiterated his agreement to said conditions on October 15 and again on October 23. 1968. See DOS, section 187.
[63] Schaffer, 213.
[64] DOS, section 136, Thanh served as the North Vietnamese Foreign Minister.

is a stockholder in this situation; that they were in power when Vietnam was divided."[65]

OCTOBER 29, 1968- IT'S A HARD RAIN THAT'S GONNA FALL

October 29

Bunker was supposed to meet Thiệu to work out arrangements for the appearance of the Saigon delegation at the November 2 negotiations in Paris. He did not expect any trouble, as Thiệu already assured him several times that he agreed with the provisions of the negotiations and would sign a joint declaration with the United States. Bunker expected to complete the formalities smoothly and then call the president with the good news. However, at the Whitehouse, the phone wasn't ringing and Johnson's people were getting nervous. The notes of the National Security Council reveal the following:

> 5:43 a.m. Bunker had not seen him (Thiệu) as late as 4:55. They are fumbling.

> 5:50 a.m. President sat around waiting for phone call.

> 6:04 a.m. Phone call to President from Dean Rusk. The President held the phone in his right hand. He held his glasses in his left hand--the sides of glasses in his mouth. George Christian was on the President's left. He says Thiệu says 3 days is too short and that he can't get delegation there. [66]

On initial glance, several days delay would appear unimportant, but the calendar gives meaning; the proposed Saigon stall would move the opening date of the negotiations after the presidential elections. Hope had turned to bitterness and recrimination; what happened, who messed this up? Addressing Saigon's request for additional time, Clifford declared, "Their objection does not have merit. They can get a man in Paris in 24 hours. It seems to me they're playing extraordinary games." Rusk added, "The under the table stuff is what may be responsible." We "got all we wanted in Paris," Clifford noted, "If they [Saigon] refuse to go along, it would be extremely serious... it is too late to turn back. It is the will of the

---

[65] Ibid., section 135.
[66] Ibid., section 140.

president and the American people." Rusk lamented, "We've invested 29,000 killed and 70 billion. The whole thing could blow up."[67]

Rostow's picture changed once again, what was the reason? Rostow, himself, supplied the answer. At 8.50 a.m., he reported to the President his findings,

> I have been considering the explosive possibilities of the information that we now have on how certain Republicans may have inflamed the South Vietnamese to behave as they have been behaving. There is no hard evidence that Mr. Nixon himself is involved. Exactly what the Republicans have been saying to Bui Diem is not wholly clear as opposed to the conclusions that Bui Diem is drawing from what they have said. Beyond that, the materials are so explosive that they could gravely damage the country whether Mr. Nixon is elected or not. If they get out in their present form, they could be the subject of one of the most acrimonious debates we have ever witnessed.[68]

He then referenced a conversation his brother, Eugene, recently had with an informant. It appears that yesterday, during a luncheon, the source spoke to a man whom,

> [W]as a member of the banking community, a colleague, a man he has known for many years, and one whose honesty he has absolute confidence. The speaker is reputed to be very close to Nixon -... the conversation was in the context of a professional discussion about the future of financial markets in the next term. The speaker said he thought the prospects of the bombing halt or a cease-fire were dim, because Nixon was playing the problem as he did the Fortas affair -- to block. He was taking public positions intended to achieve that end. They would incite Saigon to be difficult and Hanoi to wait. [69]

The Fortas reference, because of the passage of time is now obtuse, but makes sense upon examination. In June of 1968, when Chief Justice Earl Warren indicated he was retiring, Johnson nominated Abe Fortas a personal associate and friend, to fill this position, subject to Senate approval. Republican Senators and conservative Southern Democratic Senators stalled the nomination with the hope

---

[67] Ibid.
[68] Ibid., section 145.
[69] LBJ Library, the X-Envelope, "October 29, 1968 memo from Eugene Rostow to Walter Rostow," paragraph 45a.

that a new administration would come in January of 1969, and thus allow for more conservative successor to Warren. The parallel, of course, is the stall for time to allow for the change of administration.[70] Returning to the present matter, Presidential Consultant Maxwell Taylor suggested that the cause of the stall "may be sinister, or it may be ineptitude."[71] The President, adopting the sinister scenario, commented:

> It all adds up… We may give serious thought to say this would rock the world if it were said he was conniving with Republicans. We are going to get what we can out of not bombing. This is an execute order. There is a plane there to take them. Can you imagine what people would say if this were to be known; that we have all these conditions met and then Nixon's conniving with them kept us from getting it.[72]

Johnson, either hoping his impression was wrong and the delay was a result of GVN ineptitude, or more likely, believing that he could still alter the outcome, agreed to a two-day postponement to give Bunker more time to work on Thiệu. The delay would bring the meeting to November 4, one day before the election.[73] Making sure that Thiệu fully understood the ramifications of his actions, and in an attempt to place maximum pressure upon him, Johnson instructed Bunker to warn the South Vietnamese President that if he:

> [M]akes himself responsible for preventing the very peace talks, which have cost so much to obtain, the people of this country would never forget the man responsible. No American leader could rescue the position of such a person with the American people. If President Thiệu keeps us from moving at this moment of opportunity, God help South Vietnam, because no President could maintain the support of the American people.[74]

Johnson, directly addressing what he believed the actual reason for the pullout, further warned Thiệu:

---

[70] See "The United States Supreme Court: Abe Fortas," http: //wais.Stanford.edu. (accessed November 27, 2007)
[71] DOS, section 148.
[72] Ibid., section 140.
[73] Ibid., section 150.
[74] Ibid., section 151.

...there might be individuals in the South Vietnamese government who may be speculating about the internal politics of the United States. He wishes President Thiệu to understand that decisions based upon such speculation carry the gravest danger because the American people would react in fury if they should discover that lives were being lost because people of other countries were trying to intrude their own judgments into the judgments of the American people about our future leadership. The President removed himself from the internal politics of the United States on March 31 to deal with questions of war and peace on their merits; it would be intolerable if those with whom he is working should fail to adopt the same attitude.[75]

In an effort to uncover Nixon's alleged double-dealing, President Johnson instructed Bromley Smith, Executive Secretary of the National Security Council, to request FBI Deputy Director Deke DeLoach to monitor all contacts by Americans and the South Vietnamese Embassy in Washington. The situation was deteriorating, but LBJ, still hoping to pressure the South Vietnamese and discover the source of the outside influences, believed, perhaps, he could still pull it off.

LET'S TALK WIRETAPS

Because the question of the legality of the ordered wiretaps becomes relevant during subsequent decisions, and was again raised in the "Watergate" matter, the subject merits discussion now. In late October 1968, Bromley Smith, responding to the President's order contacted Deke DeLoach, Deputy Director of the F.B.I., and stated, "I'm phoning on behalf of the President and the Secretary of the National Security Council...I want to discuss a very sensitive matter in very general terms... we urgently need to know the identity of every individual who enters the South Vietnamese embassy in Washington for at least the next three days. In addition, we want an accounting of every phone conversation --, both incoming and outgoing calls." He then requested of DeLoach, "Call the Attorney General, if you need wiretap approval, also place a wiretap on Mrs. Claire Chennault at the Watergate apartments. Follow her where ever she goes."[76] After the call, DeLoach instructed the FBI to initiate physical surveillance and he placed a request to Attorney General Ramsey Clark for wiretap approval.[77] "In

[75] Ibid.
[76] Cartha "Deke" DeLoach, *Hoovers FBI: The Inside Story by Hoovers Trusted Lieutenant* (Washington, DC: Regnery Publishing, Inc., 1997), 396.
[77] Ibid., 397.

this case," DeLoach wrote in his memoirs, "I wasn't content with verbal approval. I wanted a written record."[78] Soon thereafter, Smith called DeLoach back, and in agitated manner, informed him that he spoken to Clark and he seemed somewhat reluctant to proceed. DeLoach responded, "don't worry about it, we just sent a memorandum to Clark requesting the taps. He's a born bureaucrat he's used to getting requests this way. He'll sign." Smith "expressed his relief and gratitude." [79]

Within an hour of receiving the proper paperwork, Clark approved Johnson's request which was given the code name "WF 1525 S." However, this surveillance was only directed at South Vietnamese officials. Chennault's phone was not tapped because surveilling a known representative of the Republican Party would have put the FBI "in a most untenable and embarrassing position."[80] Therefore, despite the remaining argument concerning the propriety of placing surveillance on Diem a foreign ambassador, the wiretaps received the approval of the Attorney General. One more word on this topic, there is a lingering legend that Johnson, through DeLoach, also ordered the FBI to place a wiretap on Nixon's campaign airplane. According to DeLoach, some years thereafter, he discovered that FBI Director J. Edgar Hoover embellished the Chennault surveillance episode by informing President Nixon that DeLoach once planted a bug on his campaign plane. Calling the story FBI folklore, DeLoach comments, 'I'm always surprised that anyone could believe such a tale, because the bugging of the campaign plane would have to be characterized as 'Mission Impossible.' No one could've

---

[78] Ibid.

[79] Ibid. See also, William Safire, *Before the Fall and Inside View of Pre-Water Gate White House.* Here Safire, completely contradicting DeLoach, claimed that Ramsey Clark wrote to him saying he never authorized any such tap of Anna Chennault. Safire then claimed that without the signature of then Attorney General or court order, the taps were clearly illegal. A word of warning, Safire was partly correct in that there was never an approved direct tap of Chennault's phone, but his claim is disingenuous because, if Chennault called a phone that was legally tapped, such as Diem's, then the tap of that conversation is legal. See below footnote for further discussion.

[80] United States of America. United States Senate. "Supplementary Detailed Staff Reports On Intelligence Activities and The Rights Of Americans Book III: Final Report Of The Select Committee To Study Governmental Operations With Respect To Intelligence Activities, United States Senate, (April 23 (Under Authority Of The Order Of April 14), 1976), Paragraph 10,"
http://www.icdc.com/~paulwolf/cointelpro/churchfinalreportIIIj.htm . (accessed November 27, 2007) The subcommittee clearly found that Ramsey Clark did approve the wiretap of the South Vietnamese embassy. Note, although Chennault's telephone line was not directly tapped, if she called the South Vietnamese embassy, that line indeed was tapped, therefore she was indirectly and legally surveilled.

approach such an aircraft without being apprehended and questioned by the Secret Service. You might as well try to put a bomb on board."[81]

BEHIND THE SHADOWS

To understand perhaps why Thiệu was stalling, we turn back to Chennault. Once leaving Nixon's apartment in July of 1968, Chennault felt empowered and her influence within the Nixon campaign soon became evident to others. Shortly after the Nixon meeting, Chennault met with Ambassador Diem, who complained to her that politicians of both parties had been to his office looking for information. He also expressed fear that they tapped his telephone. Asking Anna if there was anything she could do to prevent his being surveilled, she replied, "I was hardly in a position to influence the Democratic campaign workers, but I certainly would try to talk sense to the Republicans." Chennault commented that he seemed inordinately grateful. The obvious deduction is that Diem would not have come to her unless he understood her "special liaison" status, and realized if he needed action, it was best to talk to her.[82] Chennault had no problem going straight to Mitchell with Diem's complaint, because she believed that she had a "special" relationship with him, one even closer than with his top aides. She claimed that once, when she and Ambassador Robert Hill were both on a conference call with Mitchell, he said that he wanted Hill off the line so he could speak privately to Anna. This special status did not go unnoticed. Later, Hill commented, "you know, Anna, a lot of people at campaign headquarters are jealous of your intimacy with the top brass."[83] She and Mitchell were so close that, during the 1968 campaign, according to Chennault, he relied upon her to help him locate an apartment in Washington. Interestingly enough, her apartment was in the Watergate complex.[84] Exercising her specialness powers, Chennault, reacting to Diem's plea, spoke to Mitchell complaining: "Look, Bui Diem is getting fed up. Everybody's bugging him, the least we can do is leave him alone." Mitchell, annoyed, answered, "I think I know who's responsible. I'll talk to them; make sure

---

[81] DeLoach, 407.
[82] Chennault, 176.
[83] Ibid.
[84] Ibid., 179-180. Emphasizing her intimate relationship with Mitchell, Chennault related a story that after they became neighbors, Mitchell introduced her to his wife Martha stating, '"This is Anna Chennault; you've heard me talk about her." According to Chennault, Martha Mitchell looked her over in the most blatantly curious way and with a mischievous smile. "Well, well" she said, "If I had only known what a beautiful woman my husband's been working with I would have been so jealous." The irony of her living in the Watergate complex is obvious.

they stop bothering him... Tell Bui Diem It won't happen again, not from us."[85]
These anecdotes are powerful no matter how interpreted. If we believe them,
(Diem makes no mention of any such meeting in his autobiography) then it
proves her impressive power and influence within the Nixon entourage. If untrue,
then it proves her questionable credibility, an exaggerated sense of self-
importance and a pattern of blatant self-promotion. One last note, a close reading
of Mitchell's statement reveals that the republicans may have been bugging Diem
on their own!

After her July 1968 appointment in the Nixon apartment, Chennault
continued to contact Nixon but initially received nothing back other than form
letters. In September 1968, there was a change in pattern. Nixon wrote her the
following letter:

> Dear Anna:
>
> I have your letter September 16 and again was say how deeply grateful I
> am for your dedicated efforts in my behalf. You are doing just great!
>
> With the best personal regards
>
> Sincerely,
>
> Dick [86]

Unfortunately, the letter Chennault sent to Nixon has not been preserved;
therefore, the exact meaning of Nixon's response requires speculation. Her
"dedicated efforts" could mean anything from help in fund raising to furthering a
conspiracy. The personal salutation, "Dick," from an individual not known for his
warmth, does suggest the "special" status claimed by Chennault. As far as
evidence goes, though intriguing, the letter provides little else.

On October 15, 1968, Chennault sent Nixon a confidential letter on the issue
of Vietnam. Reaching beyond her special liaison status, Chennault, now acting as
an advisor, expressed to Nixon her analysis on the finer points of delicate
negotiation issues and offered her opinion that a bombing halt would adversely
affect the troops.[87] In addition to sending the letter, on October 16, Chennault
flew to Kansas City and met with Nixon to discuss its contents. On October 18,

---

[85] Chennault, 176-177.
[86] Forslund, 58.
[87] Ibid. 58.

she met with South Vietnam's Ambassador, Bui Diem.[88] According to historian Anthony Summers, at this point Chennault and Mitchell "we're now in touch by phone, almost daily."[89] Mitchell concerned about possible wiretaps always utilized a payphone; his message to Chennault was always the same, "if peace talks were announced, it was vital to persuade President Thiệu, not to take part."[90]

On October 29, 1968, a government wiretap picked up a conversation between Bui Diem and a woman, who did not identify herself, but was believed to be Anna Chennault. She commented, "she did not have an opportunity to talk with the Ambassador on the 29th, [October] in so much as there were so many people around and she thought perhaps the Ambassador would have more information this morning." When she inquired as to the situation the Ambassador responded, "just among us that he could not go into specifics, but something 'is cooking.'"[91] He did not mention the meal, but all those contacts using veiled language to suggest that it was "tasty."

In addition to flexing her muscles within the Nixon campaign domestically, Chennault also took her "special" international duties seriously. After her appointment in the Nixon apartment, she almost immediately thereafter met with President Thiệu to convey her status.[92] Attention then turns to what was said, what was promised and what was the nature of these conversations. Did Chennault just listen to the opinions of Saigon's leaders and bring them back to Nixon or did she bargain or influence? We will discover, as the evidence unfolds that there are several answers to the same questions, depending upon who answers them and when.

DIEM'S WIRE TAP DANCING

Diem was right; he was the object of surveillance by United States intelligence and their efforts did reveal two very interesting items of evidence. On October 23, the Ambassador informed President Thiệu, "Many Republican friends have contacted me and encouraged us to stand firm. They were alarmed by press reports to the effect that you have already softened your position."[93] Historian

---

[88] Anthony summers, *The Arrogance of Power: The Secret World of Richard Nixon* (New York, NY: Viking, 2000), 300.
[89] Ibid. 300.
[90] Ibid.
[91] Lyndon Baines Johnson Library, the X-Envelope "October 30, 1968, FBI memo to White House," 36.
[92] Forslund, 53.
[93] Diem, 244.

Robert Dallek claims that this message came to Diem from Chennault herself.[94] This October 23 cable may have also been intercepted by the Soviets. On that same day, Soviet diplomat, Kosharyan, expressed to his American counterpart concern that he could speak for his side and could promise that there would be no rejection of the agreement. "I can't say that we feel the same for your side" the ambassador charged, "we do not know that the government of South Vietnam will go along with any agreements... we have done our work with North Vietnam. We're not sure you've done your work in South Vietnam."[95]

In another cable, dated October 27, Diem wrote to Thiệu, "I'm regularly in touch with the Nixon entourage." Diem defined that group as consisting of Anna Chennault, John Mitchell and Senator Tower.[96] Diem has never produced these two cables in full, although he repeatedly promised author Summers "he would let him see the full text of those messages."[97] Summers believes that published version of the second cable in Diem's memoirs, "was almost certainly an exercise in damage limitation." "The actual message was more troubling" according to former State Department executive secretary, Benjamin Reed, whose notes indicate that in the October 27 cable, Diem informed Thiệu that he "explained directly to our partisan friends our firm attitude," and our "plan to adhere to that position," for "the longer the impasse continues, the more we are favored." [98]

Although only two wires were intercepted to this point, there very well may have been additional relevant contacts between Diem and Thiệu. Clifford believes "there were other messages, on other channels. Diem correctly suspected he was under surveillance by American intelligence, and tried to fool his watchers by using more secure channels."[99] Although the number of cables, and exactly what they contained, remains in dispute, it is clear that there was a two-way dialog between the Nixon campaign and the leadership of South Vietnam.

BUI DIEM THE INCREDIBLE MR. INCREDULOUS

By October 30, 1968, the Johnson administration was on full alert that individuals, in touch with the Nixon campaign, were attempting to undermine their peace efforts, and Diem was in their sights. That morning Diem visited Bill Bundy at

---

[94] Dallek, *Nixon and Kissinger: Partners in Power,* 587. This claim has to be weighed very carefully since the author did not offer any definitive evidence to back up his claim, therefore although interesting, one has to be careful making his claim conclusive.
[95] Ibid., 585.
[96] Diem, 244.
[97] Summers, 300.
[98] Ibid.
[99] Clifford, 582.

the State Department. He knew that the American administration would be upset because of Thiệu's recent actions and was preparing for a difficult meeting, but he was soon to have a rude awakening. Upon his arrival, Bundy, whom he considered a good friend, did not even ask him to sit. According to Diem, the following drama ensued,

> [Bundy] in a frigid tone, I never heard from him before, informed me bluntly that the US presidential election had nothing whatsoever to do with the negotiations in Paris. With that, he stood up at his desk, turned his back to me, as if he could not say what had to be said face-to-face. Looking at his back, I heard a mumbled growl of words, among which I distinctly made out "improper," "unethical," and "unacceptable." Then still with his back turned, he started making allusions to my connections with the Nixon camp. I was dumbfounded by the whole performance,... obviously, Bundy was laboring under a serious misapprehension about what had gone on between Nixon and me. So once I caught my breath, I told them firmly that I've done nothing that could be construed as detrimental to the good relations between our two countries. I reminded him in July, I had given my assurances that my discussions with Nixon would not touch on any specifics of the Paris negotiations. I did nothing contrary to that pledge. My relations with the Republicans consisted only of normal contacts.[100]

Diem claimed to be "dumbfounded," believing he had not violated his July 1968 pledge, to Bundy not to touch on any specifics of the Paris negotiations with the Nixon camp. However, despite his indignation, this is the same man who sent the cables on the 23rd and 27th, which clearly concerned issues at the very heart of the negotiations.

We fast-forward to November 2, 1968, to understand the incredible nature of Mr. Incredulous. By that time, as will be detailed below, Johnson already announced a bombing halt and Saigon refused to attend the negotiations. It was several days since his "good friend" Bundy accused him of treachery, and there were momentous changes in his world, yet Diem did nothing to discover the nature of the charges against him. He never contacted Bundy, or anybody else, to determine the source of his rude treatment. He never went through his papers or even soul-searched. We can only assume that either he enjoyed remaining

---

[100] Diem, 241.

"dumbfounded" or he well knew the source of Bundy's anger and did not need to do an investigation.

Diem soon received another jolt. On November 2, Saville Davis, a newspaper reporter from the *Christian Science Monitor*, came to Diem's office to question him about a story he was thinking of publishing. This article claimed that Bui Diem sent a telegram to President Thiệu, urging him not to send a delegation to the Paris peace talks. The article also noted rumors circulating that the South Vietnamese made a deal with Richard Nixon promising Saigon would not go to the Paris peace talks. The purpose of their inaction would be to sabotage the political momentum Humphrey might otherwise have gained from the negotiations. The article then alleged, "As president, Nixon, of course, would show his gratitude by providing strong support for South Vietnam." After hearing these indictments, Diem, amazingly, claimed, "I was flabbergasted. Silently, I raced through a second reading, realizing that exactly this information must have been behind Bill Bundy's angry reception a few days earlier. I knew for sure that there was no secret deal, but I cannot imagine how such a misunderstanding could start."[101] Diem decided to neither confirm nor deny the allegations in the article because anything he did or say would be misinterpreted.[102]

The author of the October 23rd and the 27th cables, which implored the South Vietnamese President not to attend the peace talks in lieu of a better deal, claimed that he left his embassy that day "perplexed, not knowing what to do" and then "sat down and tried to figure out what was behind the *Monitor* story."[103] Upon reading his memoir, one can just picture him clutching forehead with his hands muttering, "Woe is me!" Now, for the first time, several days after Bundy's angry accusations of unethical behavior, Diem, started to do some research. Upon his discovery of his cables to Thiệu, no doubt using Holmesian deduction, he "saw that they constituted circumstantial evidence for anybody ready to assume the worst."[104] To answer those individuals, "ready to assume the worst," Diem took a familiar route-he blamed others.

Diem's first strategy was to blame Averill Harriman. This interesting defense, based on the premise that on October 28, President Thiệu agreed to sign a joint declaration with the United States of America concerning the proposed agreement with North Vietnam, requires close attention. Here's the logic, even if Diem committed felonies on the 23rd and the 27th, which of course he denied, they had

---

[101] Ibid.
[102] Ibid.
[103] Ibid., 244.
[104] Ibid.

no consequence because the GVN was ready and willing to go along after those dates thus, no harm, no foul. So why did the deal fall apart? Diem claimed it was not any conspiracy, but rather a disagreement that Harriman had with Saigon's chief observer Pham Dang Lam on or about October 30, 1968, that ruined the deal. Allegedly, Lam in a conversation with Harriman, indicated that he understood that the NLF would accompany the North Vietnamese delegation, but then the two men 'began bickering over whether they (NLF) would sit apart from Hanoi delegation and whether they would be allowed to display the Vietcong flag." When Lam demanded the NLF be regarded as part of Hanoi delegation and that the negotiations be billed as a three-power conference, Harriman allegedly exploded, "All your pretensions are out of this world!" Then Harriman warned, "Your government does not represent all of South Vietnam, Mr. Ambassador, and you'd do well to remember that." Infuriated, Lam, wrote to Saigon accusing the Americans of trickery.[105] Diem claims, "Lam's report pointed out the serious inconsistencies in the American position" and as a result President Thiệu overturned his October 28 decision to sign the joint declaration.[106] Thus, if the deal fell apart, it was the fault of the Johnson administration, not the good South Vietnamese ambassador. Diem's next strategy was to blame Anna Chennault. "All though I knew I had not been involved in a deal," Diem asserted, "There were still somewhat uncomfortable ambiguities in the situation, especially concerning the role played by Anna Chennault. My impression was that she may well have played her own game in encouraging both South Vietnamese and Republicans." He further claimed that she also had different avenues open to President Thiệu, "what messages went to those people he cannot say."[107] Therefore, if you don't buy the Harriman excuse, perhaps you might accept that if there were a conspiracy, the puzzled ambassador had little if anything to do with it.[108] The title of Diem's memoir, *In the Jaws of History,* deserves mentioning here. Usually, the publisher, instead of the author, creates the title to the book in question, but whoever created this one, must have been a strong believer in irony. Poor Mr. Diem, portrayed as an innocent victim within the nasty teeth of history's accusations, was not history's prey, but rather one of its very sharp incisors.

---

[105] Jack Anderson, "Washington's Saigon Feud," *The Washington Post-Sunday,* November 17, 1968. See also Lyndon Baines Johnson Library, the X-Envelope, 74.
[106] Diem, 245.
[107] Ibid.
[108] I implore the reader to place some sort of bookmark here and come back later after you read about what transpired between Chennault and Diem after October 30, 1968.

THE CONSPIRACY BROADENS: THE APPEARANCE OF THE PROFESSOR

If Chennault was Nixon's outside co-conspirator, his inside man was Henry Kissinger. A Harvard professor, Kissinger later served from 1973 to 1977 in the Nixon and the succeeding Ford administrations, as the 56th Secretary of State while continuing to hold the position of Assistant to the President for National Security Affairs, which he first assumed in 1969 and held until 1975. He won the Nobel Prize for peace in 1973.[109] Kissinger was also a well-known and self-admitted megalomaniac. John Mitchell, a fellow member of the Nixon administration, even described him as a psychotic egomaniac.[110] Throughout his heyday in Washington, under the Nixon administration, Kissinger, hardly known for his good looks, was a popular member of the Beltway party crowd. This balding, out of shape ineloquently dressed bespectacled man was a self-described "ladies man" who would later relish in his reputation as the sex symbol of the Nixon Administration.[111] During social gatherings he would entertain with comforting "funny" one-liners such as "the illegal, we do right away; the unconstitutional takes a bit longer."[112] One can only assume that the term "we" referred to the Nixon administration.

According to Clark Clifford, Kissinger was also a liar. He traced back this assessment to an incident of October of 1965 when Johnson requested both men to travel to South Vietnam and evaluate the situation. Their mission and their findings were to be top-secret. Shortly after Clifford's return to United States, an article appeared in the *Washington Post* concerning the expedition. Clifford, keeping true to his trip's off the record nature, never discussed his trip with the press. Therefore, he was surprised that the secret assignment become public knowledge. Much to his consternation, Johnson blamed him for leaking the story, causing great acrimony between the two men. Clifford was suspicious, somebody must have talked to the press and it was not he, but Kissinger assured Clifford that he had had nothing to do with the story. Some years later, Clifford discovered, from the article's author, that Kissinger was indeed the source. Kissinger had calmly lied to him.[113]

---

[109] "Henry Kissinger, Nobel Peace Prize, 1973," http://nobelprize.org/nobel_prizes/peace/laureates/1973/kissinger-bio.html (accessed November 27, 2007)
[110] Hoff, 148 see footnote 5.
[111] "Henry Kissinger in the Swinging Seventies," http://www.wwd.com/fashion-news/fashion-features/celebrating-henry-kissinger-6967416?full=true
[112] Harold Hongju Koh, "Reflections on Kissinger," Constitution (Winter 1993): 40. Quoted in Hoff, 149.
[113] Clifford, 429, 430.

Despite their initial negative experience with the professor, the Johnson administration once again called upon Kissinger in October of 1967. The President, attempting to open up a secret communications channel with the North Vietnamese, wanted to use Kissinger as a messenger to pass information that LBJ would stop the bombing if Hanoi "would enter promptly into productive discussions with the United States."[114] The mission was a fiasco. The North Vietnamese refused to see Kissinger and replied to all his messages with strongly worded rejections. [115]

In 1968, Johnson appointed Kissinger to serve as an unofficial member of the Paris negotiating team. Unbeknownst to anyone in the administration, Kissinger was playing both sides to his own benefit. Although having recently made comments to several people that Nixon was "unfit to be president," and that a Nixon presidency would be a "disaster" for the country, Kissinger was working as Nixon's mole within the delegation. [116] Henry Kissinger, performing his dubious role, secretly informed Nixon's campaign manager John Mitchell that there "was a strong probability the Johnson administration would stop the bombing before the election." Kissinger received this information when he "met privately in Paris with Harriman, Vance, and other members of the delegation in mid-September, just before the first Harriman Vance secret meeting with the North Vietnamese and they shared with him their frustration and brought him up to date on the state of negotiations." [117] Therefore, no matter who won the election, Kissinger cleverly assured himself a position of power in that administration. Kissinger's involvement not only broadens the conspiracy but also establishes a pattern within the Nixon administration of Mitchell serving as the contact between its operators. That Mitchell served a similar role with Chennault, as he did with Kissinger, gives credibility to Chennault's claims.

Kissinger was not the only source of secret information for the Nixon camp. Bryce Harlow, a former member of the Eisenhower White House staff, and President Nixon's campaign adviser admitted he was, "a double agent working in the White House. I knew about every meeting they held... I know who attended

---

[114] Clifford, 453.
[115] Ibid.
[116] Robert Dallek, *Nixon and Kissinger Partners in Power*, 70. According to the author, Kissinger was a member Nixon's Foreign Policy Advisory Board, while supposedly serving, at the same time, as an advisor to the Paris Peace talk's delegation for the Johnson administration.
[117] Clifford, 574.

the meetings I know what their next move was going to be. I kept Nixon informed."[118]

WHEN THINGS FALL APART

October 30, 1968

While Bundy was chastising Diem, the president and his advisers were doing their best to salvage the situation. They had two goals: first, pressure Saigon to cooperate and second, buy time with the North Vietnamese who were expecting a meeting on November 2. The North Vietnamese, enemies of the United States, proved far more cooperative. DRV negotiator Thuy agreed to change the date from November 2 to November 6, but he was quick to point out that it was the US who had changed its position and "From now on, both sides should carry out their agreements correctly."[119] Thuy, also remarked, "No doubt we had realized throughout our private talks that the DRV has shown goodwill and serious intent. The DRV also wants to put aside all differences so that we can come to an agreement."[120] The change did leave Thuy somewhat suspicious as evidenced by the following comment, "The U.S. realizes that the DRV has come with a real desire to find a settlement, but this involves two sides. The US should show goodwill just as the DRV side has, and then our future work will be dealt with smoothly."[121] Events with the South Vietnamese were not going as smoothly.

LBJ was running out of time. He promised the North Vietnamese to halt the bombing on October 31, 1968, however, despite the assurances of Bunker that there was a 50/50 chance of Saigon's cooperation; Johnson needed to decide whether to proceed to the conferences without South Vietnamese participation.[122] October 31 was a long day for the Johnson administration, both literally and figuratively. Bunker applied the heavy pressure demanded by Johnson, and Thiệu "was rocked by what he was told." Nevertheless, in a surprise move, the South Vietnamese President stated that his new country's constitution required he get the opinion of the National Security Council before rendering a final decision on

---

[118] Dallek, *Nixon and Kissinger: Partners in Power*, 583. See also Ambrose, *Nixon: The Triumph of Politician 1962 - 1972*, 209.
[119] DOS, section 158.
[120] Ibid.
[121] Ibid.
[122] Ibid., section 155.

this matter.[123] Thus, the waiting game began for LBJ and his advisors. (The GVN National Security Council convened at 4:00 p.m. Saigon time)

> 5:00 a.m. EST (note all times, from now on in, will be Eastern Standard Time unless specifically referenced otherwise, see Appendix III for Vietnam to D.C time conversion).[124] Bunker reported in that he put on the administration's case in the most forceful, sympathetic but unrelenting terms, but he did not know what Thiệu's decision would be.
>
> 7:20 a.m. Presumably, after Saigon's NSC had recessed, Ambassador Bunker was asked to go to the Palace to see Foreign Minister Thanh. Still no final decision.
>
> 9:15 a.m. Bunker requested and obtained a meeting with President Thiệu. With everything on the line, Johnson sent the following telegram to Bunker to give to the South Vietnamese President,
>
> I have thought since early October that we would sit in Paris as one, determined to maintain freedom in South Vietnam and to stop the killing. We must not throw away in Paris what we have won in South Vietnam. Nor must either of our countries go it alone. I am committed to the course outlined to you by Ambassador Bunker. As you know, I went down this road this far only because I felt that you were beside me at every step--as I believe you were. I so much hope that you are not leaving me in this critical hour. [125]

Without a final decision in, the tension at the White House was thick, "We've been on a roller-coaster for days." Clifford bemoaned, "I still can't talk...a calamity if this chance gets by us... It's tough for those who've been in this for 5 or 6 years--those who have nursed SVNam [South Vietnam] on a bottle since infancy hate to see it turned down." [126] Recriminations followed, Clifford, pointing out that Bunker had told him three times that there was an agreement and

---

[123] Ibid., section 159. One should not miss the ironic humor here. The United States strongly propagandized that the Saigon Government was worth supporting because it was democratic. This time when it does act or in reality pretend to act as a democracy instead of a dictatorship, it is to the detriment of the United States' best interests. The "Pinocchio" syndrome rises up yet again.

[124] See Time Conversion Chart Attached as Appendix III.

[125] DOS, section 160.

[126] DOS, section 161.

yet there wasn't one, suddenly became suspicious of the Ambassador's loyalties claiming that he's "always urged the SVNam side" and predicts, "Thiệu will ask for more time & that Bunker will plead his case!" [127]

> 9:30 a.m. An anxious LBJ sent a telegram to the South Vietnamese embassy threatening: "If Thiệu unable to join, LBJ will do it unilaterally! U.S. says we've gone too far down the road to back off." [128] Bunker, from the United States embassy in South Vietnam, immediately flashes back 'Thiệu "rocked" by this ultimatum & pleads for time.'

> 9:45 a.m. Clifford bets right now "Thiệu won't go along! Thiệu has been arrogant & difficult all week so that finally even Rusk has had it & even Rusk came around!!" [129]

> 10:30 a.m. Ben Read, from The State Department, phones in and informs the White House: "Thiệu & SVNamese acting very badly...He (Thiệu) did go ahead & make a speech. Thiệu's comments are most serious & clearly inimical & increases LBJ's problems substantially." [130]

> 11:00 a.m. News ticker clips report that Thiệu commented to the press, "Saigon does not agree with US terms." As he reads the announcement aloud, Clifford moans, "His Gov't cannot agree!... Thiệu is playing a very dangerous game." [131]

> 11:15 a.m. For months the United States, using every diplomatic device available, and inventing new ones, pressured the North Vietnamese to accept the presence of the South Vietnamese government at the peace talks. This concession did not come easy, but now, after all this hard work, the object of their efforts had betrayed them and it is time for blame. Clifford drops "the bombshell: Bui Diem has been having conferences with leading U.S. Republicans who have told Saigon: 'Don't

---

[127] Ibid.

[128] Ibid.

[129] Ibid. The reference to Rusk is illuminating. Rusk was a strong supporter of South Vietnam from the very beginning of the United States' involvement. If this "Hawk" was fed up with the South Vietnamese government, then it becomes a strong example of the level of the Johnson administration's frustration.

[130] Ibid.

[131] Ibid.

cooperate with LBJ; he's only Pres. for 3 more months & Nixon will be in for 4 or 8 yrs. Make it hard for LBJ!'"[132]

11:30 a.m. After the anticipation and recriminations, damage control was next in order. Rostow, in a memo to the president, laid out a plan subtly suggesting blackmail. First, he recommended that they have Nixon in alone then, "Give him the evidence that the South Vietnamese are thinking that they can turn down this deal and get a better deal after the election." Then, he recommended, that LBJ explain in detail the inevitable disgust of the government, the Congress and the public would suffer if the conspiracy were exposed. He suggested that Johnson should tell Nixon, "flatly that you are confident that he has had nothing whatsoever to do with this."[133] His plan was that Nixon, as a "good American," would use his influence to bring the South Vietnamese to the table. Written, very cleverly between the lines, is the threat, "help us or we'll expose you." Rostow ends his memo, "We simply cannot let these inexperienced men snatch defeat from the jaws of victory."[134]

2:40 p.m. Ambassador Bunker called: "He had spent seven hours at the Palace with Thiệu, Ky, and Thanh" and "The GVN wants more time because their Security Council is not on board on the present draft joint announcement."[135]

6:05 p.m. Johnson decided to go ahead with his speech, that night, announcing the bombing halt and the future peace negotiations with Hanoi. He hoped that the South Vietnamese would change their minds, but he was prepared to go it alone. He next informed the presidential candidates of the events of the last several days. After placing the call and informing the candidates of the pending deal with North Vietnam, he shifted the conversation to the following statement, taking shots at Humphrey, as well as Nixon,

Now, since that time with our campaign on, we have had some minor problems develop. First, there have been some speeches that we ought to withdraw troops, or that we'd stop the bombing without any--obtaining

---

[132] Ibid.
[133] Ibid., section 163.
[134] Ibid.
[135] Ibid., 165.

anything in return, or some of our folks are--even including some of the old China lobbyists, they are going around and implying to some of the embassies and some of the others that they might get a better deal out of somebody that was not involved in this. Now that's made it difficult and it's held up things a little bit.[136]

In response, the vice president said he had no comment, but Nixon said, "Well, as you know, this is consistent with what my position has been all along and I made it very clear. I'll make no statements that will undercut the negotiations. So we'll just stay right on that and hope that this thing works out.[137] After, being informed as to the elements of the plan and Johnson's hopes for peace, Nixon responds, "We'll back you up. Thank you, Mr. President."[138] His actual reaction, which he hid from LBJ, was "anger and frustration."[139] Nixon was certain that Johnson was just playing politics. Surprise, though, was not one of his emotions. He had been kept well informed of pending developments "by a highly unusual channel," Henry Kissinger.[140]

6:40-6:50 p.m. "Because of the historical importance of this day" aides officially reported in the notes that Johnson announced to his staff the following Presidential decision.

We are ready to announce that we are going to stop bombing North Vietnam. We have always held that conferences will not be productive unless the Government of Vietnam is represented; unless the other side refrains from shelling the cities; unless there is no violation of the DMZ. Hanoi has said that it is willing for South Vietnam to sit in on the meetings. We have let them know that any violation of the DMZ will trigger an attack from us. We have talked with the Soviet Union and others and they understand this. We will test their faith and see. I am going on the air at 8 p.m. tonight to talk to the Nation. Just before that, I will order the bombing to stop at 8 a.m. tomorrow. Negotiations will resume on November 6.[141]

---

[136] Ibid, section 166.
[137] Ibid.
[138] Ibid.,
[139] Nixon, 322.
[140] Ibid.
[141] DOS, section 167.

The long day climaxed as Johnson addressed the people of United States:

> For a good many weeks, there was no movement in the talks at all. The talks appeared to really be deadlocked. Then a few weeks ago, they entered a new and a very much more hopeful phase… A regular session of the Paris talks is going to take place next Wednesday, November 6th, at which the representatives of the Government of South Vietnam are free to participate …We have reached the stage where productive talks can begin…The overriding consideration that governs us at this hour is the chance and the opportunity that we might have to save human lives, save human lives on both sides of the conflict. …There have been many long days of waiting for new steps toward peace--days that began in hope, only to end at night in disappointment. …But now that progress has come, I know that your prayers are joined with mine and with those of all humanity, that the action I announce tonight will be a major step toward a firm and an honorable peace in Southeast Asia.[142]

For those listening carefully, the phrase "the government of South Vietnam are free to participate" would generate considerable interest, but for most, there appeared to be no pending complications.[143] William Safire, Nixon's speechwriter, was somebody who was listening carefully. Although not picking up the meaning of the phrase in question on the night of the 31st, Safire commented, nevertheless, upon reflection, the next day he noticed, "impression was left that the South Vietnam would be there at the peace table, but for some reason the President had not said it outright." Safire in a memo to Nixon wrote, "strange curve in LBJ speech last night." Safire then highlighted the phrase "government of South Vietnam are free to participate" and interpreted that it meant that there was uncertainty as to their presence and "all of which could mean that all LBJ did not have all his ducks in a row." Nixon must have loved the "ducks" comment because he had Governor Finch repeat it later. Meanwhile, as if there were not enough confusion that day, Thiệu met privately with Bunker and informed him "he would not do anything to upset the President's initiative." He then stated he

---

[142] "Lyndon Johnson Speeches,"
http://millercenter.virginia.edu/scripps/digitalarchive/speeches/spe_1968_1030_johnson?P
HPSESSID=177c3b8592aab61d79416fd80ebfb660. (accessed November 27, 2007)
[143] Safire, 87.

would express his full opinions on the matter during his November 1, National Day Speech at 9:00 p.m.[144] Perhaps not all was lost, yet.

LET'S GO TO ELECTIONS CENTRAL

William Safire, who was listening very carefully to LBJ's speech, "heard the goblins of [Nixon's] defeat echoing LBJ's words, with the 'war over,' a nation wouldn't need Nixon to bring peace, and could turn to the Democrats on pocketbook issues."[145] The American voting public reacted similarly. Humphrey, early in the campaign, trailed badly in the polls, but had been making up ground since his Salt Lake speech declared his independence from Johnson and his desire for peace in Vietnam. Prior to the October 31 Johnson speech, Humphrey closed within several percentage points of Nixon. Democrats, hopeful that Johnson's speech would aid their effort, found their wishes fulfilled. Polls taken immediately thereafter, revealed a surge for Humphrey. The election, which had appeared a sure thing for Nixon, was now too close to call.[146]

A MYSTERIOUS LATE NIGHT PHONE CALL OR DESSERTUS INTERUPTUS

Anna Chennault heard Johnson's October 31, 1968 address while dining at the Sheraton Park Hotel with friends and her escort, Tommy Corcoran. As she was finishing dessert, she was summoned to the telephone, it was Mitchell.[147] "As usual," according to Chennault, "he wanted me to call him back from another more anonymous number. I jotted down his number: (914) WO7-0909 and went

---

[144] Nguyen Tien Hung and Jerrold L. Schechter, *The Palace File* (New York, NY: Harper & Row, 1986), 26.
[145] Safire, 86.
[146] "Two and a Half October Surprises -- The Last Days of the 1968 Election," http://www.americanhistoryusa.com/two-and-a-half-october-surprises-the-last-days-of-the-1968-election/ (accessed December 8, 2104)
[147] Corcoran was Chennault's significant other at that time. 'Nicknamed "Tommy the Cork" by Franklin Roosevelt, he had been FDR's chief political operative guiding much of the New Deal legislation through Congress and serving as the president's primary deal maker and talent scout. He joined Roosevelt's administration in 1933. He was recruited by Felix Frankfurter as an idealist to help "cheat the cheaters." Nevertheless, by 1941, Corcoran embarked on a career that would gain him a more dubious distinction as the prototype modern lobbyist and influence peddler. Allan Lichtman, "Tommy the Cork; the Secret World of Washington's First Modern Lobbyist. (Thomas G. Corcoran)," *Washington Monthly* (2/1/1987), http://www.encyclopedia.com/doc/1G1-4696995.html (accessed November 27, 2007). Lichtman accused "the Cork" of possessing very little integrity and very much self-interest.

to find Corcoran." [148] She left the Sheraton deciding to place the call from Corcoran's brother's apartment. Then, she did something unprecedented in all her phone calls with Mitchell; she asked Corcoran to get on the bedroom extension. Citing no rational reason for this behavior, she felt for the first time, in all of her contacts with Mitchell, she required "moral support or a witness or both." [149] "Mitchell picked up on the first ring," recalls Chennault, "Anna," he said, "I'm speaking on behalf of Mr. Nixon. It is very important that our Vietnamese friends understand our Republican position and I hope you made that clear to them." [150] Although she was accustomed to "Mitchell's vagueness, attributing it to his prior excess of caution... she detected this time a specific request behind a nonspecific tone." It was late, she was tired and not sure what she, "was to make clear to the South Vietnamese." All she knew was "that the instructions seemed to have changed from the ones (she) had been given, simply to keep Nixon informed of South Vietnamese intentions." Chennault said:

> Look, John, all I've done is relay messages. If you are talking about direct influence, I have to tell you it isn't wise for us to try to influence the South Vietnamese. Their actions have to follow their own national interests, and I'm not sure that is what will dictate Thiệu's decisions. I don't think either we or the Democrats can force them to act one way or another. They have their own politics, you know.

Unrelenting Mitchell, nervously asked her, "do you think they really have decided not to go to Paris?" Chennault replied, "I don't think they'll go. Thiệu has told me over and over again that going to Paris would be walking into a smokescreen that has nothing to do with reality." "Oh, all right," Mitchell replied with lingering anxiousness, "be sure to call me if you get any more news." [151]

Many questions arise from this alleged phone call. First, did it take place? Although Chennault remembers the entire conversation with impressive specificity, down to remembering the phone number and number of phone rings, no written document or wiretap memorialized it. Her remarkable memory and the stiff tone of her alleged responses make her rendition suspect. It appears as if she

---

[148] Chennault, 189.

[149] Ibid., 190. During this author's interview of Anna Chennault on July 26 2007, I inquired why she asked Corcoran to witness the phone call. She answered, "I was suspicious because Mitchell was so anxious to find me, and it was a hard campaign to win." When she was asked why she was suspicious on this occasion as opposed to others, she would not elaborate.

[150] Ibid.

[151] Ibid., 190-91.

suspected it was being recorded or she was carefully creating a record after the fact. We do know that she was with Corcoran on the night in question. Shortly after 6:30 p.m., federal agents observed them going to a party at the Sheraton where they watched a movie. At the conclusion of the movie, they made a "brief visit to the Corcoran home," and then attended another party thereafter. [152] Troubling, however, is that the investigation made no mention that Corcoran's brother's house was site of the alleged phone call. Thus, we are left to guess that both Chennault and Corcoran gave the agents the slip, or the agents were mistaken or the call was a fiction. The behavior of the parties, thereafter, may provide help in resolving this dilemma. In other words, if their subsequent acts relate to the alleged content of the call, then logically Chennault's claims were credible.

The next question raised by the Mitchell phone call, assuming there was one, is where was Mitchell getting his information regarding the state of negotiations? According to Thomas Hughes, head of the INR, Henry Kissinger "tipped off John Mitchell, Nixon's campaign manager, who then told Anna Chennault that it was time to advise the South Vietnamese leaders to boycott the talks and wait for a better deal from a Nixon administration." [153]

The final question concerns whether Chennault was a passive receiver of information, as suggested by her version, or whether she participated as an active involved member of the alleged conspiracy. According to the call, there appears to be no question that Mitchell, at least on October 31, 1968, considered Chennault an active member of the convincing squad, but what does the evidence suggest, at least up to this point? Diem's cables of October 23 and 27th are instructive. The first asserted that, "many Republican friends have contacted me and encouraged us to stand firm," which cements that active persuasion occurred. Nevertheless, was Chennault one of the Republican friends? In the October 27 cable, Diem stated, "I am regularly in touch with the Nixon entourage" and he includes Chennault as a member. It is logical to conclude that Chennault was one of the active actors, but this is not definitive, for other members may be the persuaders and she may have been a passive agent. Therefore, although interesting, this evidence cannot be definitive. Perhaps Chennault (in self-contradiction) may provide the answer.

During an interview on July 26, 2007, I questioned Chennault as to the nature of her role in the affair. Inscrutable defines her demeanor and response. She

---

[152] Lyndon Baines Johnson Library, the X-Envelope, "November 1, 1968 FBI memo to the President," P33.
[153] Hughes, 19.

would often either fold her arms across her chest, sit back in her chair and outright refuse to answer the question, while making it very clear that she had a secret that she wasn't about to reveal. Yet, sometimes she would give subtle hints as if they were pieces of an elaborate puzzle that the questioner had to fit together. Wading through her pool of disinformation, I was able to deduce the following. Although not mentioned in her autobiography, Chennault now claims that she had a long private conversation with Nixon during their apartment meeting in July of 1968. She would not say what, if any, promises were made during this meeting, but later she asserted that Nixon deceived and used her. She described Nixon as a complicated character, who "sometimes gave false impressions that he believed in what he was talking about, even if he didn't. He would do anything to accomplish his goals without moral basis."[154] When asked to quantify her significance in the matter she proudly admitted that she had "played a major role." [155] When asked if history would have been different without her involvement in the matter, she proudly declared, "yes." As a mere passive carrier of news, she would not have been played a major history changing role and she would not have been in a position to be deceived or used, thus her own statements logically contradict her proclaimed innocence.

One last note, when interviewed by Summers, sometime after publishing her own book, Chennault claimed that Mitchell would call her almost daily and his message "was always the same: if peace talks were announced it was vital to persuade President Thiệu not to take part."[156] Chennault claimed surprise by Mitchell October 31 telephone call request that she actively persuade the South Vietnamese. Yet, prior thereto, Mitchell on a daily basis, had been already asking her to persuade the Saigon government, thus logically how could she claim surprise? Therefore, here is another conundrum. If Chennault lied about the call, exactly what part was she lying about? If we conclude she fabricated the contents of the call, exactly what comments were true and what were false? Remembering the old adage, "false in one, false in all," If Chennault was a liar, how can we trust her claim that the call ever occurred? Can we accept the fact that the call occurred, but judge that Chennault is still lying about some or all of its contents?

That very night back in Vietnam, Thiệu was engaged in a marathon session with his National Security Council, preparing for his speech. Despite his reservations, LBJ, still hoping for South Vietnamese cooperation, sent a telegram through Bunker to Thiệu, imploring:

---

[154] Chennault, interview.
[155] Ibid.
[156] Summers, 300 (emphasis added).

I am sure that when you saw the text of what I said to our people last night, you knew that I had much in mind the interest of your people and the political problems you face. I trust that you will make every effort now--in public and in the work between our two governments--to narrow and to eliminate whatever gap there may be between us so that we can go forward as brothers in arms in Paris, as we have been so long in Vietnam.[157]

At this point, there was nothing more Johnson could do but wait.

AN AMBASSADOR BUNKERS DOWN

Ellsworth Bunker was a well-respected diplomat with a long, distinguished career.[158] Nevertheless, 74 years old and out of his element in Southeast Asia, he already made several crucial misjudgments.[159] He consistently reported overly optimistic and inaccurate information regarding the state of the war and the strength of the Saigon military and government.[160] Bunker totally missed the coming of the Tet Offensive, instead sending reassuring military evaluations almost up to the date his own embassy was captured. Bunker accused the American media of irresponsibility in reporting Tet, but never conceded that he consistently failed to provide the American public with a credible reading of the Vietnam situation (which may have been responsible for the public's negative reaction).[161] He was about to make his worst misjudgment.

On the night of 10/31/68, the Saigon government sponsored a reception for the diplomatic corps at the Independence Palace. Bunker, an honored guest, spent little time socializing, instead he wished to discuss with Thiệu the contents of his speech of the following day. GVN government cabinet member, Nguyen Tien Hung, later claimed that Thiệu recalled that, at the party, "Several times he [Bunker] asked me 'is everything okay now, Mr. President? Of course, of, of course', Thiệu said, "everything is okay.'" [162] But was it? Was Thiệu reconsidering his position, or was he harboring intentions that were more sinister?

---

[157] DOS, section 175.
[158] U.S. Department of State- Office of the Historian, http://history.state.gov/departmenthistory/people/bunker-ellsworth. (accessed December 22, 2014)
[159] Clifford, 533.
[160] Clifford, 426 & 449.
[161] Schaeffer, 196.
[162] Hung, 27.

Bunker, a strong believer in Thiệu's integrity, pleased with what he heard offered a toast to the freedom of South Vietnam.

THE CHICKENS COME HOME TO ROAST

On November 1, National Assembly Day, the government of South Vietnam, along with Ambassador Bunker, gathered to hear Thiệu's speech. The day leading up to that speech was not an easy one. Thiệu refused to see Bunker despite his urgent message that he needed to deliver a telegram from Johnson. Unable to see Thiệu personally, the Ambassador wrote him beseeching, "Victory is now within our grasp, both in the fighting which lies ahead in the South and at the conference table. I beg you not to throw away victory. I plead with you not to say anything in your speech that will cause American support of the war to be further reduced. I urge you not to say anything which will make this more difficult."[163] Bunker was able to get his message to Thanh asking him to bring it to the president. Thanh claimed he failed in his attempt to see Thiệu, but he gave the missive to the president's brother, who took it to him. Bunker, according to Hung, pleased with the preceding night's events, appeared relaxed and smiling. For whatever reason he was unfazed by his rebuff, writing it off as Thiệu trying to look strong for the local press. This demeanor was unusual for Bunker, who was usually "serious and aloof," earning him the nickname among the South Vietnamese as "the refrigerator." Despite Thiệu's earlier discouraging comments, the Ambassador expected good news. His demeanor would have been a little colder if he had known about the events that occurred earlier that morning.

While Thiệu was giving reassuring remarks to Bunker, in secret, he drafted his speech by himself, "employing three secretaries to prepare the text for delivery, each working from random pages so that no one of them could read the full text."[164] Thiệu, was worried that if his real intentions were leaked to the Americans, he might be assassinated.[165] To lessen that risk, he kept each secretary "in a small room on the second floor of Independence Palace where they typed the speech until it was finished. They were not permitted to leave the room, or

---

[163] DOS, section 178.
[164] Hung, 27.
[165] Ibid. Thiệu's fear of assassination was not without prior history. The First President of South Vietnam, Ngo Diem, (no relation to the South Vietnamese Ambassador) met a violent end. There are many who believed that the United States played a role in that assassination, or at least, did very little to prevent it once they knew in advance it would occur. Herring, 106.

even use the toilet. Thiệu, wanted to take no chances that they might try to communicate with the CIA."[166]

THE SECOND LONGEST DAY

As demonstrated above, November 1 was a day of reflection, anxiety and waiting. The stakes could not be more dire as Bunker waited for Thiệu to give his speech to his nation at 9 p.m., which would translate to 8 a.m., November 2 Washington D.C. time.[167] Bunker, encouraged by Thiệu's assurances during the embassy party, remained optimistic. The GVN president, though, did not appear in a cooperative state of mind when he commented to journalists that evening before the speech, "South Vietnam is not a truck to be attached to a locomotive which will pull it wherever it likes."[168] Further, he did not appear very compliant when he issued a communiqué that day declaring that his government "lacked any sufficiently strong reason for associating itself with the US government in this decision."[169]

Unlike the optimistic Bunker, on November 1, before Thiệu's nationwide address, LBJ was worried and did not like the signs or the language. In a telephone conversation with former Secretary of Defense McNamara, the President lamented to him that all the candidates have been playing with the South Vietnamese, that call went as follows,

> One said [Humphrey] he would stop the bombing--no comma, no semi-colon--period. So they get that and they think that if they'll wait 10 days he'll stop the bombing everything will be over with--that's what Hanoi thinks. Then Nixon comes along and his people tell them that I'm not stopping the bombing and I'm not selling you out and I'm not for letting them take you over and this crowd will sell you out just like they did China, and you better wait until I get in. Now you've got all the South Vietnamese and maybe the Koreans thinking that. The damned trouble we're going to have. We had this thing wrapped up, signed, sealed, ready to go two weeks ago, and we got this speech of stopping the bombing, period. So [Le Duc] Tho took off for Hanoi, and we couldn't get him back. Then we got this ready, and we found out that they've been playing with the South Vietnamese, and we started watching their messages. It's

---

[166] Hung, 27 Footnote #19.
[167] See Appendix III , "Saigon-Washington D.C. Time Conversion"
[168] *Keesing's Contemporary Archives*, September 6-13, 1969, pp. 23549-23550. Quoted in DOS, section 171.
[169] Ibid.

the damnedest mess you ever saw. It's just almost--well, it's just heresy. It's just unbelievable.[170]

Expecting the best outcome, Bunker took a prominent seat in the front row and waited to hear Thiệu's decision. The worst scenario was about to unfold. In clear tones Thiệu proclaimed, "The government of South Vietnam deeply regrets not being able to participate in the present exploratory talks." The chamber, Hung described, "exploded in applause with a long standing ovation." Hung asserted that Thiệu recalled to him that, "I could see Bunker trying hard to control his emotions. He began to sweat. As I looked at his face I felt sorry for him, but there was a nothing I could do. I could not accept the situation that would bring us into a coalition with the Communists." [171] Bunker, once again, profoundly miscalculated.

Johnson exploded with rage. In a conversation with James Rowe, Humphrey's campaign director, Johnson first charged that Humphrey's Salt Lake speech damaged the peace process, which took them weeks to fix, then, he turned his attention to Nixon. He accused him of tampering with the South Vietnamese alleging: "We've lost Thiệu ... because he thinks that we will sell them out, and Nixon has convinced him and this damn little old woman, Mrs. Chennault. She's been in on it." Rowe responded, "Yes, I wouldn't doubt it." The President stated, "Well, I know it. Hell, I know it. I'm not doubting it!"[172]

NOVEMBER 2, 1968: THE MAN FROM ALBUQUERQUE CARRIES A SMOKING GUN

Anna Chennault should not have been surprised by Thiệu's decision not to participate in the exploratory talks. Just one day earlier she expressed to Mitchell her opinion, "I don't think they'll go" and adding that the South Vietnamese president believed that the negotiations were nothing more than a "smokescreen." Nevertheless, in her autobiography, she described her reaction to Thiệu's speech as generating "enormous confusion, punctuated with despairing questions. How could that be? How could Saigon have agreed and then reneged? Alternatively, was it Thiệu had given his agreement without his cabinet's approval, and if so why, had he blundered, and then retracted his offer? Or had given no assurance in

---

[170] November 1-12, 1968: South Vietnamese Abstention From the Expanded Peace Conference; the Anna Chennault Affair http://2001-2009.state.gov/r/pa/ho/frus/johnsonlb/vii/21895.htm (accessed December 13, 2014)
[171] Ibid., 28
[172] Ibid.

the first place?"[173] Another question might be; why did she ask questions for which she already had the answer? Did her memory suddenly become faulty, perhaps, because, in her autobiography she completely forgot the events of November 2, 1968. That day, FBI director Hoover received the below memo from an agent in his Washington field office, reporting:

> Of November 2 instant, an informant, who had furnished reliable information in the past, reported that Mrs. Anna Chennault contacted Vietnamese ambassador, Bui Diem and advised him that she had received a message from her boss, (not identified) which her boss wanted her to give personally to the Ambassador. She said the message was that the Ambassador is to "hold on, we are going to win" and that her boss also said, "Hold on, he understands all of it." She repeated that this is the only message "he said please tell your boss to hold on" she advised that her boss had just called from New Mexico.[174]

Bui Diem, despite his soul-searching after the stinging accusations of Bundy and Saville Davis and his minimizing his level of involvement with Anna Chennault, made no mention in his memoirs of the November 2 conversation. Perhaps he suffered from the same memory malady that plagued Chennault who also failed to mention the memo in her autobiography, or more probably, his selective memory arose because the document confirming the November 2 discussions was not revealed until 1994. Diem, who wrote his memoirs in 1987, obviously felt no need to reveal contents of this damning memo, which would serve to undermine his innocent victim persona.[175] Who could blame the man wanting to hide the "smoking gun" that shoots holes in both of his theories of exculpation? Reiterating his first defense, Diem claimed that his possible misdeeds in the cables of the 23rd and the 27th were irrelevant because Thiệu agreed to sign joint

---

[173] Chennault, 189.

[174] Summers, 302.

[175] The memo was revealed as part of a group of documents is come to be known as the X-Envelope, which were compiled by Walter Rostow. On June 26, 1973, Rostow wrote a memo to Harry Middleton, then director of the LBJ Library, instructing him to seal the X-Envelope pursuant to personal instructions from President Johnson. Rostow instructed that the file: "concerns the activities of Ms. Chennault and others before and immediately after the election of 1968. At the time, President Johnson decided to handle the matter strictly as a question of national security; in retrospect, he felt the decision was correct. It is, therefore, my recommendation to you that this file should remain sealed for 50 years from the date of this memorandum." Lyndon Baines Johnson Library, the X-Envelope, "Rostow memo, June 26, 1973," 0. On July 22, 1994, pursuant to Harry Middleton instructions, the envelope was opened.

statement thereafter. The second defense was Harriman's October 29 disagreement with Lam, which caused the deal's undoing. This excuse fails because his blatant attempt at influence, captured in the November 2 wiretap, occurred after the Harriman incident. Query: why continue to attempt influence if Thiệu had already made up his mind based on the Harriman insult? [176] Finally, regarding his claim that he bore no responsibility because Chennault acted on her own, the November 2 memo destroys that fantasy.   .

WHO IS THE MAN FROM ALBUQUERQUE?

On November 2, the day of the intercepted message, Spiro Agnew, Nixon's vice presidential running mate, stopped in Albuquerque, New Mexico, during a campaign trip.[177] Immediately upon receiving the FBI wiretap, Rostow delivered it to President Johnson at his ranch and in handwriting added, "the New Mexico reference may indicate Agnew is acting."[178] On November 7, 1968, Johnson, desperate to confirm the exact identity of the man from Albuquerque instructed special assistant Jim Jones to call Deke DeLoach at the FBI. The following conversation took place,

> **Jones:** Deke, do you know about the Albuquerque thing?

> **DeLoach:** Albuquerque thing?

> **Jones:** In brief, here's what happened. Apparently, Richard Nixon phoned Chennault from Albuquerque, New Mexico on November 2. This call, as best we can tell, was in connection with a previous conversation between Mrs. Chennault and Ambassador Diem, asking the South Vietnamese to honor a request to delay participation in the Paris peace talks. The ambassador sent a coded cablegram to the government in Saigon. [November 2 memo]

---

[176] Author Lloyd Gardner offers another interesting interpretation on the "Lam" incident. He believed that it was Lam's mission to stage a disagreement with Harriman designed to produce a remark that could be used by the South Vietnamese to claim they had been insulted so as to give them wiggle room to back out of any agreement they may have made or would make in the future. Lloyd Gardner, *Pay Any Price: LBJ And The Wars For Vietnam* (Chicago, IL: Ivan R. Dee, 1995).
[177] DOS, section 188.
[178] Lyndon Baines Johnson Library, the X-Envelope, "November 2, 1968 Rostow wire to the President," 29-1.

(DeLoach describes himself as being aghast at the implications as if it were unthinkable that "an American of Nixon's stature would do such a thing.")

Jones: The president is very upset. He feels it represents a grave national security problem. The president wants additional information about this matter -- tonight!

DeLoach: What additional information?

Jones: Specifically, he wants to know what time Nixon's plane landed in Albuquerque, the length of each phone call, at what time Nixon's plane departed from Albuquerque. He also wants to know -- tonight -- if Nixon placed a call to the Secretary of State [Dean Rusk] or any other members of the Cabinet in connection with this matter. He wants to know also, whether any individuals in Nixon's party placed calls to any government officials in Washington; and if so, what persons were called and the length of each call.[179]

DeLoach was reluctant to be involved in this mess. Instead of posing a national security matter, he concluded that Johnson's requests concerned only politics.[180] In addition, he believed that Johnson's requests were impossible because if the FBI pushed the telephone companies to reveal their records, those questionable actions would be brought to the attention of the press. Sensing DeLoach's adverse position, Jones reiterated, "The president wanted the information tonight." After the phone call, DeLoach called J. Edgar Hoover [FBI director], who shared his position, commenting, "Lyndon Johnson is always asking for the impossible."[181]

After the election, on November 9, DeLoach sent Hoover a request that they perform some sort of cursory investigation to get "LBJ off our backs." According to DeLoach, Hoover "who had enjoyed a longtime friendship with the Republican

---

[179] DeLoach, 399-400.

[180] DeLoach believed that the request might have been illegal under the "Hatch Act," which forbade federal employees from engaging in partisan politics. He believed that Johnson "was angry at the Republicans and wanted to get even." Ibid., 302. DeLoach, perhaps involved in his own politics, may have forgotten that the United States was involved in serious negotiations with the Hanoi government regarding ending the war in Vietnam and that it was possible that agents were conspiring against the peace process. Such actions, if they were true, reached well beyond partisan politics and well into national security issues.

[181] Ibid., 401.

candidate, called Richard Nixon on Sunday, November 10 and tipped him off that Johnson had put us on his tail."[182] Hoover, then ordered DeLoach not to fulfill the President's request. The next day, inexplicably, he reversed that decision and instructed DeLoach to discreetly carry out the President's instructions.[183] After a summary investigation, the FBI informed Johnson that Nixon was not in Albuquerque, thus the call could not have been from him.

On November 13, Jones again called DeLoach. "The president is most anxious to receive details on whether Spiro Agnew or a member of his party actually called Mrs. Chennault from Albuquerque. In fact, the president is becoming exasperated," declared Jones. When DeLoach claimed they already provided the necessary information, Jones responded, "The president wants specifics. He isn't satisfied with what you've gotten so far." "I'm not sure we can get anything else, Jim," DeLoach told him. After concluding the conversation with Jones, DeLoach received another phone call, this time it was from Lyndon Johnson, who shouted at the top of his lungs, "Why in hell haven't you obtained the information I want?" DeLoach later acknowledged: "He knew that we were dragging our feet -- and he knew precisely why."[184] Johnson then exploded, "do you know who your commander in chief is?" "Yes sir." DeLoach responded. Johnson then made his wants clear, "all right, then. Get me the information and make it damn fast!"[185]

Because of Johnson's phone call, DeLoach called Hoover, and they both agreed to get the investigation going. Why the change of heart? DeLoach provided a fascinating explanation.

> People who live in the real world and never deal with the presidency of the United States don't understand the enormous impact of the office itself. Lyndon Johnson as a man was impressive, but hardly intimidating. I could've calmly told that man to go to hell. But President Lyndon Johnson was another matter. The office confers a special power that adds several feet to the stature of anyone who holds it. Somehow, when you're in the presence of the president (or even talking to him on the telephone) you feel the strength of millions of Americans in his eyes and voice and movements... I had come to where I felt comfortable in the presence of

---

[182] Ibid., 402.

[183] Ibid.

[184] Ibid. No doubt, DeLoach was referring to the fact that Hoover was in the Nixon camp and Johnson was well aware of that fact.

[185] Ibid., 404.

Lyndon Johnson, but it was the comfort you feel the presence of a tamed
lion. Now the lion was angry and roaring.[186]

On November 13, 1968, the same day that Johnson called, the newly motivated
DeLoach discovered the following; three calls originated from Agnew's plane. He
had a call waiting for him when he arrived at Albuquerque, and he or his aides
made five calls while he was there. One call was to Secretary of State Dean Rusk,
which lasted three minutes.[187] Kent Crane, an Agnew staff member, made the
second call to Texas. Crane then made two calls to New York City, the first to an
unidentified person and the second call was to Jim Miller. Crane also made the
fifth and last call to a Mr. Kent of the Nixon-Agnew campaign committee in
Washington, DC.[188] When he received this information, DeLoach took the
following notes: "Three phones were involved. No calls to South Vietnam
Embassy. None to Anna Chennault."[189] There is a baffling element to the
DeLoach information. It is understandable how the FBI could identify the call-ee,
because phone records would indicate the phone number, but the confounding
element is how the agency knew the identity of the caller from Agnew's plane. If
the calls were recorded, no doubt they had that information, but since there is no
record of a wiretap, how the FBI determined the identity of the caller(s), must
remain a mystery.[190]

Finally, something definitive; the man in Albuquerque was a red herring. Not
so fast, for the above was only DeLoach's account in his memoirs. He and others
presented contradictory versions. On November 12, 1968, Walt Rostow, in an
"eyes only" memo to the President, concluded after studying the FBI timeline that
the "Gentleman in Albuquerque" had "ample time to make telephone calls to the
lady (Chennault) and Secretary Rusk, while in Albuquerque." He then concluded
his memo, "The phone call to the lady was at 1:41 p.m., and Secretary Rusk at
1:55."[191] Exasperatingly, he provides no source for his conclusion that it was
Chennault who was called at 1:41 p.m.

The next version, provided by none other than the official historian of the
United States Department of State, not only contradicts Rostow, in regards to the

---

[186] Ibid., 405.
[187] This is puzzling. Whey would LBJ's cabinet member be reaching out to Nixon's camp?
[188] Ibid., 405-06.
[189] Ibid., 406.
[190] It is always possible that there was a tap, but there is no information anywhere proving
such supposition.
[191] Lyndon Baines Johnson Library, the X-Envelope, "November 12, 1968, Memo to the
President from W. Rostow," 20.

timing and order of calls, but also contradicts DeLoach's conclusion that Chennault was not involved. [192] On November 13, 1968, 5:15 p.m., Johnson and DeLoach, during a recorded telephone conversation, discussed the possible identity of the "boss" referred to in the November 2 conversation between Chennault and Diem. The transcript revealed, Johnson said, "The only thing I've got to do is see who her boss is, which we think is Agnew, because Albuquerque's the place. We ought to look at it carefully, because she talked to Agnew." In response, "DeLoach speculated that the 1:02 p.m. call to campaign headquarters actually was to Chennault from Agnew." Johnson agreed, "She got the message from Albuquerque," he noted. "That's logical that he was the one [who] gave it, because when he called Rusk, that's what we thought, because that's the only way he could get information to give her, was from Rusk." [193]

This transcript is curious in many respects. The first issue concerns the date the telephone conversation between DeLoach and LBJ occurred. As indicated above, DeLoach in his memoirs, cites his November 13 conversation with Jim Jones as the moment he clearly concluded that Chennault did not receive a call from the Agnew plane. He even made a particular effort to note that fact. Yet the above transcript reveals that, on the very same date, DeLoach concluded, in a conversation with Johnson, that she did receive such a call. DeLoach, made no mention of this contradictory conclusion in his memoirs. Second, the transcript revealed that the Rusk phone call occurred before the Chennault call, but Rostow, in his memo to the President, claimed that the Chennault call transpired first. Finally, why in the world is Rusk talking to Agnew!

Historian Anthony Summers supplied the next version of the man from Albuquerque episode. Citing "phone records," of which he provides no footnote, identification, or source, Summers concluded that they prove that an Agnew aide in Albuquerque, "the very aide responsible for briefing him on Vietnam issues, had made a call during a stopover to a Mr. Hitt at the Nixon-Agnew

---

[192] Since 1861, the Department of State's documentary series *Foreign Relations of the United States* constituted the official record of the foreign policy and diplomacy of the United States. Researchers at the Office of the Historian collect, select, arrange, and annotate the principal documents that make up the record of American foreign policy. The standards for preparation of the series and general guidelines for the publication are established by the *Foreign Relations of the United States* statute of October 28, 1991. (22 USC 4351, *et. seq.*)

[193] DOS, section 412. (Recording of Telephone Conversation Between Johnson and DeLoach, November 13, 1968, 5:15 p.m., Tape F68.09, PNO 8) The Office of the Historian, specifically for this volume, prepared these transcripts.

headquarters."[194] Hitt, an official of the Republican National Committee, then contacted his wife Patricia, a trusted Nixon friend, then serving as Cochairman of the Campaign Committee. Next Hitt's wife, who had previously served as a go-between between Chennault and Nixon, passed the message to Chennault, who then sent it to Diem in the November 2 memo.[195] Although Summers readily presents this information as accurate, it is very troubling that so many low level individuals were involved. Because conspirators tend to keep their conspiracies secret, Summers' version seems less likely.

In the end, if we remove the chaff and go directly to the wheat, the relevant facts are that somebody on Agnew's plane, likely pursuant to his orders, passed a message to Anna Chennault that the Nixon campaign desired that she convince Saigon not to attend the peace conference. Nevertheless, even this conclusion is debatable. Historian Dallek disagreed with the basic premise of the Albuquerque claim. He argued that Nixon would never have trusted Agnew with knowledge of the conspiracy. Agnew "turned out to be as much an embarrassment as an asset." He was loose with his tongue, once describing Polish-Americans as "Polacks" and a Japanese-American reporter as a "fat jap." According to Dallek, "Nixon quickly relegated Agnew to a limited role in the campaign, keeping him at arm's length and never mentioning him during public appearances." [196] Historian Catherine Forslund agrees with Dallek. She theorizes that to be the man from Albuquerque, Agnew would have had to be in possession of highly sensitive information and obviously in a strong position of trust. She concluded: "It seems implausible that Nixon would have shared his most dangerous secret and inside connection to the GVN leaders with Agnew."[197]

Summers, disagreeing with Dallek and Forslund, argued that Agnew was involved in Vietnam issues and in touch with Nixon on the subjects of the possible breakthrough in the peace talks. He pointed out that: "Nixon, in his memoirs, does refer to a conversation with Agnew in early October 1968, where he briefed him on information he learned on the subject from Secretary of State Dean Rusk." Further, demonstrating that he was in the inner circle, "on October

---

[194] Summers, 303. Note, Hitt, would later gain fame through his involvement in Watergate related wiretap procedures during Nixon's presidency. One could logically assume that the Agnew staffer identified by DeLoach, as the source of the phone calls, was Kent Crane. Again, how Summers obtained that information, from an allegedly unrecorded phone call, is unknown. Unfortunately, Summers provides no clue as to the source of his information on this point.

[195] Ibid., 303.

[196] Robert Dallek, *Nixon and Kissinger Partners in Power*, 65.

[197] Forslund, 70-71.

24, at a rally in St. Louis, Agnew said a development in the peace talks was fully expected."[198]

Still another version of the Albuquerque affair comes courtesy of Anna Chennault. She claimed that FBI wiretap technicians misunderstood what she had said during her November 2 conversation with Diem. Instead, she insisted that she said, "New Hampshire," not "New Mexico." This change in geography was significant because she claimed John Mitchell was in New Hampshire at the time, and the order came from him. Her next statement gains critical importance because it clears the fog. In relation to the source of information in the November 2, 1968 wiretap she declared, "Anything Mitchell knew or told her to do would have been known [by] or come from Nixon."

Does it really matter if the call came from Albuquerque, New Mexico, or from somewhere in New Hampshire?[199] Was it significant if Agnew, an aide upon Agnew's request, or John Mitchell made the call? What is relevant was that the order came from the Nixon campaign. Further, this information gives absolute proof that Chennault was not a passive conduit, but an active participant in the conspiracy. Albeit, no recorded conversation from anyone in the Nixon campaign directing Chennault to do anything has ever been revealed. Therefore, it is possible that she invented the October 31, 1968 phone call from Mitchell and the "boss" references in the November 2, 1968 conversation, but that argument predisposes a finding of serious mental illness upon Chennault's behalf.

JOHNSON AND NIXON-WHAT'S A LITTLE BLACKMAIL BETWEEN TWO OLD FRIENDS

On November 2, 1968, the Johnson administration, now fully aware of the contents of Thiệu's National Day speech, needed to decide its next move. Their first reaction was to get angry. That speech, lamented Clifford, "was a devastating blow to this administration and to the Humphrey candidacy. Bunker, who misread Thiệu at every step, was powerless to stop him and as was the entire Johnson administration.[200] Clifford's could not understand why Thiệu betrayed them. In response to Clifford's wonderment, Deputy Secretary of Defense Paul Nitze

---

[198] Summers, Footnote 28-Chapter 23.
[199] Forslund claims that when Chennault was directly confronted with the phone records indicating a call to her from New Mexico, she was less sure of her memory. Forslund, 71. Note, the author did not give the benefit of the source of these "phone records" I did contact professor Forslund to establish the basis of her information. She directed me to the Summers' book, which gave no reference.
[200] Clifford, 594.

declared, "it's clear as day! Thiệu is scared that Humphrey and the Democrats will force a coalition on him and the Republicans won't and he's sure this is an LBJ plot." Clifford disagreed and argued, at length, that Thiệu had no basis for double-crossing LBJ and walking away from the agreed-upon position of South Vietnam's participation at Paris. In regards to Thiệu's previous consent to sign the joint agreement, Nitze opined that it probably did not mean anything, because "Saigon never thought Hanoi would agree to their going to Paris anyway, so it was lip service."[201]

The longer they talked, the madder Clifford became, proclaiming he was disgusted with South Vietnam and ready to dump them. "Screw you!" is all he said he would tell them and then he commented angrily "I do not believe we ought to be in Vietnam... I think our being there is a mistake... this demonstrates to me why I think it was a calamity." Then turning on the "hawk" contingent, Rusk and Rostow, he sarcastically commented that "they had such an enormous personal stake in seeing a 'beautiful democracy' there; they're committed so to South Vietnam they'd let Saigon run the whole show for us."[202] Yet, unlike Clifford, Johnson was not ready to give up and still believed he had some tricks up his sleeve.

On November 2, the same day Chennault was urging the Saigon government to hold on, Johnson became proactive. At 9 p.m., The President, perhaps heeding Rostow's advice, went after Nixon. He chose Senator Everett Dirksen, who had close ties and friendship with Nixon, to be the conduit. Johnson, in a telephone call, informed the Senator of the contents of November 2 Chennault cable and that such actions negatively "impacted upon the negotiations." He then warned Dirksen that "were skirting on dangerous ground." Johnson then targeted Nixon by claiming:

> This is treason... now I can identify them because I know who's doing this. I don't want to identify it. I think it would shock America if a principled candidate was playing with a source like this on a matter this important... I know who they're talking to and I know what they're saying...if Nixon keeps the South Vietnamese away from the conference, well that's going to be his responsibility... I know this -- that they're contacting a foreign power in the middle of a war![203]

---

[201] DOS, section 180.
[202] Ibid.
[203] Ibid.

This was a brilliant maneuver. Johnson threatened Nixon with exposure unless he reversed course and focused his efforts on bringing the Saigon government to the table. On November 3, at 1:25 p.m., Johnson, continuing this strategy, called Senator George Smathers, another Nixon confidante. Smathers started the conversation by informing LBJ, that Nixon was concerned "you are getting ready to charge him with the accusation that he connived with John Tower and Anna Chennault to bring about the action of the Saigon government, not participating." [204] According to Smathers, Nixon insisted that "this was first unsupported by the truth and secondly, unfair, and thirdly unfortunate." Nevertheless, according to Smathers, Nixon vowed to offer Johnson, "His full cooperation and he would offer to go to any place that you may want him to go to bring about a successful resolution of the impasse in Paris." The president was not impressed with Nixon's promise to travel anywhere, and rather wanted Nixon to go to the same sources and tell them, "You go on [referencing Paris], I'm gonna support the president, and you better get on to that damn conference." In regards to Chennault, Smathers explained that Nixon was unaware of her efforts if any. At the end of the conversation, Smathers promised to pass on LBJ's instructions to Nixon. [205]

On November 3, Bryce Harlow received a call from Dirksen, relating his telephone conversation with the president. Dirksen warned Harlow, "something had to be done in a hurry to cool off Johnson" because he "was ready to blow his stack -- and blow the whistle on the Nixon campaign's intent to defeat his peace efforts by getting President Thiệu to hold back. Anna Chennault's name was mentioned." [206] It is very intriguing here that that level of tension, concerning the alleged involvement of Chennault was so high. It is logical to deduce that the intensity suggests that Harlow and Dirksen were aware to the conspiracy and apprehensive about its reveal. Whether it was due to Harlow's recommendation or because of the Smathers' call or both, several minutes after Johnson finished his conversation with Smathers, he received a call from Richard Nixon. After stating how strongly he believed that the GVN should go to Paris, Nixon then informed Johnson: "rumblings around about somebody trying to sabotage the Saigon government's attitude certainly-- have no--absolutely no credibility, as far as I am

---

[204] Query, how did Smathers know about the supposed Nixon Chennault allegation? LBJ had not gone to the press on this matter

[205] DOS, section 186.

[206] Safire, 93. It is interesting that there was no outrage directed at LBJ's accusations by either party to the conversation. Logically if there were no basis for such outrageous indictments, Dirksen and Harlow would have shown some indignation.

concerned."[207] Nixon, appalled by the allegations, affirmed, "My God, I would never do anything to encourage Hanoi--I mean Saigon--not to come to the table, because basically that was what you got out of the bombing pause. Good God, we want them over in Paris. We've got to get them to Paris, or you can't have a peace." [208] Although the call started with allegations, it ended with friendly conversation and no further threats.

The implications of the LBJ/Nixon phone call cannot be understated. The timing is critical because it took place before the elections. Had Johnson wished to, he could have gone to the press and revealed his allegation that Nixon sabotaged the peace process. The damage resulting from such exposure would have been unprecedented. On the other hand, if the allegations were made without proper evidence, it would have backfired on Johnson, damaging his reputation and the credibility of his party. Journalist Jeffrey Hodgson, in a March 1969 analysis of the Nixon/LBJ phone call, highlighted its stakes. His sources revealed that:

> The President himself brought up Mrs. Chennault's name and appeared well informed about her phone calls. Finally, Mr. Nixon was able to convince him that her activities had not been licensed by him or his staff and the President changed the subject. When he finally hung up, Mr. Nixon and his friends collapsed with laughter. It was partly in sheer relief that the victory had not been taken from them at the 11th hour.[209]

William Safire had a somewhat similar recollection. After the phone call was finished, Nixon, sitting among his staff, which included Safire and Pat Buchanan, leaned back smiled and entertained the boys with the following analogy, "you fellows ever eat lamb fries? I did, 20 years ago, helping some congressman in Missouri. We all ordered 'em- tasted like veal, breaded, you know?" Safire then asked what they were, Nixon responded, "They told me we'd been eating sheep's nuts, that the farmers bite 'em off. When this is over, we'll go out and have a mess

---

[207] DOS, section 187.

[208] Ibid., There were no reports of lightening hitting the room at any time during Nixon's conversation with Johnson, however it is fascinating that Nixon does confirm the necessity of Saigon's presence at the negotiations..

[209] Godfrey Hodgson, "The Woman Who Scared Nixon," *The Spectrum,* (March 1969), Contained in Lyndon Baines Johnson Library, The X-Envelope, 60. The author's newspaper article does not reveal the source of his information. I attempted to contact Hodgson to ask him this question, but he did not return my e-mail. The credibility of the story is strengthened by the fact that the article, in regards to the nature and content of the phone call, was fairly dead on.

of them."[210] Nixon dodged the bullet. No question, he saw himself as the farmer, and Johnson was the sheep.

To Disclose or Not Disclose That Is the Question

It was still several days before the election. Johnson, in possession of information, that if credible, could blow the lid off the election, needed to make a decision. Should he bring it to the public, and how much, if anything, should he tell Hubert Humphrey? The situation was brought to a head when *Christian Science Monitor* reporter Saville Davis, contacted Walter Rostow asking him if he could confirm the allegations in his story that Nixon got Thiệu to change his attitude on the Paris peace talks. On November 4 1968, the President, Rusk, Clifford and Rostow met by phone to discuss the article and, as they coined it, "the China Matter." They first discussed the parameters of the Monitor's article aptly titled *"Recalcitrant Saigon Hopes for a Better Deal."* Davis' story, they concluded, was along lines familiar to the president, although its sources were Vietnamese, and not from the US government. The three of them discussed whether they should confirm this story and reveal the plot to the public. "I think that some elements of the story are so shocking in their nature," Clifford argued, "that I'm wondering whether it would be good for the country to disclose the story, and then possibly to have a certain individual elected. It could cast his whole administration under such doubts that I would think it would be inimical to our country's interests." "Well, I have no doubt about that" the President responded, "But what about the story being published and our knowing of it, and our being charged with hushing it up or something?" Clifford answered, "Oh, on that, Mr. President, I don't believe that would bother me. I think that the amount of information that we have--that we don't think we should publicize--it has to do with the sensitivity of the sources, it has to do with the absences of absolute proof."[211] In the end, the common recommendation was the administration should not encourage such stories and hold tight to their data. They based their decision on their conclusions that they did not have an open and shut case, it was just too late to have a significant impact on the election and the viability of the man elected as president was involved as well as subsequent relations between Johnson and him.[212] Later, in his memoirs, Clifford added further considerations claiming they withheld the information because Bunker continued to predict progress and disclosure could

---

[210] Safire, 93.
[211] DOS, section 192.
[212] Ibid. See also Lyndon Baines Johnson Library, the X-Envelope, "November 4, 1968 memo to the President from W. Rostow," 27.

impede that progress. Further, there was fear that if Hanoi discovered the strains between Saigon and Washington, it would lead to a disruption in negotiations.[213]

Author Stephen Ambrose offered several other versions of why the administration did not disclose the alleged Nixon/Chennault connection to the public. One version claims that Johnson forbade it because it would reveal the illegal telephone tap on Chennault. It must be remembered that these were pre-Watergate, and most certainly pre-Patriot Act/NSA times, and the public was not used to hearing that its government recorded the conversations of its citizens. Ambrose's version fails, however, because neither the Johnson administration nor the FBI directly tapped Chennault's phone. Rather, as indicated previously, Attorney General Ramsey Clark issued proper permission to wiretap the South Vietnamese embassy and all recorded Chennault conversations were through that authorized source.

Ambrose, alternatively offers, "Johnson was angry at Humphrey for breaking with him on the war during the Salt Lake speech, and thus had no interest in defeating Nixon. He wasn't going do anything for the purpose of seeing Nixon discredited." [214] Clifford also agrees with this assessment, labeling it perhaps one of the most important considerations. He commented, "Throughout the campaign, the President treated his Vice President badly, excluding him from national security meetings and threatening to break with him over the platform planks on Vietnam. What mattered to President Johnson, at that moment, was not who would succeed him, but what his place in history would be."[215] This explanation appears unlikely. Johnson was furious with Nixon upon discovering that he meddled with his careful peace plans. Before that point, LBJ may have secretly supported Nixon and treated Humphrey poorly, but thereafter, he openly supported Humphrey, even appearing at his final day rallies exhorting the candidate as "a progressive and compassionate American" who strongly deserved his endorsement.[216] More important, if Johnson did not want to help Humphrey, he would have not disclosed the conspiracy to James Rowe, Humphrey's campaign manager. On the other hand, Johnson did not disclose all the information to Humphrey. He had not informed him of the "smoking gun" type

---

[213] Clifford, 583.

[214] Ambrose, *Nixon: The Triumph of Politician 1962 – 1972*, 214. This claim is confounding in light of Ambrose's declaration that Johnson's peace efforts were a gambit to get Humphrey elected. If this were true, no question LBJ would have exposed the conspiracy.

[215] Clifford, 583. Note this evidence also strongly disputes the allegations that LBJ was in the peace business just to aid Humphrey's election as discussed in Section I above.

[216] Solberg, 399.

information found in the November 2 wiretap intercept from Chennault to Diem. Which leads to the next question, in light to the information he did have, albeit somewhat limited, why didn't Humphrey disclose the information of a possible conspiracy?

Washington columnist Jules Whitcover, when asked to comment upon Humphrey's decision not to disclose the conspiracy, remarked, "The decision was either one of the noblest in American political history, or one of the greatest tactical blunders. Possibly it was both."[217] Author Theodore White, writing about Humphrey's forbearance, commented, "I know of no more essentially decent story in American politics than Humphrey's refusal to [exploit it]; his instinct was that Richard Nixon personally had no knowledge of Mrs. Chennault activities, had no hand in them and would have forbidden them had he known."[218] Pushing aside White's musings, which are nothing more than thinly disguised adulation of Nixon, the reality of the situation presents a different scenario.

On November 1, 1968, Humphrey, while on his campaign plane, learned that attempts to get Thiệu to the conference before the election were of no use. His aide told him: "Well the old 'China Lobby's' coming back one more time." Upon hearing this comment, "Humphrey leaped from his seat, pounded his fist on the table and shouted, I'll be damned if I'm going to let the China lobby of all people steal this election from me." At that point, he dictated the following statement; "As President, I would sever all relations with the South Vietnamese and leave them on their own." It was his intention to publish that statement once the plane landed. The Vice President, however, did not issue that statement and issued a far more toned down version indicating the United States would go on with the conference without the South Vietnamese.[219] Solberg, Humphrey's biographer, concluded that Humphrey decided not to disclose the conspiracy because he did not have the necessary proof, the November 2 wiretap. Indeed, even without the benefit of the "smoking gun" Humphrey, in his diary, wrote,

> I wonder if I should have blown the whistle on Anna Chennault and Nixon. He must have known about her call to Thiệu. I wish I could have been sure. Damn Thiệu, dragging his feet this past weekend hurt us. I

---

[217] Bundy, 43.
[218] Solberg, 401.
[219] Solberg, 401.

wonder if that call did it. If Nixon knew. Maybe I should've blasted them anyway.[220]

Had Humphrey possessed the necessary information, it is reasonable to assume that Theodore White might have changed his opinion on his Humphrey's "decency."

ELECTION NIGHT NOVEMBER 5, 1968

Just after the president's speech, support for Humphrey surged. Nevertheless, twenty-four hours later, when it became apparent that Thiệu balked and there would be no instant peace, the support ebbed. One fact was certain; the race was going to be tight.[221] Chennault was one of 73 million Americans who voted for president. No doubt, she cast her ballot for Nixon. After voting, she claimed that she reported to Mitchell. Although a number of people were waiting to see him, due to her "special" status, he skillfully placated them and was able to meet her privately. "You look confident" she commented, "I am" he agreed, "He's going to win." Then, "he put on his somber banker's face," according to Chennault, " the one he wore whenever something personal needed to be said" and then commented, "The whole campaign has emphasized Vietnam, and you've done a great deal to help Mr. Nixon. You have done a great job, he will never forget that. I'm sure Mr. Nixon will want to see you after the election. So let's keep in touch the rest of the day."[222]

There are several relevant aspects to the above, unwitnessed, undocumented, conversation. If Chennault, in this affair, were merely a passive actor just relaying information, that action would hardly encompass a "great job" accomplishing a "great deal" that Nixon would "never forget." There are several other problems. First, this quote appears in Chennault's autobiography, in which she took the clear position that she did not get involved in trying to persuade the South Vietnamese not to participate. Yet, in the same book, she does not attempt to contradict Mitchell's above statement. A possible answer is that the November 2 memo to Diem, conveniently left out of Chennault's autobiography, occurring 3 days before her encounter with Mitchell, documented her active participation. At

---

[220] Herbert Parmet, *Richard Nixon and his America* (Boston, MA: Little, Brown & Co., 1989)

[221] On October 21, the Gallup poll gave Nixon an eight point (44% to 36%) lead over Humphrey. By the time Gallup completed the poll on November 2, two days after Johnson's speech, Nixon led Humphrey by only two points (42% to 40%). Theodore White, *The Making of The President* 1968 (New York, NY: Athenaeum, 1969), 446.

[222] Chennault, 191.

the time of the publication of her autobiography, in 1981, the memo was still secretly ensconced in the Johnson Library, thus she was playing both sides of the issue, just in case. Second, in light of the contents of Mitchell's puzzling October 31, phone call and his Election Day statement, if Chennault held the opinion that she only relayed information, why didn't she take the opportunity to question Mitchell as to what he meant? Such a line of questions appeared natural at that juncture. Just like Diem, either she enjoyed remaining dumbfounded or possessed little need to ask questions, when she already knew the answers.

On the night of the election, enjoying her "special" status, Chennault, allowed into the campaign's inner sanctum, checked with Mitchell for the latest election returns.[223] The returns were in; Nixon by a very narrow margin of .7% or approximately 500,000 votes was elected President of the United States.[224] After Nixon declared victory, Mitchell told Chennault that the president-elect wanted to see her "immediately after his victory announcement." Her "special status" confirmed again. Nevertheless, because of the chaos, Nixon was unable to see her and Mitchell postponed the meeting for the following week.[225] Chennault, ready to enjoy the fruits of her labors, whatever those were, was in for a surprise.

THE MAN FROM FLORIDA

Until November 7, 1968, no documents directly connected Nixon talking to Chennault concerning the alleged conspiracy, but according to Anthony Summers, a wiretap that day established the link when the FBI overheard Chennault's conversation with the South Vietnamese embassy. According to Summers, she initially called the Ambassador (referring to Diem) to say she had "made contacts already" and would phone later. Then, speaking with the ambassador's secretary, she passed word that she had talked to "him," and had been "talking to Florida and has to make a few other calls before she can move." After Chennault and the ambassador lunched together, they spoke on the phone that evening, "she now told Bui Diem the message from President Thiệu to "our boss" was "all right." The FBI report noted, she said:

---

[223] Chennault, 192.

[224] The exact results were as follows,

Nixon Humphrey Wallace

	Nixon	Humphrey	Wallace
Popular Vote	31,783,783	31,271,839	9,901,118
Percentage	43.4%	42.7%	13.5%

"President Elect 1968", http://www.presidentelect.org/e1968.html (accessed November 27, 2007)

[225] Chennault, 192.

the person she had mentioned to Diem, who might be thinking about "the trip" went on vacation this afternoon and will be returning Monday morning at which time she will be in touch again will have more news for Diem... they are still planning things but I'm not letting people know too much because they want to be careful to avoid embarrassing you, themselves, or the present US government.[226]

Summers claims that the "boss" was clearly Nixon, because it was confirmed that he was vacationing in Florida at that time. If the contents of the call are credible, it becomes especially damning evidence, yet one must look closely before reaching conclusions. Like the man from Albuquerque, the existence of the man from Florida comes from the mouth of Chennault. If the wiretap was between Nixon and Chennault, as opposed to Chennault and Diem, it would have far more weight. It is also still possible that Chennault fictiously created these connections trying to inflate her importance, a trait distinctly highlighted in the previously mentioned 1969 *Washingtonian* personality profile It is also possible that the man from Florida was not Nixon, but rather somebody in his entourage with authority, such as Mitchell. Therefore, although tantalizing, the November 7 wiretap is not as compelling as Summers contends.

CHENNAULT RECEIVES AN UNUSUAL REQUEST

The election passed, but Nixon remained in jeopardy. He made promises to Johnson and now he needed to give at least the appearance of fulfilling them. During the Monday following the election, Chennault received a call from Mitchell's office requesting she meet him in New York on November 13. Upon her arrival, Mitchell was quick to get to the point. "Nixon," he said, "had agreed with Johnson to come out with a joint statement announcing a Vietnam policy...we need to do something about our friends in Saigon." "Do what about our friends in Saigon?" She replied, not yet understanding. "Well, persuade them to go to Paris," he said. Flabbergasted, she declared, "You must be joking; two weeks ago Nixon and you were worried that they might succumb to pressure to go to Paris, what makes you change your mind all of a sudden?" Mitchell, according to Chennault, just shook his head "Anna you're no newcomer to politics. This, whether you like it or not, is politics." "I don't play that kind of politics," she exclaimed, "You go and tell them yourself!"[227]

---

[226] Summers, 305.
[227] Chennault, 192-193.

The above exchange is relevant in two ways. First, it proves that Nixon, through Mitchell, was convinced that Chennault had the connections and the ability to persuade the South Vietnamese to act or not to act. He could only have this impression if she performed such tasks in the past. Second, the ferocity of her rejection of Mitchell's request proves Chennault's emotional investment in the South Vietnamese non-attendance at the meetings. A final note; although there is no documentation that this meeting took place, nevertheless, Chennault's memory here is reasonably credible since it is consistent with the promise of cooperation Nixon gave to Johnson in their previous telephone conversation.

Where There is Smoke There is Hot Water?

The Mitchell meeting with Chennault was not the end of it. According to Chennault, later that evening, she received a call from Herbert Klein, Manager of Communications for Nixon's presidential campaign. "Anna," he said, "I'm not going to beat around the bush, you must promise to say to the press that our friend does not know about our arrangements with President Thiệu." Chennault responded, "What arrangements are you talking about? I know of no arrangements; I never made any arrangements." Chennault then claims that Klein went on as if he had not heard her response and said, "we know you're a good soldier; we just want to be sure our 'friend' is protected." She responded, "Why should your friend need protection?" Chennault describes she was talking like them, referring to her use of the phrase "friend" (Nixon) despite herself and she "couldn't understand why they were behaving as though they feared their own shadows."[228]

The confusing barrage from Nixon's confidantes was still not finished. According to Chennault, Tom Evans, Nixon's former law partner, now called her, which made her furious. Poor Chennault, she was being harassed and she had no understanding why. With "impressive audacity," Chennault claims Evans requested, "we want you to deliver a message to the Vietnamese Ambassador urging President Thiệu to send a delegate to the Paris peace talks, and also to tell them that Nixon won't have time to visit Vietnam just yet." Chennault now answering back, through bared teeth, barked, "Look, you don't seem to understand I'm on my way back to Washington. Give the assignment to somebody else."[229] In a scene worthy of any cheesy soap opera, Chennault described that the Evan's conversation rendered her nauseous, requiring her to

---

[228] Ibid., 193.
[229] Ibid., 194.

seek the sanctuary of the shower stall. "First the hot water. Then the cold," She
recalled, "Before the right temperature had been mixed. I could taste the salt
running down my face in painful tears."[230]

Still, the torture was not over. The next day, when she was in Washington,
she received a call from Senator Dirksen, requesting they meet. She agreed,
because she "was powerless to resist." During this meeting, he mentioned that
Nixon informed him that she would not carry on the new mission. The Senator
implored Chennault that she should not "let anger get the better of me
[Chennault] by talking to the press." [231] She finished the story, in her
autobiography, with the anecdote that sometime later she visited Dirksen, as he
lay dying in a hospital. On his deathbed, she told him, "Senator, I'm not angry
anymore at what happened, but I'm going to tell the story someday."[232] Despite all
their attempts, none of Nixon's entourage convinced Chennault to reverse course
and contact the South Vietnamese urging them to change their minds and attend
the conferences. Because Chennault refused to act on his behalf, Nixon himself
wrote to Thiệu to encourage him to go to Paris.[233]

Chennault's gauntlet has relevance beyond its obvious entertainment value.
Before our analysis begins, it must again be emphasized; there are no documents,
no wiretaps, and no confirmation of the substance of the alleged conversations.
Further, all these events memorialized in her 1980 autobiography transpired 12
years before. Nevertheless, Chennault was able to remember entire conversations
verbatim and describe even the minute detail of these confrontations. One must
be either impressed by Chennault's precise memories, or suspicious of her
credibility.[234] Perhaps she included these stories because she visualized herself,
like Diem, a poor victim of the machinations of others, seeking her reader's
sympathy as she cries in the shower stall. Yet, by including these tales, she
undermines her own attempted exculpation. Why would Mitchell, Klein, Evan's
and Dirksen, all powerful and intelligent men, be under the same impression that

---

[230] Ibid.
[231] Ibid.
[232] Chennault, 194-95.
[233] Ambrose, *Nixon: The Triumph of Politician 1962 - 1972,* 230.
[234] Any analysis of Chennault's memory ability must include its disingenuous variability.
There are instances where she either exhibits excellent recall or, in the alternative, total
blackout. For example, she remembers the temperature of the shower water and Mitchell's
phone number, but then has memory failure concerning whether the man from
Albuquerque called from New Hampshire or New Mexico. Further, she completely
"forgot" to mention, in her autobiography, the November 2, 1968 and the man from
Florida conversations. Chennault may have excellent memory and her forgetting of
information that she would or should not forget, is evidence of selective memory, which
becomes a credibility issue more than a memory deficit problem.

Chennault had, not only the ability to influence the South Vietnamese, but also the power of harboring a dangerous secret? As Queen Gertrude told Hamlet, "The lady doth protest too much, methinks."[235]

Chennault's stories not only implicate her, but also establish a direct Nixon connection. Why are Mitchell, Klein, Evans and Dirksen, so concerned with Anna Chennault talking to the press if there was nothing to hide? All these men, extremely close to Nixon, would likely know of a conspiracy, if one existed, and their actions with Chennault prove their complicity. Again, no documentation of these meetings has surfaced, but there was reasonable confirmation of their content by Senator John Tower. After the election, a reporter confronted Tower with the possibility of the Nixon Chennault connection to Thiệu. He specifically denied any existed before the election, but he claimed after the election, pursuant to President-elect Nixon's request, "Chennault did … ask the Saigon government to cooperate with the American officials in getting to the peace table." [236] Although Tower directly contradicted Chennault's account of her intentions, the critical factor here is that he verifies the request of all the President-elect's men. Additionally, by confirming the request, he established the direct Nixon-Chennault connection to the Saigon government designed to influence their choice of attending the peace talks. To borrow another phrase, "where there's smoke there's fire" and there was a lot of smoke. On last note, with all the murmurings in the press about a possible Nixon /Chennault nefarious connection during the election it boggles the mind that Nixon would associate with her at all at this point. One possible explanation is that perhaps he feared possible exposure by LBJ unless things were righted with Thiệu.

Extra, Extra, Read All About It

As the date of Nixon's inauguration approached, the St. Louis Post-Dispatch requested Chennault to grant them an interview. Despite her recent rage and tears inspired by the visits of Mitchell, Klein Evans and Dirksen, she had no clue why they would want to talk to her, but she agreed. When Reporter Tom Ottenad came to her office, he showed her his story alleging, "Humphrey's defeat could be attributed to the South Vietnamese government's refusal, ten days before the US presidential elections, to join the Paris Peace Talks - an act of sabotage traceable to Republican skullduggery." According to Chennault, the reporter studied her

---

[235] William Shakespeare, *Hamlet.*
[236] Ymelda Dixon and Joy Billington, "Tower Denies Dragon Lady Role," *The Evening Star, Washington, DC,* February 11, 1969.

carefully as she read the piece, and then accused her, "I've been told that it was you who carried out the assignment to influence the Vietnamese leaders, that President Nixon sent you to Saigon, a month before the elections. Do you have any comment?" "Yes, I have a comment," she said, handing him his story with the secret impulse to fling it in his face. "Your story is rubbish!" She then claims she never found out whether the article was published. If we believe Chennault's version of this meeting it was angry, short and uncomfortable. It should come as no surprise that the author of that article had quite a different recollection.[237]

The article, published in the *St. Louis Dispatch* on January 6, 1969, claimed that Anna Chennault, a top Nixon official, contacted the South Vietnamese government in an attempt to delay them from going to the peace talks. The article further alleged, according to a source in the Saigon government, that his colleagues "had been in touch with a lot of our friends both Democrats and Republicans." Ottenad reported that the Nixon campaign stated that any contact Chennault made with South Vietnam was an individual unauthorized action. Referring to Chennault, an unidentified Nixon staff aide claimed, "She is pretty freewheeling. She took a number of independent actions in this campaign." Timeout! We have to stop here before continuing forward. The staffer's remark must be studied closely because it might be the subtle smoking gun. What it does reveal is that the Nixon campaign did know that Chennault was out there, and they did know what she was doing and they did know it was inappropriate. In light of the stakes, peace, and of Nixon's supposed support of same according to the LBJ phone calls, if he was an innocent why then didn't he take a stronger stance in making sure that he NOT connected with Chennault's efforts. The failure to take affirmative action serves as very strong proof that the Nixon campaign was behind her actions. In any event, back to the article. According to it, when interviewed, Chennault declined to confirm or deny reports that she had been in frequent touch with representatives of the South Vietnamese embassy before the election and responded, with a half-smile, "Who told you that?" Later she commented, "you're going to get me in a lot of trouble... I can't say anything... come back and ask me after the inauguration. We're at a very sensitive time... I know so much and can say so little." When confronted with the Nixon disclaimer, she remarked while laughing, "you've covered politics. What would

---

[237] Tom Ottenad, "Was Saigon's Peace Talk delay Due to Republican Promises," *St. Louis Dispatch*, January 6, 1969, Contained in Lyndon Baines Johnson Library, the X-Envelope, 11a.

you expect? In politics, nothing is fair." When asked whether others may have made contact she replied, "I certainly was not alone at that time."[238]

It is safe to say that there were "slight" differences in the Ottenad and Chennault versions of their encounter. In hers, she was raging and offended, in his, she acted sly, and coyly suggested there was a great story out there but she was not telling. Obviously, this author has no personal knowledge of their meeting, but I can attest that Ottenad's description of her sly half smile attitude ["I know something you don't know"] was evident in my 2007 interview just as it was in 1969. This same demeanor was present during Herbert Parmet's 1985 interview with Chennault. [239] During their discussion, Parmet recalls, "she added the tantalizing suggestion that the full story was far from known, but then refused to provide further information."[240] Therefore, because of personal experience, and Parmet's similar encounter, this author is far more inclined to recommend the reporter's version of events.[241]

THE LADY REMAINS OPERATIONAL

Despite her protestations, Chennault continued her activities with the South Vietnamese. Shortly after the election, Nixon made public statements, which "revealed that there were no significant differences between Nixon's views and those of the [Johnson] administration." [242] Thereafter, Nixon gave public and private support for Clifford's program of pressuring Thiệu to go to Paris, causing no doubt, some serious consternation among those in Saigon. On December 10, 1968, Chennault contacted Nguyên Hoan at the South Vietnamese Embassy, offering words of comfort to an apparently agitated colleague; she informed him that Nixon's appointment of Melvin Laird, as Secretary of Defense was good for the Vietnamese and "not to be too concerned about the press' reference about a coalition government."[243] This note has great importance in several respects. First, it represents Chennault's continued attempts to convince the South

---

[238] Ibid.

[239] Chennault certainly enjoys being interviewed and has been interviewed. It did bother me that, without any substantial credentials, I was able to interview her shortly after making the request. Perhaps she enjoys the attention.

[240] Parmet, 522.

[241] If Chennault reads this book, and I have a good suspicion she will, I implore her, time is running short, if you have something to say on this topic, stop playing games and say it. Your continued silence proves that you care more for the acclaim that comes from the mystery than about the truth.

[242] Clifford, 600.

[243] Lyndon Baines Johnson Library, the X-Envelope, "December 10, 1968 FBI memo to White House," 15a.

Vietnamese.[244] More important, it is evidence of the nature of the Nixon deal she may have offered to Thiệu. During this author's interview with Chennault in July 2007, she would not directly comment as to what, if anything were offered to the South Vietnamese by the Nixon campaign in exchange for their non-participation in the peace talks. Yet, she did volunteer that her vision was of a separate South Vietnam government without the formation of a coalition. Her statement to the South Vietnamese ambassador, not to be concerned about a coalition government, logically means that Nixon pledged he would not support such a policy. The purpose of Chennault's memo was to reassure Saigon that Nixon had not gone back on that promise.

On December 14, 1968, another FBI intercept revealed that a Vietnamese official left a message and a present with Chennault to give to Nixon. Although seemingly innocuous, this contact is evidential in our analysis because it suggests that the South Vietnamese were convinced of the existence of a direct connection between Chennault and Nixon. [245] Why leave it with her as opposed to anyone else unless they were convinced, by prior circumstances, of the close relationship.

THE UGLY AFTERMATH

On November 12, 1968, South Vietnamese information Minister Thien stated publicly that the Johnson administration "had both halted the bombing of North Vietnam and agreed to the Paris talks without Saigon's approval." An enraged Johnson asked Clifford to rebut these charges at a press conference. Clifford described his demeanor at press conference as deliberately angry. He said, "We had a full and complete understanding with Saigon until the very last instant, when suddenly... Saigon changed its mind and decided not to go ahead." [246] Clifford surmised that his charge must have shocked many Americans, because up until that point, the public was not aware of differences between Saigon and the administration.[247]

Clifford's remarks filled the Saigon government with paranoid dread. Thiệu confided in his closest associates that he feared Clifford "would attempt to

---

[244] This conversation was picked up by an FBI wiretap. Walter Rostow sent the contents of the intercepted message to the President's attention with a note informing LBJ, "the Lady is still operational." Further, a handwritten addition contains the reference "keep all these in one file for ready reference." The importance of this suggestion is that Rostow and the President believed that Chennault's activities were serious enough to merit the creation of a separate folder, which indeed happened by the creation of the X- Envelope.

[245] Lyndon Baines Johnson Library, the X-Envelope, "F.B.I. memo to Whitehouse," 15a.

[246] Clifford, 601.

[247] Ibid.

overthrow or assassinate him, like Ngo Diem."[248] Clifford later appeared on the CBS television program *Face the Nation* stating the same charges against Saigon causing greater anger among the South Vietnamese. Indeed, on November 18, 1968, Thiệu characterized the United States' treatment of South Vietnam, "As a betrayal comparable to the US abandonment of Chiang Kai-shek."[249] Ten days after his appearance, Clifford received an amusing letter from the Face *the Nation's* producer describing the fuss South Vietnamese Vice President Nguyen Kao Ky put up when he was a guest on the same program one week later. According to the producer, when asked to sign the program's guestbook immediately below Clifford's name, "Ky at first refused. Someone suggested that he draw a line between our names. 'No!' Ky replied. Then he carefully drew too thick black lines on the page wrote 'DMZ' between the two lines and then signed his name."[250] It is safe to say, at this point, the relationship between the Johnson administration and the South Vietnamese became strained.

Not until January 16, 1969, did all parties, including the GVN agree to the simplest basics for the talks, such as the size of the table, use of flags or nameplates, and speaking order. On January 18, 1969, just two days before the Johnson administration left office, the peace talks officially began. Clifford believes that the "famously stupid argument over the shape of the table in Paris," was the product of a deliberate attempt by Saigon to delay the start of the talks until January 25, when Nixon officially was sworn in as president. "How could diplomats argue over the shape of the table in Paris when young men were dying in Southeast Asia," the former Secretary of Defense asked.[251] The possible answer to his question is simple and cold. Saigon, given a promise, was not about to do anything until it was time to collect.

---

[248] Hung, 27. It is commonly believed that the Kennedy administration, fed up with President Ngo Diem, was complicit in his assassination. See John Prados, "JFK and the Diem Coup," http://www2.gwu.edu/~nsarchiv/NSAEBB/NSAEBB101/index.htm (accessed December 22, 2014).
[249] Lyndon Baines Johnson Library, the X-Envelope, "November 18, 1968, C. I. An intelligence information cable," 71a. It is interesting to note here that Thiệu was parroting a familiar Chennault scenario. Although it is logical that he drew the analogy himself, however in light of his discussions with Chennault, it is also sensible that he picked this phrasing up from her. The China argument might have been one of the stronger persuading arguments used by Chennault when she spoke with officials of the Saigon government. Thiệu's use of the China analogy also argues that instead of being a mere messenger, Chennault was a persuader.
[250] Clifford, 603.
[251] Clifford, 604.

THE CONSPIRACY OF GREATER PROPORTION

To explore a different spin on the alleged Nixon conspiracy, we need to return to October 31, 1968, when Johnson just finished his speech announcing the bombing halt. Nguyên Hung, a close associate of Thiệu's correctly surmised that Humphrey must have been elated by Johnson's speech, because prospects for peace could only help his candidacy. He then logically concluded that, "Nixon should have been saddened; but this was not the case." Hung, based on his post event discussions with President Thiệu, alleged that Nixon, "with intimate knowledge of what Thiệu was contemplating in Saigon, was glad to see the Democrats sinking into a self-created trap. Nixon knew that Thiệu would not go to Paris, yet the Democrats were inflating the prospects for peace by linking the bombing pause to expanded Paris peace talks."[252] Nixon, according to Hung, "turned this seeming disadvantage to his favor. He inflated peace hopes even higher, knowing they would be deflated by Thiệu and he would benefit politically from the disillusion and doubt over President Johnson's initiative."[253] Indeed, Nixon did speak at a Madison Square Garden rally immediately after LBJ's speech telling the crowd that he trusted that the bombing halt would "bring some progress" toward peace when, all along, he well knew that Thiệu would not participate. Hung, though, goes further, (without the support of any documents), and concluded: "Thiệu's National Day speech was the key move **Nixon had plotted** and anticipated to compound confusion over President Johnson's action."[254] Hung provides a new interpretation, one far darker, which requires careful analysis. Simply, he alleges that Nixon went beyond using Chennault and others to convince Thiệu not to go to the peace talks. Rather, Nixon plotted the entire scenario from the beginning. Going back to the "Clue" analogy at the beginning of this section, if we assume that the conspiracy occurred, one scenario is that Saigon was either undecided about going to the meetings and Chennault convinced them not to go, or second, they decided to go and Chennault changed their minds. The third scenario is that they never intended to go and Nixon's actions were irrelevant. However, the final scenario suggested by Hung is that Thiệu actively conspired with Nixon, from the beginning, to create the appearance of a possible peace and fraudulently build expectations for a process they never intended to be a part. This is the plan; first build peace expectations to a crescendo level through Thiệu's "three agreements with Bunker. Next, Nixon further builds the possibility peace in his speeches. Then at the preplanned right

---

[252] Hung, 26.
[253] Ibid., 27.
[254] Ibid., 28 (emphasis added).

moment, dash hopes for peace dramatically, publicly, and at the last minute right before Election Day. Through this plot, Nixon achieves multiple benefits. First, the voting public, their hopes built up not only by Johnson, but also by Nixon, becomes angry with the Democrats due to their serious disappointment. Second, Nixon secures another benefit by blaming the incompetence of the Johnson administration for the failed peace attempt. Finally, he claims that the Johnson administration attempted to manipulate the American public by pushing a phony peace effort, further stoking anger against the Democrats. The purpose of these machinations? Nixon gets elected to president and the South Vietnamese benefit by the election of an American president that is burdened with a deep debt owed to the Saigon government.

Hung's intriguing idea is not buttressed by any document, but that does not mean that there were not incidences of strange behavior by Thiệu that would support such a plot. Saigon agreed, three times, to the terms of the US agreement with Hanoi, but waited to the last minute to "change" their minds. Further, Thiệu played Bunker up to the very moment of the speech of November 1, still feeding him information that he would cooperate while knowing all along he would not. This sort of behavior would make sense within a "build expectations" scenario.

Nixon also demonstrated behavior consistent with Hung's plot. As indicated above, he intentionally inflated peace hopes during his Madison Square Garden speech, well knowing it would not occur. Further, on the eve of the election, he relied heavily on the strategy that Johnson's attempts were nothing more than fraudulent acts designed to aid the Humphrey campaign. On November 4, 1968, Nixon, employing classic "technique," utilized aide Robert Finch as his stooge mouthpiece to accuse the Johnson administration of lying. In a story reported by the New York Times, "a highly placed aide to Nixon today said the South Vietnamese decision to boycott the Paris talks did not jibe with the assurances given the major presidential candidates by Johnson." The story continued, "Nixon said the advisor felt that Saigon's refusal to attend the expanded negotiations could jeopardize the military and diplomatic situation in Vietnam and domestically reflect the credibility of the administration's action to halt the bombing of North Vietnam."[255] Thus, Nixon pushed the idea that the Johnson administration's "fraudulent" attempts at peace were actually damaging the peace process.

There is still further proof that Nixon strategized the darker scenario from the beginning. On October 24, Nixon received information from Harlow (the former Eisenhower aide serving as the conduit between the White House mole and the

---

[255] DOS, section 187.

Republican Party) that their source within the White House revealed that an
agreement had been reached with Hanoi.[256] Nixon now believed it was time for
him to comment on the peace talks. In a draft, released on October 26, he started
by praising Johnson for "resisting pressure to contrive a fake peace." On must
admire how he gets the word "fake" in the mix without actually claiming it. Then
he claimed, however, "in the last 36 hours I have been advised of a flurry of
meetings in the White House... I am told that top officials... have been driving
very hard for the agreements on a bombing halt... I'm also told that the spurt of
activity is a cynical, last-minute attempt by President Johnson to salvage the
candidacy of Mr. Humphrey... this I do not believe."[257] In typical Nixon style, he
put forward the dirty allegations that the peace attempt was fraudulent, but
remained clean by denying he believed the charges. Query, how could he be so
certain these attempts were fraudulent if he was not in on the conspiracy with the
South Vietnamese President? As indicated above, Clifford, the US Paris
delegation and even the Soviets were certain that peace was at hand. Thiệu was a
week away from the November 1 speech, yet while Bunker was still convinced of
Thiệu's cooperation, Nixon appeared to have the inside information. Nixon also
gained the added benefit of instigating Johnson to accuse him of making "ugly
and unfair charges and of being "a man who distorts the history of his time."[258]
Nevertheless, it appears reasonable to conclude that all along Nixon knew that
Thiệu would not attend the conference.

TALKING HEADS—START MAKING SENSE?

Welcome to "History Center." Today, on our show, we will be interviewing
authors, politicians and historians who have given their opinions regarding the
conspiracy in question and whether or not Nixon was involved.[259] First, I would
like to introduce our very distinguished panel. For the audience's benefit, we will
be sitting at a roundtable and all our guests will be identified by the nameplate in
front of them. Flags are not necessary. To my right is former Secretary of Defense
under the Johnson administration, and former presidential adviser and powerful
Washington attorney, Clark Clifford. Also joining him, on our panel, are Walter

---

[256] This mole could not have been very reliable or connected because the leaked
information was blatantly false.

[257] Ambrose, *Nixon: The Triumph of Politician 1962 – 1972,* 209. See also Safire, 85-86.
The above is classic Nixon technique demonstrated by his use of the phrase "This do not
believe."

[258] Ibid., 210.

[259] Of course the talk show is a fiction, however although the questions are a recent
creation, the answers to those questions are actual and are properly footnoted for source.

Rostow, Special Assistant for National Security Affairs during the Kennedy and Johnson administrations; Bryce Harlow, former member of the Eisenhower White House staff, and President Nixon's campaign adviser; renowned author and historian Theodore White; H.R. "Bob" Haldeman, President Nixon's White House Chief of Staff and fellow Watergate co-conspirator; British politician, convicted perjurer and author of "Nixon, a Life," Jonathan Aitken; economist Nguyen Tien Hung, author of the book "*The Palace Files*," based on his experiences as special assistant to South Vietnamese President Thiệu; William Bundy, assistant Secretary of State under Johnson and author of "A Tangled Web, The Making Of Foreign Policy In The Nixon Presidency;" Nixon's speechwriter and columnist for the New York Times, William Safire; and New Dealist, lobbyist and Chennault escort, Tommy Corcoran.

Clifford

> **Laine:** Mr. Clifford, as the month of October 1968 was ending; did you believe there would be any issue regarding the South Vietnamese's agreement to the deal the administration worked out with Hanoi regarding the peace negotiations?

> **Clifford:** The South Vietnamese were kept informed on a daily basis as to exactly what was going on. They knew every facet of it. The Saigon government was kept posted all the time and as we were making progress, we could begin to see that finally we're going to get to some point to where we could agree. So, a statement was prepared for release in Saigon and release in Washington, exactly the same wording, announcing the day that the bombing was to stop and that the substantive talks were to begin and that the Saigon government was to have a representative there.[260]

> **Laine:** Did the South Vietnamese change their intentions in the last week of October?

> **Clifford:** Suddenly out of a clear sky, the Saigon government says no.[261] I cannot understand what has happened in the last week. I thought we had an agreement. There [was] a missing factor here. We [were] facing

[260] Transcript, Clark Clifford Oral History Interview III, 7/14/69, by Joe B. Frantz LBJ Library. Online.
[261] Ibid.

an utter debacle.[262] The cable arrived that he had reneged on everything to which he had previously agreed. It was a shattering message -- after a sleepless night, this unexpected disaster. I was furious. Their objection [did] not have merit. It seems to me they are playing extraordinary games.[263]

Laine: What games are you talking about and who is to blame?

Clifford: Gradually we realized that the South Vietnamese growing resistance to the agreement in Paris was being encouraged and indeed, stimulated by the republicans and especially by Anna Chennault, who we referred to as the "Little Flower."[264]

Laine: Did you believe there were improprieties in the republican's actions?

Clifford: The activities of the Nixon team went far beyond the bounds of justifiable political combat. They constituted direct interference in the activities of the executive branch and [in] the responsibilities of the chief executive, the only people with authority to negotiate on behalf of the nation. The activities of the Nixon campaign constituted gross, even potentially illegal, interference in the security affairs of the nation by private individuals.[265]

Laine: I understand your allegations against the Republican Party, but do you believe that Nixon, himself, was involved in this activity?

Clifford: No smoking gun has ever turned up linking Nixon directly to the secret messages. There are no self-incriminating tapes from the campaign, and the whole incident has been relegated to the status of an unsolved mystery. On the other hand, this chain of events undeniably began in Richard Nixon's apartment in New York and his closest adviser, John Mitchell, ran the Chennault channel personally with full understanding of its sensitivity. Given the importance of these events, I have always thought it was reasonable to assume that Mitchell told

---

[262] Clifford, 578.
[263] Ibid., 587.
[264] Ibid., 583.
[265] Ibid., 582

Nixon about them, and that Nixon knew, and approved, what was going on in his name.[266]

Rostow

Laine: Mr. Rostow what was the South Vietnamese's position regarding the proposed agreement with Hanoi?

Rostow: As late as October 28, Thiệu, despite the uneasiness, of which we were aware, told Ambassador Bunker he would proceed as he had agreed to two weeks earlier. [267]

Laine: Was there a change in their beliefs and when did this happen?

Rostow: In the early hours of October 29, the President and his advisers met with [General Creighton] Abrams. Before going to that meeting, I was telephoned at home by my brother, Eugene Rostow. He reported the first of his messages from New York on Republican strategy during the meeting with Abrams, word came from Bunker of Thiệu's sudden intransigence.[268]

Laine: How did the administration react?

Rostow: President Johnson,…instructed Bromley Smith, to get in touch with… Deke DeLoach and arrange that contacts by Americans and the South Vietnamese Embassy in Washington be monitored.

Laine: After reviewing the surveillance, your own actions and the President's, what did you conclude?

Rostow: I am inclined to believe the Republican operation in 1968 relates in two ways to the Watergate affair of 1972. First, the election of 1968, proved to be close and there was some reason for those involved on the Republican side to believe their enterprise with the South Vietnamese and Thiệu's reluctance may have sufficiently blunted the impact on US politics of the total bombing halt and agreement to

---

[266] Ibid., 584
[267] Lyndon Baines Johnson Library, the X-Envelope, "Rostow Memo to File," 39.
[268] Ibid. Note, Deputy Chief of Staff Creighton Abrams, replaced William Westmoreland as Commander of Forces in Vietnam at that point.

negotiate to constitute the margin of victory. Second, they got away with it... Thus, as the same men faced the election in 1972, there was nothing in their previous experience with the operation of doubtful propriety (or, even legality) to warn them off; and there were memories of how close elections could get and the possible utility of pressing to the limit -- -- or beyond. [269]

White

Laine: Mr. White you have written in your book, *The Making of the President 1968*, that Nixon had no involvement in the alleged Chennault conspiracy. What do you base that on?

White: When the Nixon camp first heard the story, (his) aides investigated, and found out about Mrs. Chennault's activities, and were appalled. The fury and dismay at Nixon's headquarters, when his aides discovered the (Chennault) report were so intense that they could not have been feigned simply for the benefit of this reporter.[270]

Aitken

Laine: Mr. Aitken you stated in your book that it is your belief that the White House and the Kremlin collaborated to stop Nixon's presidential bid in 1968 and that the peace negotiations were to ensure that they would have maximum impact on the election. You even allege that the FBI placed bugs on the Nixon campaign plane. Do you have an opinion whether or not Nixon was in a conspiracy with Chennault to stall the peace process?

Aitken: He was certainly not a guilty party to the breakdown of the peace talks. Nixon was far too experienced a practitioner in national security affairs to involve himself in a conspiracy to derail a bombing

---

[269] Ibid.

[270] White, 381. Author's comment, White just has to be kidding. Is he that naïve and/or stupid to believe that Nixon would share his plans with low-level campaign aides? Such information, if true, obviously would be shared with only his closest and trusted associates. His logic can be compared to a jury finding OJ Simpson not guilty of double homicide because the water boy, without any evidence, said he didn't do it.

halt for political purposes. Advanced knowledge of such activity would have appalled Nixon as a patriot and alarmed him as a politician.[271]

Laine: What document do you rely upon to support your conclusion here?

Aitken: On May 25, 1991, Nixon sent me a memorandum indicating he would have been the first to realize that his electoral prospects could be severely damaged if any connection between his staff and Mrs. Chennault's maneuvers had been exposed.[272]

Safire

Laine: Mr. Safire my question to you is did Anna Chennault act as Nixon's proxy to urge South Vietnam's leaders to refuse to come to the Paris peace table under the terms offered by President Johnson just before the Election Day?

Safire: Dammit, the answer appears to be yes and no. I cannot positively assert that she did so, or if she did, that it was asked at the direction of Mr. Nixon or his aides.[273] Perhaps there is more to that story that would make a clear cut answer possible; in all likelihood, it was a fuzzy situation and will remain so for years. Did Nixon direct an agent of his to get the South Vietnamese to hang back? No evidence of that; he only did not discourage her. [274]

Summers

Laine: Mr. Summers you claim that Nixon was directly involved in this conspiracy. But, didn't Johnson, in his memoirs, disagree with your conclusion?

---

[271] Aitken, 362.

[272] Note, in the interest of clarity this footnote was converted into a declarative statement; however, the contents of the remark are verbatim. Curiously, Aitken does not question that Nixon focused his answer on exposure instead of denial. The fact that somebody does not want something divulged does not mean he did not do it. Few bank robbers advertise their actions. Further, his allegation concerning the bug on the plane was wrong as indicated herein and evidence of sloppy research or bias. On more comment, Nixon's "patriotism" and experience did not prevent his deeper involvement in the very sordid Watergate affair.

[273] Safire, 88.

[274] Ibid., 90.

Summers: In his memoirs, Johnson would write that he had "no reason to think that Republican candidate Nixon was himself involved in this maneuvering, but a few individuals active in his campaign were." I agree with historian Herbert Parmet, who believes, that "Johnson was dissembling because he knew more than he would or could let on." To be forthright, the former President would have had to have revealed what he had learned from intelligence sources, some of which remain secret to this day. In 1971 when the memoirs were published, to have exposed Nixon would have been to expose a sitting president, himself still wrestling with Vietnam's impact.[275]

Hung

Laine: Mr. Hung, what was President Thiệu's impression of Anna Chennault?

Hung: Thiệu was fascinated by Anna Chennault…an intelligent stunning woman.[276]

Laine: Did she visit him and if so what did she tell him?

Hung: She visited Saigon frequently in 1968, to advise Thiệu on Nixon's candidacy and his views on Vietnam. She told him then that Nixon would be a stronger supporter of Vietnam than Humphrey.[277]

Laine: Thiệu, as I understand it, was under heavy pressure from the Democrats to change his mind about not attending the conferences, did Chennault say anything to him regarding that pressure?

Hung: Chennault said, "My job was to hold him back and prevent him from changing his mind."[278]

Corcoran

Laine: Mr. Corcoran you probably knew Anna longer and better than any of the gentlemen in town, and she claims you were are on the phone

---

[275] Summers, Chapter 22-footnote #17.
[276] Hung, 23.
[277] Ibid.
[278] Ibid.

once when she spoke to Mitchell. Did you ever ask her what exactly was up with the peace negotiations?

Corcoran: I was very careful not to ask her... if I had been Anna, I'd have done what they say she did. But I'd have been a goddamn careful, I didn't do it without orders from the top.[279]

Laine: Mr. Corcoran could you be more direct, I'm not sure what you're implying.

Corcoran: People have used Anna scandalously, Nixon in particular. I know exactly what Nixon said to her and then he repudiated her and Anna said nothing. She kept her mouth shut.[280]

Haldeman

Laine: Mr. Haldeman, after the inauguration, anticipating a problem in the Chennault affair, you reviewed highly confidential information relating to the alleged affair. What did you conclude?

Haldeman: There was nothing in the FBI files or the messages intercepted in Saigon that showed Nixon personally used his influence to kill the Paris peace talks. There is, however, sufficient information to demonstrate that he was far from uninvolved. Looking back upon those events, he certainly was indiscreet about his meetings with Chennault and Diem. [281]

Harlow

Laine: Mr. Harlow, you served the Republican candidate as a conduit for their double agent within the Johnson administration, informing

---

[279] Judith Viorst, "The Three Faces of Anna Chennault" *The Washingtonian,* September 1969, 27. Quoted in Lyndon Baines Johnson Library, the X-Envelope, 53. This is a fascinating quote, because Corcoran did suggest that to justify Chennault actions, the orders would have to have come from the top, therefore, he implied a connection to Nixon. He did not mention anything about the Mitchell phone call, but he was not asked.

[280] *Washington Post,* February 18, 1981. M2. Quoted in Bundy, 45

[281] Parmet, 522-23. Because Nixon completely denied any involvement, it is of strong interest here that Haldeman his old colleague suggested a connection. It should be noted, however, that Parmet's interview of Haldeman took place in 1983, well after the Watergate unpleasantness, which led to a criminal conviction for Haldeman. Perhaps he wasn't feeling so solicitous about Mr. Nixon at that point.

Nixon of the inner goings-on within the White House. You actively supported Nixon in the 1968 presidential election. What do you think about allegations that Nixon was behind the conspiracy?

Harlow: I'm not convinced that it was not true, it was too tempting a target. I wouldn't be a bit surprised if there was some shenanigans going on... but at any rate, Nixon told him [Johnson] no and Johnson put down his pistol, except Johnson probably didn't believe it.[282]

Bundy

Laine: Mr. Bundy, you are aware that Nixon responded to charges of his involvement with a categorical denial, saying flatly that whatever Chennault did it had to have been on her own with no connection or knowledge on his part. What is your response?

Bundy: This barefaced lie was his only tenable line of defense and the word must've gone out to top campaign people accounting for the vehement denials Theodore White encountered at the Republican campaign offices.[283]

Laine: How would you describe the Nixon strategy?

Bundy: In selecting Anna Chennault as his emissary, he made it possible to disassociate the Republican Party from the enterprise, if it were detected. But by keeping himself at a distance, working only through totally discreet John Mitchell, he can achieve what the covert action trade always wants, "plausible deniability," that no action can be definitely linked to the key individual. He was thus, of course, much better able to deny convincingly it was anything but an unauthorized caper by a head-strong lady who happened to be also involved in his campaign organization.[284]

---

[282] Dallek, *Nixon and Kissinger: Partners in Power,* 590. The "pistol" Harlow referred to was the Johnson-Nixon phone conversation where Johnson directly accused Nixon of the impropriety and Nixon denied it with Johnson seemingly backing down. This conversation allegedly ended with Nixon laughing upon hanging up.
[283] Bundy, 43.
[284] Bundy, 44.

Laine: Well there you have it. However, before we wrap up first a word from our sponsor.

Commercial: The show was brought to you by Vietnam Business Services (VBS) - remember we arrange business links with Vietnam – direct, efficient and friendly. If you need to do business in Vietnam, we can make it happen. Vietnam is your place to do business, since Jan. 1, 2004; foreign economic organizations and individuals has enjoyed a tax exemption for transporting profits abroad. V.B.S is officially recognized by the Chambers of Commerce and Industry in Hanoi, Ho Chi Minh (formerly Saigon) and other cities throughout Vietnam. Contact us through our website *http://www.vietnambusiness.com/contact.htm.*[285]

Laine: Before we close the show, a word about experts. Experts are funny people. My experience as a lawyer taught me there are many pitfalls to be aware of when we wander into the world of "Expertdom." In almost every civil trial I participated in, there were experts. Whether the subject was safety codes, medicine, or economics, one fact remained certain, each side has an expert saying the exact opposite. Here's the game, one expert takes a stand with a long list of credentials from impressive universities and states their opinion on the standard of care. Then, opposing counsel calls a different expert, with just as many outstanding credentials, and they testify that the first expert was totally off base. On some occasions, especially in medical malpractice cases, an honest difference of opinion derives from contrary schools of thought. More often, the expert's opinion depends on who is paying them, which reveals a sad, but important truth; experts lie, sometimes unintentionally

---

[285] This pro-capitalist website is not a creation. The United States has become one of Vietnam's major trading partners. Jason Folkmanis, "Trade Partners Push Vietnam Was World Trade Organization," *Herald Tribune* ,March 12, 2006, http://www.iht.com/articles/2006/03/12/bloomberg/sxdong.php (accessed November 29, 2007)

and sometimes intentionally.[286] Every expert who has written a book must be subject to the question of whether their claims are true for the sake of history or contrived for the sake of book sales and increased fees in the lecture circuit, or maybe both! Beyond money, the next most important cloud in expert world is self-interest, and the above panel was polluted with it. Perhaps the best example provided is Clark Clifford whose indignation and opinions regarding blame are clear. Nevertheless, Clifford personalized the Vietnam disaster. He failed to prevent the escalation when he knew it was wrong in 1965, and then provided enthusiastic "hawk-like' support during the failed policy of escalation, which he knew was based on improper foundations. In 1968, negotiations gave him a chance to fix those glaring marks on his otherwise sterling career. With the chance of redemption taken from him, so tantalizingly close at the last moment, he was furious. It should come as no surprise that he would readily blame others such as Chennault or Nixon for the failure in Vietnam, rather than accept personal responsibility for the debacle, which he obviously felt dearly. In his autobiography, when summing up the Vietnam War, Clifford made an amazing statement. He declared that in 1973 the hawks caved in and reached an agreement "that doomed Saigon's chances of surviving and blamed the outcome on the antiwar movement, Congress and the American press, whom they accused of biased reporting." He then argued: "in fact it was the hawks, not the doves who weakened America by pursuing the war for so long... then after the failure of their policies they sought to blame America's defeat on those who opposed the war, instead of accepting responsibility for the poor strategy and poor leadership they themselves had offered in Vietnam." In this sad and revealing observation, Clifford condemned himself.

---

[286] Some of our experts are convicted liars. Aitken a former British government Cabinet minister. He was convicted of perjury in 1999 and received an 18-month prison sentence, of which he served seven months. "Aitken's Downfall Complete," http://news.bbc.co.uk/2/hi/uk_news/politics/364174.stm (accessed December 24, 2014). Mr. Haldeman resigned as was convicted of perjury, conspiracy and obstruction of justice in trying to cover up the Nixon Administration's involvement in the Watergate scandal. "H. R. Haldeman, Nixon Aide Who Had Central Role in Watergate, Is Dead at 67," http://www.nytimes.com/1993/11/13/obituaries/h-r-haldeman-nixon-aide-who-had-central-role-in-watergate-is-dead-at-67.html. Clifford, as will be discussed in the Epilogue herein, at the age of 85, was charged with very serious economic crimes before his death.

The same avoidance of blame applies to Rostow, a known "hawk" and strong supporter of the South Vietnamese throughout his career. William Safire, Hung, Bundy, Corcoran, and Harlow were all involved in some way or another with the disaster known as the Vietnam War and would be more than pleased to shed any personal responsibility. Others not involved like Summers and Aitken may have political agendas or books they are trying to push. Still, others like Haldeman may have had personal vendettas. Judges, recognizing this problem with experts instruct a jury: "An expert witness may be able to assist you in understanding the evidence in this case or in performing your duties as a fact finder. But I want to emphasize to you that the determination of the facts in this case rests solely with you as jurors."[287] I give you the same advice. Thanks for listening to my show, good night.

CLOSING ARGUMENTS

Anna Chennault

If we choose to believe Richard Nixon, Anna Chennault acted as an independent agent on a mission of her own, when she attempted to convince the South Vietnamese not to attend the peace conference. Certainly, Chennault had the personal motivation. She was strongly against any dealings with communists based upon her own personal experiences. She blamed the United States for losing China to communism, and believed the same failure was about to repeat itself in Vietnam. She was certain that no deals could be made with communists because they only respected strength. Motivated to fulfill the destiny of her hero dead husband and pushed by personal demons that demanded she be somebody "special," Chennault possessed the necessary motivation to act alone. She retained independent strong connections with leaders in Southeast Asia, who respected her due to her personal accomplishments and those of the General. Nevertheless, motivation and means, although compelling, do not determine guilt. We must turn to the evidence.

Anna Chennault is the prime witness claiming Nixon was behind the conspiracy, but was she credible? She failed to mention the critical November 2, 1968 intercept in her memoirs. Her recollections of events are often internally contradictory and often at odds with the recollections of others. She conveniently

---

[287] New Jersey Civil Model Jury Charge 1:15. See also *N.J. Rules of Evidence* sections 702, 703, 704 and *Landrigan* v. Celotex, Corp., 127 N.J. 404 (1992).

failed in her autobiography to mention the "man from Florida" conversation, the October 23 and 27th conversations with Diem that became subject of the intercepted wiretaps and presented a very fuzzy version of the "man from Albuquerque" scenario. On the other hand, her recollection was bizarrely clear in other circumstances, such as remembering telephone numbers and word for word conversations that occurred over a dozen years before she wrote her memoir. Her side of the October 31, 1968, Mitchell telephone conversation reeks of artificial post-hoc self-protection. Based on the above, her entire interpretation of events becomes suspect. She claimed, in her memoirs, that she never attempted to convince and only relayed messages. She reinforced this position by the surprise she demonstrated during the Mitchell phone call of October 31 and the visits from, and demands of, Mitchell, Klein, Evans and Dirksen. Did she really expect her readers to believe that all four men were similarly wrong regarding the role she played? Yet, Chennault claimed that she spoke to Mitchell every day and the subject of conversation was preventing the South Vietnamese from coming to the negotiations. According to Hung, Chennault believed that convincing Thiệu was "her job." She maintains, to this very day, the "I know something you don't know" attitude. It is understandable that when Nixon and his cronies were alive she might have been fearful of retribution. That fear does not exist today; there is no reason for this 80-plus year old woman to harbor secrets.

Here lies the problem. Often in civilized society, it is anathema to directly challenge somebody else's credibility. Often we dance around the issue, giving excuses such as failure of memory, the statement was taken out of context, there was a misunderstanding or misquote, etc. Nevertheless, I will risk this scorn and pose the question; is Anna Chennault is a liar? There is an old legal principle, *falsis in unum, falsis in omnibus* or false in one thing, false in all things. This means that if jurors determine that a witness was untruthful in one material statement, they are justified in dismissing the witness's entire testimony. [288] Nevertheless, does that principal of law apply here, or are we able to accept some of Chennault's allegations but dismiss others? The answer to our question will come after examining the nature of her alleged fabrications and whether other statements or events corroborate her claims. We will first address her situation in 1968. Did she possess "special" status within the Nixon campaign? It is logical that the more power she had, the more likely it would be that she enjoyed a direct connection to Nixon. There was evidence this may have been true. Nixon's aides

---

[288] Sheldon Richman. "Commentaries: False In One, False In All," *The Future Of Freedom Foundation*, July 14, 2003, http://www.fff.org/comment/com0307i.asp (accessed November 29, 2007)

strongly recommended that he not meet with Chennault in his apartment during the summer of 1968, yet he still met with her. It is logical that Nixon went against the advice of staff because he envisioned a grander role for Chennault. Further, Diem confirmed the apartment appointment separately. Admittedly, his credibility is hardly solid; however, he does not benefit from this information and therefore he becomes more believable. She did receive personally signed letters from Nixon and did meet with him in Kansas City to discuss strategy, but that could just be good people management on Nixon's part. The South Vietnamese believed she was speaking on Nixon's behalf and passed the messages to him through her. Nevertheless, their trust may have been encouraged by Chennault's statements. Therefore, more likely than not, Chennault did enjoy special status within the Nixon campaign, but this hardly proves Nixon was responsible for the conspiracy.

The strongest evidence of Nixon's involvement is the intercepted wiretaps of November 2, 1968 and a supposedly exculpatory statement by Senator John Tower and the "four horsemen." (A term I use to describe those incredibly stressful contacts made to Chennault by Nixon's agents Mitchell, Klein, Evans and Dirksen). We have good evidence that Chennault received a call from New Mexico. Yet, we have no direct information about what was said. The fact she did receive calls from the Nixon campaign does support her "special" status. On the same day, we do have corroborating information that she contacted Diem, informing him that she spoke to "the boss" who called her from New Mexico, directing her to instruct Diem to tell the South Vietnamese government to "hold firm." Chennault made it clear that she was acting upon the direction of Nixon, thinly disguised as the "boss." Is it possible that Chennault was lying about the source of the instructions when she spoke to the ambassador? Could she have constructed an elaborate story that she was acting upon Nixon's behalf while actually conducting a mission of her own? Yes, it is possible; she has lied before, but is it probable? This is where we turn to Senator Tower and the "four horsemen."

After the election, Tower confronted with Chennault's alleged acts, specifically denied any Nixon connection. Still, he did volunteer that Nixon contacted her after he was elected, for the purpose of having her convince the South Vietnamese to attend the peace talks. Tower unknowingly may have given away the secret. Question: Why would Nixon go to Chennault, of all the people in the entire world, to convince the South Vietnamese to go to the peace talks? Answer: Because he previously used her in that role. Nixon already knew she had the trust of the South Vietnamese and the ability to convince them. Tower's statement confirmed that pipeline.

In a move that must be admired for sheer audacity, Nixon in 1972 reconfirmed the Chennault-Thiệu pipeline. Once again, there was a possibility for settlement with Hanoi. Once again, the South Vietnamese president stood in the way of any agreement. Furthermore, consecutive votes of Congress to cut off funding for the war added additional pressure on Nixon to find a solution. Nixon needed to convince Thiệu to agree to the provisions that then Secretary of State Kissinger, was working out with Hanoi to end the war. Who did he contact using Mitchell as an intermediary? Anna Chennault, of course. According to presidential adviser Haldeman, Nixon attempted to persuade Chennault to influence the South Vietnamese, but she refused.[289] Nixon's going back to the well serves as strong proof that he was the one who dug it.

Tower also gave credibility to Chennault's story of the "four horsemen." There are no documents confirming their visits, however because their purpose was consistent with Tower's assertion, it becomes extremely unlikely that Chennault fabricated these stories. There is still another fascinating point about the "four horsemen." As Chennault presented it, all were consistent in their fear that Chennault would somehow publish information that could become hurtful to Nixon. Why would there be so much concern if there were no direct Nixon connection? Chennault argued that she would not have been involved in anything that would have led to Nixon's embarrassment and used the stories as devices proving her victimization. After all, she never attempted to convince the South Vietnamese, she was a mere messenger. Undoubtedly, when she wrote the story she believed that her stories exculpated her. Nevertheless, by presenting evidence that four separate individuals feared disclosure of her acts could be harmful to Nixon only provides proof that their concerns were accurate. Chennault's own version of the "four horsemen" conversations proves contrary to her assertions that she was a mere pawn.

Richard Nixon

The chief witness claiming that Nixon was not behind the conspiracy is Richard Nixon, but was he credible? Was Nixon the type of man who would perform such heinous acts? We turn to Nixon's reputation for truth and his past behavior to assist in answering the above questions. The 1968 election was critical for Nixon,

---

[289] War Presidents Materials Project – Haldeman notes, January 4, 1973. Quoted in Stephen Ambrose, *Nixon Ruined and Recovery 1973 to 1990*, (New York: Simon & Schuster, 1991), 46

because, the man who needed to win was on a very public losing streak. In 1960, he lost the presidency to a John F. Kennedy practically unknown, at that time. His subsequent embarrassing loss during the 1962 California governorship race prompted his famous remark, "For 16 years, ... you've had a lot of—a lot of fun—that you've had an opportunity to attack me and I think I've given as good as I've taken.....But as I leave you I want you to know—just think how much you're going to be missing. You won't have Nixon to kick around anymore."[290] Nixon demonstrated in his past that his overwhelming desire, if not obsession to win, at all costs, rendered him capable of doing whatever was necessary to effect the outcome of the close 1968 race. He created false evidence in his 1946 congressional campaign. When confronted with this impropriety by a friend, he candidly stated, "Sometimes you have to do this to be a candidate." He falsely accused Helen Gahagan Douglas of being a communist. He surreptitiously fanned the flames of anti-Semitism in that same Senate bid. The 1968 pre-election polls, although favoring Nixon, did not indicate a landslide lead and that lead steadily dissipated over the summer. Question: Would this "aprincipled man" be the author of a conspiracy to prevent peace in South East Asia to ensure his election to the presidency of the United States? Before attempting to answer to this question, we must first take a step back to appreciate the gravity of our effort. The law often treads very carefully when attempts are undertaken to find an individual guilty of a crime based on their prior bad acts. It would appear that an accused's history of similar bad behavior should be relevant, but because it can be overwhelmingly prejudicial, such testimony is inadmissible to prove new bad conduct.[291] Nevertheless, the inquiry does not end there. The law, much like Harriman and Vance during the negotiation process, becomes creative in the use of language. Prior bad acts can be admissible if they go to the credibility of the witness. [292] Therefore, in the credibility challenge between Nixon and Chennault, it is proper to consider Nixon's past alleged acts of untruthfulness during prior

---

[290]"The Nixon Era Center," http://www.nixonera.com/welcome.asp (accessed November 29, 2007)
[291] In the State of New Jersey, the admission of evidence into court is controlled by the Court approved "Rules of Evidence," which are largely modeled on the Federal version. Under Rule 404 (b): Other crimes, wrongs, or acts. Evidence of other crimes, wrongs, or acts is not admissible to prove the disposition of a person in order to show that he acted in conformity therewith. Such evidence may be admitted for other purposes, such as proof of motive, opportunity, intent, preparation, plan, knowledge, identity or absence of mistake or accident when such matters are relevant to a material issue in dispute.
[292] Under New Jersey and Federal Rule of Evidence, section 608. Evidence of Character for Truthfulness or Untruthfulness: The credibility of a witness may be attacked or supported by evidence in the form of opinion or reputation, provided, however, that the evidence relates only to the witness' character for truthfulness or untruthfulness.

election campaigns while judging the believability of his denial of complicity in this matter.

The law also allows a jury to consider the habit and custom of an individual to prove that his behavior in another circumstance was in conformity with that pattern. [293] Nixon's campaign manager during his run for Senate, Murray Chotimer, described Nixon as a perfectionist employing complete control of his campaign. Is it unlikely that this type of personality would be unaware that Anna Chennault was running around the world making claims in his name without him having knowledge? Further, it is reasonably arguable that the conspiracy was also consistent with Nixon's technique, or in legal terms, custom and habit. Nixon, as learned previously, was the master of plausible deniability. It was his well-honed method to have others do his dirty work and deny his involvement thereafter. Setting up Chennault as the fall person in this matter was perfectly consistent with his *modus operandi*.

If Chennault was Nixon's sole co-conspirator that would be less damaging in the case against Nixon, but that was not the situation. One individual acting out may make sense, but so many of Nixon's cronies knew about and cooperated in Chennault's activities. We learned that Kissinger, an unidentified mole in the White House reporting to Bryce Harlow, his law partner Tom Evans, his campaign manager Mitchell and Senators Dirksen and Tower all appeared to be somewhat involved or at least knowledgeable . Mitchell served as a conduit for Kissinger's secret information just as he served as a conduit for Chennault. The above network and pattern of deceit only strengthens the supposition that Nixon was the master conspirator.

Nixon's behavior during the accusatory phone call with Johnson was also troubling. He lacked indignation when accused of hatching the conspiracy, but that could be just the fruits of his finely honed skill to mislead. More troubling, however, were his actions after he hung up. According to one source, the entire room broke up with laughter, having dodged a bullet. If Nixon were innocent, such behavior would not make any sense. If there was no bullet, why would he need to dodge anything? Critically, William Safire confirmed the story. In the room during the phone call, his former speechwriter confirmed the laughter,

---

[293] Under New Jersey and Federal Rule of Evidence, section 406. Habit; Routine Practice: Evidence of the habit of a person or of the routine practice of an organization, whether corroborated or not and regardless of the presence of eyewitnesses, is relevant to prove that the conduct of the person or organization on a particular occasion was in conformity with the habit or routine practice.

along with Nixon's immediate bizarre analogy about biting off your opponent's "nuts." Would Nixon make such a remark if he were innocent?

You now have before you the scales of justice. You have been presented with the evidence and your decision is difficult because both principals lack credibility. You now must answer the following question. Does the quality of evidence supporting the allegation that Nixon was involved in a conspiracy to prevent the South Vietnamese from attending the peace conference weigh more, even if ever so slightly, than the evidence supporting that he had no involvement, if so vote YES on the verdict sheet to question #2, if not answer No. If you answer affirmatively, the race moves on. If not, read ahead anyway, you may still change your mind.

CHAPTER 3

Choices versus Preferences

In 1972, Academy Award-winning director Franklin J. Schaffner released his extraordinary film *Papillion* that portrayed the adventures of incarcerated French criminal Henri Charrière, a/k/a Papillion, while serving his sentence banished to Devil's Island. The prison's topography and isolation rendered escape virtually impossible. Any jump from its high cliffs into the water below would result in certain death. Papillion, nevertheless, believed there must be an alternative. One day he discovered an alcove on the island where the water, during particular times, was deep enough to allow a successful jump. However, surviving the jump did not mean safe escape. He had to ensure that the ocean currents would allow him to safely swim away from the island instead of smashing him against the rocks below. Over the years, he meticulously studied the movements of the waves. He lashed together coconuts that approximated his size and weight and threw them into the water below to calculate the effects of the tide. After long periods of observation and experimentation, he arrived at a conclusion; he had a reasonable alternative. He jumped. Papillion escaped and survived.

The tale of Papillion it is about the availability of reasonable choice. As we approach the third hurdle, assuming a Nixon conspiracy, we will encounter the "so what" issue. Did Nixon's conspiracy, if you so find, effectively convince the South Vietnamese not to attend the peace conferences or did they make this decision on their own, outside of his influence? If Thiệu's decision was independent or inevitable, with or without, as Ambrose puts it, "that rather silly woman [Chennault] whispering in his ear," then we fail this hurdle and our story, although enlightening as to character, becomes historically insignificant. On the other hand, if Nixon offered Thiệu a previously non-existent, reasonable alternative upon which he based his "jump," in whole or part, then our runner clears this hurdle, and the race continues.

THERE WAS A DECISION TO GO BUT THEY CHANGED THEIR MIND

We start with examining the credibility of the premise that before October 31, 1968, Saigon officials made a decision to attend the peace conferences and then changed their minds for whatever reason. Before October 31, 1968, on at least three occasions, Bunker assured Johnson that the South Vietnamese were on board with the US-Hanoi deal. Although up to this point, Bunker made serious miscalculations and was about to make another the following night, he still had some understanding of the South Vietnamese and their sensitivities. He did inform the president that he had concern about Saigon's apprehension about being abandoned to communism. He also worried about the impact of the impending negotiations on the South Vietnamese leadership. [1] Because of his understanding of the scenario's complications, it is reasonable to assume that he announced the South Vietnamese agreement, on those three occasions, only after he and Saigon leadership fully debated/discussed the issue. Simply, Thiệu did not offer an off-the-cuff agreement and Bunker, before reporting their consent to LBJ, understood any reservations the GVN might have had. Consequently, there is reasonable evidence to support the original premise that Saigon legitimately decided to attend the conferences, but later changed its mind. Our friend, Ambassador Diem, the incredible Mr. Incredulous, presents an alternative explanation.

THEY WERE NEVER CONVINCED TO CHANGE THEIR MIND BECAUSE THEY NEVER INTENDED TO GO

According to Ambassador Diem, Thiệu was well informed about the negotiation process that led to the US-Hanoi deal. He knew the United States was ready to accept expanded talks that would include the NLF, with a vague "our side-your side formula." He also "believed the North Vietnamese offer was nothing but a ploy to influence the presidential race in favor of Humphrey, whom they much preferred to Nixon, the renowned anti-communist. By accepting the American offer, the North Vietnamese were achieving both a bombing halt and the potential ability to affect the election." However, despite his misgivings, "Feeling pressured by the Americans, Thiệu had acquiesced to these conditions back in July, but with profound inner reservations. He hoped -- and believed -- that the North Vietnamese would never agree to such an offer."[2] It is difficult to believe anything Diem offers in light of his questionable, at best, credibility. Still, his

---

[1] Schaffer, 199.
[2] Diem, 239.

memories of the situation highlight some intriguing possibilities. First, he confirmed that there was an acceptance, therefore whatever his shortcomings, Bunker reported accurately to the President. Next, a troubled man such as Thiệu, with inner reservations, would be a prime target for Chennault's whisperings about better options. Further, if Thiệu's "yes" was only to placate the Americans, gambling that the North Vietnamese would never accept the United States offer, this supports the argument that he never intended to go. The problem with accepting this interpretation is that it stretches logic. Thiệu could only think that the North Vietnamese would not accept the United States' deal because it was not in their best interest. If they accepted this "bad" deal, then it would have to be a good deal for the South Vietnamese, which they would naturally support. Admittedly, this criticism makes the possible false presumption that Thiệu acted logically.

Clark Clifford, one might assume, would be a strong believer in the proposition that there was a change of mind by the South Vietnamese. After all, he exclaimed that Thiệu's decision on November 1, not to attend the conference came "suddenly out of a clear sky."[3] He labeled Saigon's actions an "unexpected disaster."[4] He could not "understand what ha[d] happened in the last week."[5] In his own memoirs he wrote, referring to Chennault, "there is no doubt that she conveyed a simple and authoritative message of the Nixon camp that was probably decisive in convincing President Thiệu to defy President Johnson, thus delaying the negotiations and prolonging the war."[6] Clifford was convinced the South Vietnamese would attend the meetings. Yet if one examines his predisposition as to what Saigon would do, what is truly shocking was his failure to predict their actions. During July 1968, Clifford visited South Vietnam. Thereafter he informed a "shocked" president that he "was now absolutely certain that the South Vietnamese government did not want the war to end-not while they were protected by 500,000 American troops and a golden flow of money."[7] On October 17, 1968, Saigon stated their concern to Bunker that the NLF would be treated as a sovereign separate government during the Paris talks. Clifford, upon receiving this information believed: "It was clear that we sought different objectives from a bombing halt: we wanted to ensure that it did not lead to increased deaths of American and South Vietnamese soldiers, whereas Thiệu sought to prevent the NLF from gaining political advantage through the

---

[3] Transcript, Clark Clifford Oral History Interview III, 7/14/69.
[4] Clifford, 578.
[5] Ibid.
[6] Ibid., 522.
[7] Ibid., 551. The South Vietnamese seem to bring out the shock in all.

negotiations by obtaining recognition as a separate delegation." Notwithstanding these differences, the administration, including Clifford, accepted Bunker's assurances that these were "minor problems that would be cleared up quickly."[8] Clifford's amazement at Saigon's ultimate lack of cooperation proves that despite his strong pre-existing misgivings, this intelligent world experienced man must have possessed rock solid evidence that the South Vietnamese were going to attend which supports the proposition in above chapter.

Yet, after the fact, though, Clifford completely reverses himself and returns to his previous assessment that Saigon was never going to come. In a 1969 oral interview Clifford explained,

> What I had come to see as clearly as any equation I have ever seen, and that is by the end of 1968 the goal of the Saigon government was utterly antithetical to the goal of the United States. One, the Saigon government did not want the war to end. Number two; they did not want the Americans to pull out. Number three, they did not want to make any settlement of any kind with Hanoi or with the Viet Cong or the NLF. They preferred it the way they were. With 540,000 American troops-- they were in no danger whatsoever, and if we stayed... In addition to that, when you've got 540,000 troops in a country and thousands of civilians, it's just as though you had a golden pump running, and were pumping the money in there, and they certainly all liked that fine.[9]

Clifford's assessment has become representative for the position that Saigon was never going to attend. Yet, Clifford's epiphany was not original. He held that exact belief in July of 1968, yet he was convinced in October 1968 that the South Vietnamese would consent to the peace process as proven by emphatic response to their withdrawal and his spirited argument with Nitze. There was no question that Clifford was furious with the South Vietnamese and absolutely shocked by their withdrawal. Yet, despite his clear position, he completed a 180-degree position change. Is it that he received new information or was it more personal? His need to throw the blame off himself may have motivated him to re-embrace his earlier policy. After all, if one accepts that the South Vietnamese were corrupt, lying, no good, misleading miscreants, the failure of the war was not Clifford's responsibility, rather it was Saigon's. Therefore, relying on Clifford for the premise that the South Vietnamese were never going to attend the conference

---

[8] Ibid., 577-578.
[9] Transcript, Clark Clifford Oral History Interview III, 7/14/69.

because it was never in their best interests, may not be the wisest course. If anything, Clifford stands for the proposition that they were going to attend the conference but then there was a change of mind.

The Bureau of Intelligence and Research (INR), a less passionate and an arguably more objective source, concluded that even if the South Vietnamese attended the peace negotiations they would most likely have stalled them, with or without Nixon's interference. On May 3, 1968, the INR, exploring how the South Vietnamese would react to possible peace negotiation, concluded, "Saigon would probably acquiesce to the holding of talks, but would continue to resist the total halt of bombing, any reduction of US forces, and any expansion of the subject matter in the bilateral talks to include the present or future situation in the South." Further, they predicted there "will, undoubtedly, be a progressive rise in South Vietnamese suspicions of US intentions and with it may come an increased possibility of a military takeover in Saigon." Their analysis presciently concluded that South Vietnam would hope to delay any stage where they perceived that the NLF might substantively participate in the proceedings.[10] What the INR ignores is that with the election of Humphrey and his known predisposition against the Thiệu government, it is reasonable to postulate that support from the US would end and his government would cease to exist. Realistically what power did Thiệu have to oppose any reduction of US forces or oppose a bombing halt? No doubt, what the INR report concluded would be what the GVN would prefer, but if given no reasonable alternative preferences do not necessarily determine choices.

THREE LIKELY SCENARIOS, THE GAME OF RISK

If we accept the premise that the South Vietnamese never intended go to the conferences, no matter what Nixon did or did not do, our analysis stops here. No doubt, the South Vietnamese did not want to go to the peace conferences. No doubt, they would have preferred to continue to enjoy the products of the "golden pump." Further, Saigon did fear that "disastrous consequences" would occur if the NLF participated in a conference, especially if their participation was as a distinct entity from the DRV.[11] At that time, Thiệu and Ky had only been in power a short time following a long parade of failed incompetent governments.

---

[10] The National Security Archive. (INR) "Intelligence and Vietnam: The Top Secret 1969 State Department Study. Review of Judgments in INR Reports A.(VII)the search for peace, April -- December, 1968,"
http://www.gwu.edu/~nsarchiv/NSAEBB/NSAEBB121/A-VII.pdf, 5 (accessed November 29, 2007)
[11] DOS, section 89.

Pacification, a program to sway South Vietnamese Villagers away from the Viet Cong and to the Saigon government, was an abject failure.[12] Thiệu had reason to fear that the tenuous grip his government had on the country could slip if the NLF achieved international legitimacy.[13] Nevertheless, the gulf between wants or preferences and availabilities or alternatives is wide, and the degree and nature of risk determines the integrity of the bridge. The risk facing the South Vietnamese if they decided not to attend the peace conferences can be broken into three scenarios.

> **First case:** *Humphrey is elected.* Humphrey, never a strong supporter of the Saigon government, would react with great negativity upon discovering their attempt to sabotage the possibility of peace. It is reasonable to conclude that he would have begun withdrawing United States troops from Vietnam, thus exposing the Saigon government to almost certain extinction. As mentioned herein, while on his campaign plane Humphrey wrote a press release indicating his intention to dump the South Vietnamese, only changing his mind at the last minute. His potential action of pulling the troops and shutting the "golden pump" would certainly have enjoyed the support of the American people. As Bundy aptly concluded: "To walk back from the deal, [that]both Saigon and Hanoi had agreed to would've been difficult under any circumstances; to do so on the basis that Saigon had to be accepted as the preeminent South Vietnamese representative would have been impossible to explain to the American people, let alone Hanoi."[14] To

---

[12] For an excellent discussion of "pacification" see "The American And South Vietnamese Pacification Efforts During
The Vietnam War," http://etd.lsu.edu/docs/available/etd-0419102-103048/unrestricted/Pinard_thesis.pdf (accessed December 22, 2014)
[13] The National Security Archive. (INR) "Intelligence and Vietnam: The Top Secret 1969 State Department Study. Review of Judgments in INR Reports A. (VII) the search for peace April -- December, 1968," 19.
[14] Bundy, 33.

borrow a term from the George W. Bush administration, the risk faced by the South Vietnamese would have been at the red level.[15]

Second case: Nixon is elected, but there was no conspiracy and no promises or assurances given concerning any different policy other than that already proposed by the Johnson administration. In this scenario, the risk level remains the same as in the first. Putting it simply, if there were no other alternatives available to Saigon, then there was no other reasonable choice available other than cooperation with the US peace efforts. South Vietnamese Vice President Ky added critical input to this argument when in his book he claimed; "I had reservations about the support we might get from Humphrey if he became president. Then out of the blue Nixon's supporters stepped into the picture."[16] The "out of the blue" language surely suggests that the Nixon alternative came as a surprise, albeit a welcome one, for the South Vietnamese.

Third case: Nixon is elected and he has made promises and assurances to the South Vietnamese that he would ensure their survival. With this safe harbor, Thiệu's decision not to attend the peace conferences, poses significantly less risk. As William Bundy explained, if Thiệu,

[H]ad not been told they would have Nixon's support in holding back, he would surely have given greater weight to what refusing to go along could do to his chances of full support from any American president. He was in effect, assured that the top Republicans would soften any immediate criticism of him, and would themselves hold him in greater favor for holding back.[17]

---

[15] President George W. Bush's administration assigned various colors to correspond to the risk of terrorist attack. The palette of relative danger starts at green, which is low risk. It progresses to blue, the hue of general risk. Then it's yellow - the color of significant risk of attack. Then to orange, symbolic of high risk. Finally, red means severe risk of attack. See 'Color Us Frightened, No More Reassured A Rainbow Of Risk Tells Us The Likelihood Of A Terrorist Act. So Now What?"
 http://articles.philly.com/2002-03-13/news/25341936_1_color-linda-trent-kodachrome (Accessed December 5, 2014)
[16] Nguyen Cao Ky, *How We Lost The Vietnam War*, (New York, NY: Stein, and Day, 1976). Quoted in Berman, 33.
[17] Bundy, 47.

If Nixon made a promise, what was it? All writers, when discussing this question speak in vague terms such as, "things would be better with the Republicans" or "Nixon offered a better deal." It is fair to assume that if Thiệu took the great risk of changing his mind and not cooperating with the Johnson administration, he must have had a concrete offer. Based upon this author's July 2007 interview of Chennault and simple reasoning, the offer must have been assured survival. South Vietnam, as the INR study concluded, feared coalition. They believed a coalition government eventually meant communist rule and an end to their power. Nixon, through Chennault, must have offered them support to sustain the status quo. Indeed, Nixon may have inadvertently disclosed his earlier promise during his first meeting with Thiệu as President, when Nixon promised him "eight years of strong support - four years of military support, during his first term in office and four years of economic support during his second term." [18] Putting it in other terms, faced with no other alternative, the South Vietnamese logically would have cooperated with the Johnson administration's policy. However, if Nixon came along and offered a parachute for the "jump," ensuring that the waters were deep enough and the tide and currents were safe, then Saigon, given this safety of the alternative, could decide not to cooperate with the Democrats. However, without any other alternatives, whether it was Nixon or Humphrey as the new US president, logic predetermined that they had to attend the peace conferences.

If we assume the above was the nature of the "offer," our focus then shifts to whether it had credibility. As revealed herein, Thiệu was quite nervous over whatever Nixon promised and required constant assurances, from multiple sources, that there was a deal on the table. The purpose of this section is more about Nixon and his character and credibility than it is about the South Vietnamese, who either due to their need to believe or Nixon's well-honed duplicity and his skillful manipulation of Chennault or both, believed the alternative was real.

Before the election, Nixon never disclosed what he planned for Vietnam, other than to claim that he supported the president. He did imply, nevertheless, that he possessed a secret plan that would end the war. Nixon would even resort to dramatically "touching his breast pocket as if the plan were right there in the jacket and implying that to say what was in it might jeopardize secrecy." At the same time, Nixon told speechwriter Richard Whelan, "I've come to the conclusion that there is no way to win the war. We can't say that, of course."[19] After the election, it became apparent that Nixon's breast pocket was empty.

---

[18] Summers, 307.
[19] Summers, 294.

According to Bundy, Henry Kissinger's proposal for peace on behalf of the Nixon administration, "matched almost exactly what Johnson's negotiators would have suggested." In a December 1968 issue of the magazine *Foreign Affairs,* written months earlier, and published a few days after his appointment by Nixon as Secretary of State and chief adviser on foreign affairs, Kissinger set forth his own evaluation of the Vietnam negotiations. "On every point of substance he agreed with the line taken in Paris by the Johnson/Humphrey negotiators." In response to this revelation author Christopher Hitchens lamented, "One had to pause for an instant to comprehend the enormity of this, Kissinger helped elect a man who had surreptitiously promised the South Vietnamese could do a better deal than they would get from the Democrats." [20] Yet there was no better deal. On November 11, Nixon, at a briefing with the Johnson administration concerning foreign policy, "revealed that there were no significant differences between Nixon's views and those of the administration." As stated previously, thereafter, Nixon gave public and private support for Clifford's program pressuring Thiệu to go to Paris. When Chennault refused to act on his behalf, Nixon himself wrote to Thiệu to encourage him to go to Paris. [21] One can only reasonably conclude there never was a parachute, the waters were never deep enough and the tide was not safe. Nixon lied when he said he had a secret plan for peace and lied to the South Vietnamese and Chennault about the existence of a reasonable alternative.

If "reasonable" thinking is applied, our conclusion must be that the conspiracy significantly influenced the GVN because without a reasonably safe harbor, the extraordinary risk would have determined that they had no choice but to attend the conferences. Choice depending on the availabilities of options as opposed to preferences is well recognized in the field of psychology When analyzing existing models of decision making in high level negotiation processes Social Scientist Michael Watkins summed up this phenomena well when he opined,

> [p]arties make choices by evaluating their alternatives through the lens of their interests: agreement is reached only when available terms are more attractive than no-agreement alternatives. … Negotiators make hard choices only when they lack more attractive alternatives and doing nothing is not an option. [22]

---

[20] Christopher Hitchens, *The Trial of Henry Kissinger* (New York, NY: Verso, 2001), 15.
[21] Stephen Ambrose, *Nixon: The Triumph of a Politician 1962 – 1972*, 231.
[22] Michael Watkins, "Building Momentum in Negotiations: Time-Related Costs and Action-Forcing Events." *Negotiation Journal* Volume 14 Issue 3 (July 1998): 241-256.

With Humphrey as the potential president, Thiệu had no other options other than to agree with the peace process, but Nixon's alleged offer introduced the more attractive alternative.

We have to be careful though, reason does not always determine action. Often ego leads one down the path of destruction that was otherwise avoidable. Thiệu, Bunker's "great statesman," was not without great ego. He grew weary of the references that he was nothing more than a puppet of the United States. His brother Nguyen Van Kieu, who often spoke on Thiệu's behalf stated, "My brother would never concede to the Americans and was prepared to leave the presidency if the Americans cut off financial aid to the GVN or to die if there was an attempt against his life." He further claimed his brother's preference was for "a respected name in history to living shamelessly like a dog obeying his master's every command." [23] Thiệu, himself declared South Vietnam "is not a truck to be attached to a locomotive which will pull it wherever it likes." [24]

Unreasonable behavior can also be a product of emotion. Thiệu did not like Humphrey. According to Hung, their first meeting in 1967 at Thiệu's inauguration did not go well. During this meeting, Humphrey informed him "you need to know the political picture in America: Time is running out and the transition is needed to greater Vietnamese self-help." "Yes, we understand," Thiệu responded, "but we also understand it will be necessary for you to remain here at present levels." Humphrey then repeated his concerns and told Thiệu, "Several years more of the same aid levels, militarily and economically, are not in the cards." After that exchange, according to Hung, "Thiệu and Humphrey had become enemies." [25]

How then do we solve this puzzle? We return to the evidence. If there is proof, the South Vietnamese behaved as if they were getting and needing assurances from the republicans then that is strong evidence that they relied upon these assurances in making their decision not to come to the peace talks. When the risk of the jump is high, one would want to make it absolutely sure that the parachute is there, the water is deep enough and the current is flowing in the right direction. We already know of the numerous contacts through Diem to the South Vietnamese expressing the Republican position. Thiệu, apparently nervous that he might not be getting the correct information upon which to base his choices, made sure he had independent contacts to the Republicans other than Ambassador

---

[23] DOS, section 148.
[24] *Keesing's Contemporary Archives*, September 6-13, 1969, pp. 23549-23550. Quoted in DOS, section 171.
[25] Hung, 21.

Diem. Hung claimed that Thiệu was leery of Bui Diem whom he considered primarily loyal to Vice President Ky.[26] Because he feared he might be receiving falsified intelligence, Thiệu sent his own messengers to Washington to contact Mrs. Chennault, and he relied heavily on his brother Nguyen Van Kieu, who was South Vietnamese ambassador to Taiwan.[27] In her interview with author Parmet, Chennault also claimed that confidential messages from Washington to Saigon went through additional carriers other than Ambassador Bui Diem.[28] This information was confirmed by the CIA report to the President: "Thiệu during the US election campaign [redaction] had sent two secret emissaries to the US to contact Richard Nixon."[29] All this communication, back and forth, between the Republicans and the South Vietnamese, only makes sense in light of a conspiracy scenario. After all, what else could they be talking about?

The South Vietnamese also exhibited other behavior suggesting that they based their decisions on promises given by the Nixon team. As the election neared, Hung described Thiệu as being, "extremely nervous, fearing that Humphrey might still win"[30] His behavior in the last week before the election could be reasonably explained as a calculated attempt to make sure that Nixon won the election. By building anticipation for peace and dashing it at the last minute, Thiệu did all he could to avoid the disaster of a Humphrey election.

When Thiệu received word of Nixon's election, he stated with relief, "This is nice. Now at least we have bought ourselves some time. When the new president comes in... we have some more rope to play with."[31] During the election, other than pointing to his breast pocket and talking about secret formulas, Nixon had not disclosed his future Vietnam policy. How could Thiệu know "how much rope" he had to play with unless Nixon and/or his co-conspirators had showed him its length and supposed integrity? Further, Thiệu's statement reveals that he well understood that he had no rope to play with if Humphrey was elected.

---

[26] In a confidential memo prepared for the President exploring Diem's background, it was revealed that he served as a prime advisor for Vice President Ky. This is relevant because although Thiệu and Ky ran on the same ticket for president and vice-president in 1967, they were often seen as opponents rather than as cooperative government officials. Because Diem was aligned with Ky, "many influential Vietnamese regard[ed] him with suspicion as an alleged opportunist and schemer" See Confidential Bui Diem Viet-Nan E.O 12956, Sec 3.6, NL: 93-183 NARA date 6-16-98, source LBJ Library. See also Parmet , 522.

[27] Hung 21.

[28] Parmet, 522

[29] Lyndon Baines Johnson Library, the X-Envelope, "November 18, 1968, C. I. A Intelligence Information Cable," 71a.

[30] Hung, 29.

[31] Ibid.

Ambassador Diem was also nervous, "he was keeping his fingers crossed due to his emotional involvement." Despite his respect for Humphrey, Diem claimed that, "he had to side with those people who gave the Vietnamese the maximum of conditions." [32] How would he know what the conditions were unless he had received prior information? Even after the election, the South Vietnamese sought assurances that Nixon's promise would be kept. They were especially nervous in light of Nixon's new actions aimed at pressuring South Vietnam to attend the conference. It deserves repeating here that Chennault contacted officials at the South Vietnamese Embassy to inform them that Melvin Laird's appointment as Secretary of Defense was good for the Vietnamese and "not to be too concerned about the press' reference about a coalition government." [33] No doubt, this was her attempt to calm down some much frayed nerves.

CLOSING ARGUMENT

Once again, we arrive at a decision point. Does the runner clear the third hurdle? This section presents the first of our "so what" inquiries. Our dilemma is that we have separate actors contributing to a single outcome, that being the no-show at the peace conferences. Assuming the Nixon conspiracy, we must weigh how its influence contributed to the outcome, if at all. To aid in decision-making, we again turn to the civil law and the parameters it has established to sort out such challenges.[34]

---

[32] Lyndon Baines Johnson Library, the X-Envelope, "November 6, 1968 Memo to President from W. Rostow," 25.

[33] Ibid., 15a.

[34] It is worth repeating my statement from the Introduction that it is not my purpose to have the reader consider whether or not Nixon committed a violation of the criminal or civil codes. It is not that I do not believe a conviction is possible, but rather I believe that such a focus would reduce, not increase, the significance of these alleged acts. Perhaps an analogy is helpful. Recently, an emotionally distraught teenage girl committed suicide because she was duped to believe that an individual, with whom she was corresponding with on-line, took a romantic interest in her and then cruelly rejected her. It turned out that this "individual" was a mean hoax concocted by her adult neighbors. See http://www.foxnews.com/story/2007/11/16/mom-myspace-hoax-led-to-daughter-suicide/ (accessed December 15, 2014). The neighbor's acts, no question were heinous, but to present date they remain uncharged because there was no specific violation of the criminal code. The lack of a technical penalty does not make their act any less despicable. The same logic applies to this matter. I am not interested in whether there were technical violations of the law in the present case. My references to the civil law are to provide only a proven and accepted method of dispute resolution. Here, no doubt, since there is a dispute concerning historical significance, civil law is provided as a framework or a tool to solve this dispute.

In most civil trials, the jury must determine if the alleged acts of the defendant caused the claimed damages of the plaintiff, this task is known as determining "causation." As society became more complex, the civil law concept of "causation" also evolved. One of the most important contributors to the development of this law is the American Law Institute (ALI).[35] Over the years, the ALI publishes its opinions on what the law is, or should be, in an authoritative and widely accepted work known as the Restatement of Torts. We will rely upon the third, version to assist in our analysis. We begin with the most basic statement. Under section 26 of the Restatement of Torts 3rd, causation is determined to exist when,

An actor's tortious conduct must be a factual cause of another's physical harm for liability to be imposed. Conduct is a factual cause of harm when the harm would not have occurred absent the conduct.[36]

Simply stated, but complicated in application. The first question that arises is whether the conduct must be the "only" cause of the harm or "a" cause to be actionable. The ALI, responding to this issue, commented, "An actor's tortious conduct need only be 'a' factual cause of the other's harm. The existence of other causes of the harm does not affect whether the specified improper conduct can be the legal cause of the harm in question." [37] In our matter, we are particularly concerned with a scenario where there are multiple causes for one effect. The ALI addresses this complexity in several ways. In some cases, two causal sets may exist, one or the other of which was the cause of harm. In the alternative, the effects of multiple acts combine to produce or cause the ultimate event. The following example is helpful to understand the differences between the two possibilities

Plaintiff claims that a vaccination caused subsequent seizures, and the defendant claims that the seizures were caused not by the vaccination but by a preexisting traumatic injury to the plaintiff, the causal set including

---

[35] The ALI, founded in 1923, has a membership consisting of judges, practicing lawyers, and legal scholars from all areas of the United States as well as some foreign countries, selected on the basis of professional achievement and demonstrated interest in the improvement of the law. ALI, through a careful and deliberative process, drafts and then publishes various Restatements of the Law, model codes, and legal studies to promote the clarification and simplification of the law and its better adaptation to social needs, to secure the better administration of justice, and to encourage and carry on scholarly and scientific legal work. http://www.ali.org. (accessed November 29, 2007)

[36] "American Law Institute Restatement of Torts 3[rd Section] 26," http://www.ali.org/ali/2-22-tort.pdf, 337(accessed November 29, 2007). Note a tortious act is one that violates the standard of care as defined under the civil law.

[37] Ibid., Comments to section 26, 339.

the vaccination and the causal set including the traumatic injury are such alternative causes. If sufficient evidence to support each of these causal sets is introduced, the fact finder will have to determine which one is better supported by the evidence. On the other hand, if the evidence revealed that a traumatic injury and a vaccination could interact and cause seizures, then the vaccination and the trauma may each be a factual cause (both elements of the causal set) of the plaintiff's seizures.[38]

An exception to the combination scenario applies when one contribution is deemed *deminimus,* such as throwing a match into a raging bonfire. The match contributes to the flames, but the effect is without consequence and thus not a causative element.

Still, there is still another scenario; how is the issue of causation addressed when there are multiple acts and any of them could have led to the ultimate event. This is addressed under section 27 of the Restatement of Torts 3rd:

If multiple acts exist, each of which alone would have been a factual cause under § 26 of the physical harm at the same time, each act is regarded as a factual cause of the harm.[39]

The ALI offers another excellent illustration to simplify the above,

Rosaria and Vincenzo were independently camping in a heavily forested campground. Each one had a campfire, and each negligently failed to ensure that the fire was extinguished upon retiring for the night. Due to unusually dry forest conditions and a stiff wind, both campfires escaped their sites and began a forest fire. The two fires, burning out of control, joined together and engulfed Centurion Company's hunting lodge, destroying it. Either fire alone would have destroyed the lodge. Each of Rosaria's and Vincenzo's negligence is a factual cause of the destruction of Centurion's hunting lodge.[40]

In the above example, both Rosaria and Vincenzo are liable for damages.

It is simple to apply the above formulas to the instant matter. The harm is the failure to attend the conferences. The events contributing to the event are the pre-existing position of the South Vietnamese and the whispers and promises of the

---

[38] Ibid., 339.
[39] Ibid., 371.
[40] Ibid., 371.

alleged Nixon conspiracy. Did they combine to lead to the harm? Would they have independently led to the ultimate decision or was the Nixon contribution deminimus, like the match in the bonfire? I promised, in the introduction, to provide evidence and let the reader decide, therefore, like any juror in any civil case, you must respond to the below jury verdict sheet. Note, you are only answering question #3 at this point. One last note, the preponderance of the evidence standard also applies to this question as well. Remember, one grain of sand on the scale of justice weighing in favor of causation is sufficient to disturb the equipoise in favor of a positive verdict.

CHAPTER 4

Lost Opportunity?

A PROPER STANDARD

If we accept that all necessary sides to peace were sincere and that Nixon orchestrated a conspiracy to destroy peace, and that these actions were effective in influencing the GVN decisions, our last question, and perhaps most important one is whether there was a reasonable opportunity for peace. Had the GVN lived up to the promises it made to Bunker and the Johnson administration, could peace have been reached in 1968 or shortly thereafter? The above scenario is known in civil law as "lost opportunity" and again we turn again to civil law. To clarify we start with an example; a woman visits her OB/GYN for her normal checkup. The physician performs a breast examination and finds a lump; believing it somewhat suspicious, she sends her patient for mammography testing. The study revealed that the patient had stage one carcinoma of the right breast. The testing facility transmitted the report to the doctor's office, but unfortunately, filed it in the wrong patient folder. The patient never calls the physician for the results because it has been her previous experience, that unless the result is positive, she was not notified. A year goes by, she returns to the doctor and again the physician palpates her breasts, now discovering additional changes. Puzzled the doctor searches for the results and finally, upon locating the study, realizes that her office failed to warn their patient of the positive finding. The physician performs a biopsy revealing confirmed advanced stage four carcinoma, giving the patient very little chance of survival. The woman dies six months thereafter of complications from the disease. Did the failure to timely diagnose and treat the cancer amount to a lost opportunity or was the outcome already predetermined?

In 1968, was there a lost opportunity for peace? South Vietnam did not attend the conferences as originally planned, and the negotiations, when they eventually began, were exercises in futility. The war raged on for five long bloody years. Was there a realistic chance that all or some of the devastation and carnage could have been avoided? As we approach the fourth hurdle in the race for historical significance, we face our toughest challenge, when, once again, we are confronted with the "so what" issue. Our favorite party-quipping sex symbol professor, Henry Kissinger, summarized the "so what" position in a letter to the editor he prepared, after reading, as he put it, Anthony Summers' "tendentious" *Arrogance of Power*. In his missive, addressing the issue of whether the alleged conspiracy had any effect on the peace process, Kissinger opined that "the expanded peace talks began in early November, and any delay was therefore very brief... it also needs to be borne in mind that the expanded peace talks, once they began, were about procedure, not substance. Those talks immediately deadlocked." [1] Put simply, the talks were doomed to fail from the beginning and nothing Nixon did or did not do had any effect on the ultimate outcome. Simply, no harm -no foul.

The good professor made his conclusion based upon outcomes. His analysis, seemingly sensible upon first glance, becomes disingenuous after study because he failed to allow for the effect of lost opportunity. In our cancer analogy above, the patient died. Using Kissinger's outcome- focused approach, it proves irrelevant that she did not receive the positive mammogram finding one year earlier. After all, dead is dead. Nevertheless, this approach ignores the possibility that if informed, she may have sought treatment, which could have been effective during the earliest stages of her disease. In other words, her outcome was not predetermined, for there were alternative paths available at that earlier time, perhaps unavailable later on. The purpose of this section is to determine whether there was a reasonable chance of peace during the 1968 peace talks as opposed to the ultimate outcome of failure. We will examine what effect, if any, the South Vietnamese late attendance to the talks had on the process and the participants. To assist us, we once again seek the advice of the civil courts. In the cancer scenario above, the courts have wrestled successfully with the problem of how to handle lawsuits based on claims for lost opportunities. Therefore, we will start with the court's formula in such matters to give us a framework to apply the evidence and theory, supplied thereafter.

In the cancer case above, the judge would charge, or instruct the jury, on the law they are to apply when determining a lost opportunity case. In the below, I took the Model Jury Charge from the State of New Jersey on this very issue and substituted, therein, changes rendering it relevant to this action. [2] In Appendix III,

---

[1] Hitchens, 137. It is not my purpose at this point to debate Kissinger's statements, since his opinion is given as an example of an accepted argument. However, it would be irresponsible to ignore that in the very same letter, he wrote that he was not associated with Richard Nixon during the 1968 election campaign. Since it is obvious that he was involved with Nixon, his statement was a falsehood. Also, note that Kissinger was being slick in his remark. It is true that the peace talks began in early November but they began without the South Vietnamese and that situation was the very purpose of the alleged conspiracy.

[2] The model charges were created in New Jersey for the purposes of applying uniform identical law. The judge must apply the model charge in all cases. Often attorneys will attempt to supplement or change the model charge based upon the peculiarities or

I attach the exact wording of that charge for comparison purposes. When you analyze the remaining evidence in this chapter, apply the below standard in your decision making process.

LADY'S AND GENTLEMAN OF THE JURY;

In this case, peace talks were set up for November, 1968 with the participants to be the United States, the Government of South Vietnam, North Vietnam and the NLF utilizing a "your side our side formula" for organization. It is alleged that the South Vietnamese did not attend this conference in a timely fashion due to the action of a Nixon-led conspiracy. You need to determine what the chance was that if the conferences had been timely held they would have been successful in shortening the war in Vietnam that lasted for 5 years thereafter? You then must decide to what extent was the conference's failure caused by the preexisting political conditions and to what extent was its failure caused by the acts of the alleged conspirators.

All parties invited to the peace conference had pre-existing political interests, which by themselves had a risk of causing the conference to be an abject failure. However, it is claimed here that the alleged Nixon conspiracy increased that risk of that failure and contributed to the non-efficacy of the conferences. To establish that the alleged conspiracy was a cause of the conference failure, it must first be proven that the conspiracy increased the risk of harm posed by South Vietnam's leader's preexisting political state.

Second, the plaintiff must prove that the increased risk was a substantial factor in producing the conference failure. If the alleged conspiracy was only remotely or insignificantly related to the failure, then it does not constitute a substantial factor.[3]

---

particularities of their case. The supplementation procedure is performed with the judge outside of the hearing of the jury in a hearing called a "charge conference." The Model Jury Charge has been adopted as authoritative by the New Jersey courts.

[3] The hardest task in these matters is setting the definition of "substantial factor." The State of New Jersey has defined this term in the following cases which are cited here as illustrative (that is, good law to be followed by the jury) by the Model Jury Charge. The determination of what constitutes a "substantial factor" was analyzed in Velazquez v. Jiminez, 336 N.J. Super. 10 (App. Div. 2000), *aff'd.* 172 *N.J.* 240 (2002), where the jury

However, the alleged conspiracy need not be the only cause, or even a primary cause, to be a substantial factor in producing the failure. If under all of the circumstances here you find that the conference may have shortened or lessened the carnage of the war had there not been a conspiracy, then the conspirators are liable for the failure of the conference. On the other hand, if you find that the conference was doomed to fail even if there were no conspiracy, then the alleged conspirators are not liable for the failure of the conference.[4]

To sum up the above, fault is found in this lost opportunity case if; 1) Nixon's conspiracy increased the risk that the conference would fail and 2) that increased risk was a substantial factor in producing the conference failure.

THE PLAYING FIELD

This was the playing field before Thiệu's November 2, 1968 National Day speech. The North Vietnamese were facing a unified enemy. This enemy defeated their all-out gambit during Tet causing tremendous losses to the NLF and NVN armed forces. In addition, subsequent NVN spring and fall offenses failed. The South Vietnamese army performed far more effectively than expected. The bombing of North Vietnam seriously affected Hanoi's ability to supply the war. The Soviets, its main supplier of munitions and food, were strongly pushing peace and the Chinese, for the first time, were not actively opposing the process. In a word, the United States had leverage, and in negotiations, leverage equals power.[5]

After November 2, the playing field changed. The North Vietnamese now looked at a divided enemy. Clark Clifford made it very clear, in his press conference and television appearances that a substantial rift developed between

---

found that 5% of the ultimate injury resulted from a preexisting condition, that a settling defendant contributed to 92% of the ultimate injury and that the non-settling defendant was 3% responsible. The jury awarded damages totaling $2,500,000.00. The trial judge then ruled, *sua sponte*, that the non-settling defendant was not negligent as a matter of law. In reversing, the Appellate Division held that the jury's finding that a defendant was 3% negligent satisfies the substantial factor test. The Velazquez Court cited Dubak v. Burdette Tomlin Memorial Hospital, 233 *N.J. Super.* 441, 452 (App. Div.) certif. denied 117 *N.J.* 48 (1989) which held that a finding of 10% fault satisfied the substantial factor test. Velazquez, 336 N.J. Super. at 31-32.
[4] New Jersey Model Jury Charge Section 5.36(E) Medical Negligence: Pre-Existing Condition - Increased Risk/Loss of Chance.
[5] Patrick J. Cleary, *The Negotiation Handbook,* (Armonk, NY: M.E. Sharpe, Inc. 2001), 17. Cleary having served as a federal mediator for 20 years and as Chair of the National Mediation Board is a recognized expert in negotiations and dispute resolution.

the two allies. It was reasonably possible that the United States could pull out of Vietnam or substantially reduce support in all areas. It was also possible, in light of not too distant events, that the United States might attempt a South Vietnamese regime change. Further, the North Vietnamese, always aware of American public reaction, could only delight in the effect that the South Vietnamese action would have on the already powerful and growing antiwar movement. In addition, South Vietnamese troops, who had been seen as an increasingly substantial force, were now regarded by the North Vietnamese as dispirited by the failed peace attempt. This perception was voiced in an intercepted November 17, 1968 conversation between NLF leader Nguyen Van Linh and Mao Zedong, where Linh declared,

> Saigon troops are very discouraged. Many of them openly oppose Thiệu, saying, "If Mr. Thiệu wants to fight, just let him go to Khe Sanh and do it." The morale of the Saigon troops and government officials is very low. Our people, cadres, and troops in the South are encouraged and determined to fight harder. We see that because we are strong, we can force the US to stop bombing the North. Therefore, [this] is the time we should fight more, thus defeating them. This is the common aspiration and spirit of our people, cadres, and troops in the South, Uncle Mao.[6]

Whether there was indeed an actual negative effect on the South Vietnamese troops, the key element was that such belief was now part of the North Vietnamese discourse. The North Vietnamese negotiators now saw opportunity. The bickering between South Vietnam and the United States, because of Saigon's betrayal, could only benefit their cause. When the South Vietnamese ultimately attended the conferences, whether it was one day, one month or one year after originally scheduled, it became irrelevant because leverage was lost. Kissinger, a supposedly experienced negotiator, ignored this crucial concept when he commented that whatever Nixon was alleged to have done was irrelevant. Does Kissinger seriously believe that once a balloon bursts it is a simple task to re-inflate it to its pervious state?

---

[6] Cold War, International History Project, virtual Archive, "Discussion between Mao Zedong and Pham Van Dong November 17 1968," http://www.wilsoncenter.org/index.cfm?topic_id=1409&fuseaction=va2.document&identifier=5034CD31-96B6-175C-94B8985ED02AB324&sort=Collection&item=The%20Vietnam%20(Indochina)%20War(s) (accessed November 29, 2007). It is obvious that this comment could be just mere propaganda, but the fact that it was now part of the discourse whether true or not, makes this comment significant.

A Loss of Momentum

According to negotiation expert Patrick Cleary, momentum in the negotiation process often favors resolution.[7] It is understood that positive momentum in and during a negotiations process raises expectations of a favorable outcome. The presence of strong momentum makes it more likely for the parties to be able to breach the points of resistance in the negotiation agenda and achieve breakthroughs.[8] A critical metric for capturing the negotiation momentum is the level of interest of the parties in attending the negotiations. According to Oxford Professor Corneliu Bjola, "the larger the number of participants to international negotiations, the greater the importance that parties attach to these negotiations and by extension the stronger their motivations to achieve certain results or to avoid others in the final agreement."[9]

The evidence supporting that momentum for a settlement was strong until the point the GVN pulled out of the negotiations consists of the following,

> *a. Anecdotal-* As indicated above, participants in the process were excited by the prospects for peace. Daniel Davidson, a key member of the US team, expressed that optimism was so high that when they believed all parties where going to attend the conference, they broke out bottles of champagne to celebrate what they hoped would be an impending peace. Soviet Ambassador Kosygin was also optimistic as demonstrated by his June 1968 note to LBJ declaring "a real possibility to find a way out of the situation, which has developed in Vietnam with the aim of halting the many years old and bloody war being conducted there." Clifford strongly reacted to that note expressing he was "certain that the Soviet Union, which was giving Hanoi vast amounts of aid, could help settle the war."[10] Even a highly skeptical LBJ was convinced towards the end of October that real peace could be achieved. Clifford's and LBJ's, and indeed the entire administration's palpable anger and shock upon discovering the Thiệu's betrayal certainly served as evidence of their high expectations. Clifford's immediate statement that the South

---

[7] Clearly, 135
[8] Dr. Corneliu Bjola, "How To Use Momentum Analysis To Explain And Forecast the Outcome Of International Negotiations?"
http://www.academia.edu/7678187/How_to_use_Momentum_Analysis_to_Explain_and_F orecast_the_Outcome_of_International_Negotiations (accessed December 14, 2014)
[9] Ibid.
[10] Clifford, 546.

Vietnamese betrayal was an "unexpected disaster" captured the mood of the Johnson administration perfectly.[11]

b. *The situation was ripe*- The concept of "ripeness" in regard to negotiations of conflicts, as advanced by political scientist I. William Zartman and sociologist Louis Kriesberg, claims that, like the maturation of fruit on the vine, there is a certain best or right moment to pluck a conflict or to wait. According to these scholars,

To pluck the fruit of a conflict too soon is to risk the greenness that comes from having insufficient motivation on the part of one or more of the interested parties; without the motivation to take their dispute seriously, and to do whatever may be necessary to bring about a settlement, the disputants are unlikely to engage in the exchange of views that can create a negotiated agreement.[12]

For" ripeness" to exist there must the perception by involved parties that they are in a "mutually hurting stalemate and a sense that a negotiated solution is possible."[13] As indicated above the GVN was hurting. Tet was an enormously costly failure resulting in, for all purposes, the complete destruction of the NLF. Over the years the bombing campaign destroyed North Vietnam's' manufacturing capability. Their spring campaign was a disaster and for the first time the GVN army were actually winning battles. China and the USSR, North Vietnam's allies and chief sources of critical supplies, were on the on the same page urging a cessation in hostilities. The USSR had been urging a solution for years. China, always the stalwart foe of negotiations, performed a 180-degree turn. More anxious of the Soviets than ever after the Czechoslovakian invasion and Soviet proclamation of dominance, they believed that better relations with the United States might be in their best interest. Indeed, after Johnson's March 1968 speech initiated the peace talk process, China "began to pull back its support troops from the DRV."[14] The lack of the voice of aggression whispering into the ears of the

---

[11] In a court of law an excited utterance, which is a "statement relating to a startling event or condition, made while the declarant was under the stress of excitement that it caused," is often given great credibility since the declarant had no time to fabricate or strategize a response See U.S. Federal Rules of Evidence Rule 803. Exceptions to the Rule Against Hearsay.

[12] E. O'Kane, "When Can Conflicts be Resolved? A Critique of Ripeness." *Civil Wars* 8, 3/4 (Sept. 2006): 268-284.

[13] Ibid.

[14] Zhai, 179.

North Vietnamese could only have aided in the final peaceful resolution of the conflict. Realizing that they had lost their former ally to the Soviets, China would continue their de-escalation of support for the North Vietnamese war effort. Thus, coupled with their military defeats and the crumbling of indispensable allies support, the North Vietnamese were hurting.

The "hurting" was not limited to the NVM. In the US, especially after Tet, there was strong opposition to the war. The burgeoning peace movement, the Chicago Convention riots and even Walter Cronkite were symbolic of the public's opposition to the war. Up to that point, over 30,000 Americans died and scores were seriously wounded. LBJ's chief generals advised of the need for even more men without any guarantees for success. Thus, it is clear all parties were at a "mutually hurting stalemate" but was there a sense that a negotiated solution was possible?

> c.   *Building Momentum-* Social Scientist Morton Deutsch observed, in regard to conflict resolution that
>
> [w]hen simple acts of cessation of overt conflict are coupled with other such acts, the results may generate the momentum necessary to move antagonists out of stalemate toward a settlement of their differences. In other words, a string of behavioral changes over time may produce the basis for subsequent attitude change.[15]

For Deutsch "the focus of negotiation is not attitude change *per se* but an agreement to change behavior in ways that make settlement possible."[16] A fair review of the evidence provided above demonstrates a clear change in behavior. The US agreed to a bombing halt without express conditions, LBJ withdrew from the presidential race to concentrate on peace, the US agreed to sit at the table with the NLF, all sides agreed to the "Facts of Life," the NVM agreed to accept "definitions" and sit down with the GVN, the "your side my side" philosophy was adopted. All of these concessions and agreements transpired only after long hard negotiation and written assurances not only backed by the involved warring parties, but others, China and the USSR, who also had strong interest in resolution.

---

[15] Jeffrey Z. Rubin and Carol M. Rubin, Conflict, *Negotiation, and Change* (New York, N.Y: Springer, 1991), 5.
[16] Ibid.

Returning to Deutsch's theory, it is reasonable to conclude that in light of not only attitude change but also demonstrable significant behavioral changes, there was a sense that a negotiated solution was possible.

> d. *Foot in the door* – In addition to ripeness theory, a reasonable possibility for peace is also supported by "foot in the door" and cognitive dissonance theories. In Section 1, I documented the long and slow process of negotiation between Washington and Hanoi, where minor agreements eventually led to more substantial agreements, such as the acceptance of the "Facts of Life" and the presence of the Saigon government at the peace table. The progress timeline, attached as Appendix II, documents this forward march. The process of small agreements leading eventually to larger agreements is a documented psychological phenomenon known as "foot in the door."[17] In the words of social psychologist Robert Cialdini, "to get people to agree to something big, start small and build."[18] Because the negotiation history leading to November 1968 fits this phenomenon perfectly, there was further evidence of positive momentum towards a resolution of the larger issue of peace.

Forward momentum to support eventual resolution, was also a product of the extensive time and effort expended by the parties in the process. Psychologist Leon Festinger investigated how one's actions affect attitudes. He found that where thoughts and actions do not coincide, the individual experiences unpleasant tension called cognitive dissonance. According to cognitive dissonance theory, to relieve this tension, "people will bring their attitudes into line with their actions. It's as if people rationalize, if I choose to do it (or say it), I must believe in it."[19] To put it another way, the more time and effort that is expended on a project, the more investment in the outcome an individual experiences. In a goal-directed process, one naturally seeks the achievement of that goal to justify the time and effort expended during the process, thus lessening dissonance. In the present matter, negotiators on behalf of Hanoi and the United States were working for months, sometimes around-the-clock, to reach an agreement. It is reasonable to believe that a certain degree of cognitive dissonance resolution stimulated both sides to offer gradually greater compromises to justify their efforts. Further, it

---

[17] David G. Myers, *Psychology 3rd Edition* (New York, NY: Worth Publishing 1992), 555. See also John W. Santrock, *Psychology 6th Ed* (New York, NY: McGraw-Hill 2000), 556.
[18] Meyers, 555.
[19] Ibid., 556-557.

wasn't only the investment of time but the shared purpose between all parties that strengthens this argument According to Festinger's *social comparison* theory, individuals are driven to evaluate their beliefs in terms of their correctness or validity, which is often accomplished through social comparison with the beliefs of others.[20] Here, it was perceived at least, that all parties made major concessions in a very public forum with very high stakes, acting to reinforce their belief in the peace process. In other words, each participant's buy in to the peace process was predicated and strengthened by the other's buy in, thus increasing the expectation of positive outcome. When the GVN pulled out of the negotiations in such a public and abrupt matter, the social reality of the group radically changed.

Up until November 2, 1968, the peace process had momentum. Returning to the dance analogy, Hanoi and the United States were in each other's embrace. They may have arrived in that situation by choice or by circumstance; nevertheless, once embraced it was difficult to release. If North Vietnam pulled away from the peace process, it would have risked losing the psychological advantage they had gained by manipulating world opinion, and the American public, to believe the US was an imperialist, war-mongering aggressor and they were its innocent victims. The United States could not separate from the dance due to political pressure at home. The music was playing and all were watching. However, on November 2, 1968, when Saigon announced it would not be part of the negotiations, it acted as if it had removed the needle from the record and stopped the music. Now both sides had the opportunity to leave the dance without taking personal responsibility. The North Vietnamese could become more intransigent, blaming their behavior on the betrayal of trust that occurred when the United States could not back up its promises to produce Saigon at the table. Similarly, the United States had an excuse to back away from the table without taking blame for that action. Saigon's acts not only changed the field but also reversed the momentum.

CREDIBILITY

When our friend Kissinger concluded that the GVN's withdrawal from the conferences had no effect on the ultimate outcome, he conveniently failed to recognize the critical effect that credibility maintains in negotiations. According to Cleary, "your only stock in trade is your word. It must not be forgotten that the

---

[20] Leon Festinger, "A Theory of Social Comparison Processes," https://www.humanscience.org/docs/Festinger%20%281954%29%20A%20Theory%20of %20Social%20Comparison%20Processes.pdf. (accessed December 22, 2014)

US could not have had a strong stock of credibility with the North Vietnamese. Roosevelt promised the Vietnamese people independence in exchange for their support in WWII, yet the US government supported France's reentry into the region after the end of the war. Despite the fact that the Vietnamese people undoubtedly defeated the French and the Geneva Accords clearly set forth the road to independence through a nationwide vote, the US claiming it did not sign the agreement, obstructed this vote, installed a despotic leader in the south and a civil war resulted. To say the word of the US had little weight is stating the obvious. However, through long negotiating and skillful creation of personal relationships and a coming together of many factors, a degree of trust was rebuilt only soon to be destroyed.

US negotiators hurt their credibility in two main ways: by making promises they don't keep and making threats that they don't keep."[21] The United States promised to bring South Vietnam to the table. This was no minor pledge; months of difficult negotiations were spent achieving that objective. The Soviet Union, after intercepting the October 23, 1968 Diem cable to Thiệu, became noticeably concerned that the United States could not control its ally. When Johnson shifted the initial conference date from November 2 to November 6, the North Vietnamese were visibly annoyed and warned that future failures to live up to promises would lead to their doubting the good faith of the United States. In previous negotiations with the North Vietnamese and in discussions with the Soviets, US representatives repeatedly emphasized that it was "unthinkable for the United States to stop bombing without the inclusion of South Vietnamese representatives in Paris negotiations."[22] When Johnson could not deliver the South Vietnamese to the table, especially after lobbying so hard for their presence, it had to act as a serious blow against the credibility of the United States. Further, by going to the conferences, without the South Vietnamese being present, the United States performed what officials had previously termed the "unthinkable."

Saigon's failing to attend the conferences on time, put the United States in the position of making promises it could not keep and reneging on threats it could not fulfill. This loss of credibility may have had an additional negative effect in light of the culture of the North Vietnamese. Mao advised Pham Van Dong (North Vietnamese Prime Minister) that a negotiated end to the war would be difficult because the Americans "did not keep their word."[23] The United States'

---

[21] Cleary, 84.
[22] Gaiduk, 178.
[23] Zhai, 173.

failure to keep their end of the bargain could only have reinforced his point. According to Roger Dawson, an expert negotiator and writer on the topic, successful dialogue with South-East Asians relies primarily on trust. Written contracts mean little; rather trust between the parties is the key to problem resolution. [24] Surely aware of their loss of face, the United States' chief negotiators, Vance and Harriman, were very embarrassed by the South Vietnamese situation and found Hanoi gloating over the situation.[25]

SOME EXPERT INPUT

We come into the arena of experts pre-warned; nevertheless, their opinions are unavoidable. We turn first to William Bundy who asked the question to himself: "was a chance for peace lost?" After pondering, he answered,

> Here again one must be tentative. If North Vietnam was as hard pressed as Johnson's advisers believed and said at the decisive meeting of October 14, immediate and serious peace negotiations might have produced useful concessions. Yet as Dean Rusk pointed out, complete negotiations would have taken months and Hanoi might have reverted to a very hard line. My conclusion is that probably no great chance was lost.[26]

According to Bundy, one of the major obstacles for peace was that for "North Vietnam to agree on reciprocal withdrawals would be to admit that its forces did not belong in the South, undercutting its claim that the conflict was a civil war in which only the United States was truly foreign."[27] He concluded that although an early agreement was "not in the cards... what might have been hoped for, however, was an early negotiation aimed initially at reducing the level fighting, then the level of forces." [28] This point of view is consistent with that held by others closest to the action. Harriman and Vance, based on the suggestions of Le Duc Tho in September 1968, believed that the Vietnamese were seriously ready to discuss reciprocal troop withdrawals.[29]

---

[24] Roger Dawson, *Secrets Of Power Negotiating* (Franklin Lakes, NJ: Career Press. 1995), 195
[25] DOS, section 188.
[26] Bundy, 47.
[27] Ibid., 51.
[28] Ibid.
[29] Ibid., 50.

Author George Herring supplied the negative view. Basing his conclusion on the lack of any proof that Hanoi was ready to make any substantive compromises, he believed nothing short of an American withdrawal and a coalition government would have brought a peace agreement, and such terms would not have been acceptable to the United States. Thus, even if Thiệu had attended the conference on time, Herring concluded: "It appears highly unlikely that any meaningful peace settlement could have been reached in 1968." [30] This point of view, however, ignored the possibility of de-escalation. The war raged for many years after 1968, gradually dwindling down by 1973. A complete and prompt peace agreement, with total withdrawal of American troops may not have been possible in 1968, but the Bundy, Harriman and Vance view of de-escalation with substantial troop withdrawals, offered a much better alternative than full out engaged war. One more point, Herring believed that in October 1968, under "extreme pressure from Democratic politicos, he [Johnson] finally backed a bombing halt as a way to salvage Hubert Humphrey's faltering presidential campaign." [31] In this tale of confusing and alternative versions, we can be reasonably certain that Herring was significantly off the mark on this conclusion and this can only negatively affect the credibility of his other opinions.

Finally, we turn to Professor Ambrose, who offered the most cynical and unsettling conclusion. Ambrose did not believe that de-escalation was a possibility; only victory could have fulfilled the enormous egos of Nixon and Johnson. "No law prevented Johnson from accepting the onus of abandoning South Vietnam and pulling the fighting troops out before Nixon took office," Ambrose claims, "The United States would have survived, and Nixon would have begun his presidency with a clean slate. He could have muted his criticism of Johnson." Still, this scenario was not going to happen, because both Nixon and Johnson "swore publicly and with deeply felt emotion, 'I'm not going to be the first president to lose a war.'" [32] If one accepts the above premise, then the talks were doomed. Yet, Ambrose missed one important element. On January 15, 1973, Nixon announced the suspension of offensive action against North Vietnam. The Paris Peace Accords on "Ending the War and Restoring Peace in Vietnam" were signed on January 27, 1973, officially ending direct U.S involvement in the

---

[30] Herring, 216.

[31] George C. Herring, edited by David L. Anderson, Shadow *on the White House: Presidents and the Vietnam War, 1945-1975* (Lawrence, KN: University Press of Kansas, 1993), 107.

[32] Ambrose, *Nixon: The Triumph of Politician 1962 – 1972,* 231.

Vietnam War.[33] Even the most optimistic of accounts could not argue that the US was the victor at this point. Yet the troops came home. After January 1969, LBJ was out of the picture. Certainly, some option yielding less than victory, but not all out defeat would have been available to Humphrey had he been elected President. This, let us not forget, may very well have happened without the Nixon conspiracy and Humphrey, hardly a supporter of the Thiệu government, may very likely have pulled support at any time not suffering the same burdens that may have influenced LBJ's judgment.

CLOSING ARGUMENT

We have come to the end of the race. It is of no matter that the runner cleared the three previous hurdles, because if he trips here, the race for historical significance is over. The only way the runner clears the final hurdle is if you believe that the Nixon Conspiracy increased the risk that the peace conferences would fail and you find that this increased risk was a substantial factor in producing that harm. If the conspiracy was remotely or insignificantly related to the failure, there can be no finding of fault. You should consider the arguments of "the change in the playing field," the "loss of momentum," and the "loss of credibility." As previously stated in the above sections, you must respond by way of a jury verdict sheet. Note, now you are only answering question #4. Remember, one grain of sand on the scale of justice weighing in favor of Nixon's liability is sufficient to disturb the equipoise in favor of a positive answer to this question.

THE AUTHOR WEIGHS IN

At the beginning of this book I promised that I would present the reader with the facts and deconstruct the evidence allowing for an independent conclusion on this very important issue, and I hope I lived up to that promise. Now that you have entered your verdict, I believe the time is ripe to give my opinion on this particular question only. I hearken back to William Bundy's conclusion that there was a chance, albeit not a great chance, of peace. With this in mind, I give you the final pieces of evidence I considered before arriving at my decision.

Richard Edward Cyran was born February 17, 1949. His home was in Clifton, NJ. Cyran had one brother, John Jr., and three sisters. He attended Clifton public schools and Clifton High School and liked football, baseball and all kinds

---

[33] Peter Church, ed., *A Short History of South-East Asia.* (Singapore: John Wiley & Sons, 2006), 193–94.

of sports. He received his GED while in the service. Cyran entered the US Army in June of 1968 and arrived in Vietnam on November 22, 1968, where he was assigned to the 25th Infantry Division as a driver. He attained the rank of Specialist 4 (SP4). On June 6, 1969, while serving with Company B, 4th Battalion, 23rd Infantry, 25th Infantry Division, Cyran was killed in action.[34]

Jay Thomas Dandurand was born in Kankakee, IL, on November 11, 1948, and attended grade school and West Junior High there before his family moved to Kinnelon, NJ. He was a 1966 graduate of Kinnelon High School and he went on to complete one year of college at Newark State College before enlisting. He enjoyed motorcycling and played the saxophone. On the afternoon of 12 March 1970, Jay was flying a troop lift mission approximately 52 miles southeast of Saigon, Republic of Vietnam. His UH-1D helicopter experienced an operational malfunction and crashed into a heavily wooded area, instantly killing all aboard.[35]

Finally, Mike P. is 59 years old. He survived. After January 1969, he served with the Army in Vietnam as a helicopter gunner. Shot down three times, he suffered serious injuries requiring extensive reconstructive surgeries. I know Mike, he is a friend and I interviewed him for this book. He now suffers from a debilitating neurological disease that is most likely related to the multiple physical traumas suffered in the war. He cannot even hold his new granddaughter. He told me, (when he could talk, he can barely speak now due to his disease), that the physical wounds healed, but his psychological pain is relentless. He never feels safe even when surrounded by his loving family. He is always wary of sounds and movements. He, like thousands of his fellow veterans of the Vietnam War suffers from Post-Traumatic Stress Disorder (PTSD). [36] The PTSD is the ever present unrelenting "monkey on his back," that dampers even the happiest of

---

[34] New Jersey Vietnam Veterans Memorial Foundation,
http://www.njvvmf.org/results_acmx.cfm (accessed November 29, 2007)
[35] Ibid.
[36] PTSD is defined is a recognized psychological disease. It is caused by exposure to traumatic events and symptoms manifest in severe anxiety, reliving the traumatic event, avoidance, and emotional numbing. According to a major study conducted by The National Vietnam Veterans' Readjustment Study (NVVRS) in response to a 1983 congressional mandate, using these assessment tools, an estimated 15.2% of male and 8.5% of female Vietnam theater veterans met criteria for current PTSD. Those with high levels of war-zone exposure had significantly higher rates, with 35.8% of men and 17.5% of women meeting criteria for current PTSD. Rates of PTSD were consistently higher for Vietnam theater veterans than for Vietnam era veterans and civilians. United States Government. Department of Veteran Affairs. Jennifer L. Price, Ph.D., "Findings from the National Vietnam Veterans' Readjustment Study"
http://www.ncptsd.va.gov/ncmain/ncdocs/fact_shts/fs_nvvrs.html (accessed December 4, 2007)

occasions. He could be in the middle of a family barbeque and if there is a loud noise, he is seized with panic. He prays for medical science to find a drug that works so that he "can feel normal again, like he was before the war."[37] Mike never heard about Anna Chennault or Nixon's shenanigans of 1968. When I informed him of the results of the research in this book, he initially had no reaction. He took it in slowly, and then he shook his head and said quietly he was "damn mad."

Either one of the above gentlemen, and any of the thousands of soldiers killed or injured after November 1968, if given the opportunity, would have gladly opted for any chance of peace, or at least a significant de-escalation, but they could not, because it was erased due to the personal ambitions of one man. Bundy said that there was a chance, and that is enough for me.

---

[37] Mike P., interview by author, December 3, 2007

Epilogue

Assuming the conspiracy occurred; the damage it caused continued to haunt the Nixon administration and the nation. Nixon owed his presidency to the South Vietnamese President and Thiệu's "favors" did not come without a price. Nguyen Hung, who served as Thiệu's special assistant declared, "Thiệu believed that Richard Nixon owed him a political debt as a result of his refusal to support President Lyndon Johnson's peace initiative just before the US 1968 election.[1] This debt would have great consequences. According to William Bundy, "in most cultures, but perhaps especially in East Asia and in Vietnam, the sense of such a debt raises profound questions of loyalty and honor. Even at the expense of other obligations."[2] According to Dallek, the greatest actual consequence of Nixon's actions was the obligation he incurred to Thiệu. This debt "would become a significant impediment to Nixon's freedom to influence Thiệu's conduct of the war and reduce Vietnam's dependence on the United States for security and autonomy."[3] Bundy, agreeing with Dallek, claimed: "a new American president starting with a heavy and recognized debt to the leader he had, above all to influence, was surely a great handicap brought on by Nixon."[4] Every soldier who died or was injured because of the debt their President owed to Thiệu paid the heavy price of Nixon's trespasses.

NIXON

In January 1973, a Democratic-controlled Senate threatened to investigate a purported Republican break-in of the Democratic National Headquarters at Watergate Office Complex. According to Dallek, Nixon tried to intimidate Johnson to urge the Democrats to call off the investigation. Nixon hoped that the threat of a press leak about FBI bugs ordered by LBJ on his and Agnew's 1968 campaign planes during the Chennault affair would persuade Johnson to pressure congressional Democrats into dropping the Watergate probe.[5] On January 9, Nixon asked Attorney General John Mitchell to request Deke DeLoach to dig up information they could use as fodder for blackmail against Johnson to protect

---

[1] Hung, 21.
[2] Bundy, 48.
[3] Dallek, *Nixon and Kissinger: Partners in Power,* 78.
[4] Bundy, 48.
[5] Again , this was nothing more than urban legend and widely disputed due to a complete lack of evidence and logic, but of course why should that impact Nixon.

their own hides.[6] At the same time, LBJ was aware the Washington *Evening Star* was doing a story on wiretapping. Johnson called DeLoach at home informing him: "I received a call from the Washington Evening Star this afternoon. The reporter says he's writing an article on Mrs. Claire [Anna] Chennault and he claims I ordered the FBI to place surveillance on her because of some requests she supposedly made to the South Vietnamese ambassador. I never did anything like that, did I?" DeLoach was confused and was not sure if Johnson had forgotten or was looking somehow to get off the hook. DeLoach answered: "Yes, you did, Mr. President, I vividly recall the matter." Johnson, after a sigh, answered: "Well, if you say I did, there must be something to it. But if they try to give me any trouble, I'll pull out that cable from my files and turn the tables on them."[7] According to DeLoach, LBJ was looking to see if the Chennault affair had been remembered or if he had any deniable plausibility. The "they" he referred to was Nixon and his cronies. Feeling threatened by their move, LBJ was going to countermove with the heavy artillery, the November 2, 1968 cable documenting the Chennault-Nixon conspiracy. After all, what is wrong with a little blackmail between friends? However all activity in this regards stopped because a few days later, LBJ died of a heart attack.

In January 1972, Nixon called Chennault to his office to express her opinions about China and Taiwan. To no one's surprise, she advocated supporting the Taiwanese position and strongly condemned the Chinese Communists. After their little meeting, Kissinger joined the two of them for a smiling photo-op. The snapshot of these three cheery companions appeared in the newspapers across the world implying a camaraderie and agreement among friends. Ten days later, Nixon announced his historic upcoming visit to mainland China. He did not bother to mention this "inconsequential" plan during their meeting. Nixon, no doubt, used the photo to give the false impression to the public that Chennault and the "China Lobby" endorsed his policy of acceptance towards the communist Chinese. When asked how she felt about being once again used by Nixon, Chennault, with bitter resignation, replied, "When you're in Washington long enough you assume that you're lied to, and he [Nixon] was no different maybe even worse."[8]

Pressured by impending impeachment, on August 9, 1974, Nixon, resigned, the office of President of the United States in disgrace. After saying goodbye to

---

[6] Dallek, *Nixon and Kissinger: Partners in Power,* 616.
[7] DeLoach, 409. Again, it must be reiterated that at least pursuant to available information at this time, Chennault's phone was never tapped.
[8] Chennault, interview.

his staff in a rambling speech in which he appointed himself a victim who would once again rise up, he walked to the presidential helicopter and oblivious to the shame he brought upon himself, his family, his administration and his nation, his last act was to raise his arms in triumph and give the victory sign.[9] To his dying day, Nixon still denied any involvement in the entire ordeal. In the years leading to his death in 1994, Nixon enjoyed a resurrection of his reputation. He became the respected elder statesman. Even President Bill Clinton consulted with him. At his funeral, attended by many powerful individuals, California Governor, Pete Wilson remarked,

> It's hard to imagine a world without Richard Nixon. For half a century, he played a leading role in shaping the events that have shaped our lives. It's not just that he served for three decades in high office; it's not just that he garnered more votes than any candidate in American history; it was because his intellect, his insight and his indomitable will could not be ignored.[10]

Rolling Stone Magazine writer Hunter Thompson was not invited to the funeral, but, had he have been there, he would have given this "slightly" different eulogy entitled "Notes on the Passing of an American Monster,"

> Richard Nixon is gone now and I am poorer for it. He was the real thing--a political monster straight out of Grendel and a very dangerous enemy. He could shake your hand and stab you in the back at the same time. He lied to his friends and betrayed the trust of his family. Not even Gerald Ford, the unhappy ex-president who pardoned Nixon and kept him out of prison, was immune to the evil fallout. Ford, who believes strongly in Heaven and Hell, has told more than one of his celebrity golf partners that I know I will go to hell, because I pardoned Richard Nixon.[11]

---

[9] President Nixon's Farewell to the White House Staff, https://www.youtube.com/watch?v=32GaowQnGRw (accessed December 15, 2014)
[10] Remarks by Governor Pete Wilson of California at Richard Nixon's Funeral. (April 27, 1994) http://www.watergate.info/nixon/94-04-27_funeral-wilson.shtml. (accessed November 27, 2007)
[11] "The Nine Lives of Richard Nixon: Nine Obituaries," http://teaching.arts.usyd.edu.au/history/hsty3080/StudentWebSites/Nixon%20Obits/source 9 (accessed November 27, 2007)

CLIFFORD

After Nixon's election, Clifford returned to private practice as senior partner in the firm of Clifford & Warnke. One of his clients was the Bank of Credit and Commerce International (BCCI). In July of 1991, the bank was accused of fraud, drug money laundering and bribing bank regulators. Over $20 billion in assets could not be accounted for. It was soon discovered that Clifford made about $6 million in profits from bank stock that he bought with an unsecured loan from BCCI.[12] Clifford, at the age of 85, was indicted for bank fraud. This distinguished advisor to presidents and former Secretary of Defense was booked and fingerprinted like a common criminal. When questioned about his activities, with pained earnestness he explained, "I have been deceived and I view this all with a deep sense of grief …This is the first time in 62 years that I've had any doubt cast on my character, any cloud attached to my behavior."[13] On April 7, 1992, all charges were dropped due to his failing health. In 1999, Clifford died of respiratory failure at his home.[14]

CHENNAULT

Presently, Anna Chennault is alive and well and has a beautiful office/shrine in Georgetown. She is still, to the best of my knowledge, harboring the "full" story and probably loving every minute of it.

---

[12] "Clark Clifford" http://www.spartacus.schoolnet.co.uk/JFKcliffordC.htm. (accessed November 27, 2007)
[13] Neil A. Lewis, "Washington at Work; Clark Clifford, Symbol of the Permanent Capital, Is Faced With a Dilemma." *New York Times,* April 6 1991.
http://query.nytimes.com/gst/fullpage.html?res=9D0CE4DD1639F936A35757C0A967958 260. (accessed November 27, 2007)
[14] Bart Barnes, *Washington Insider Clark M. Clifford Dies*
http://www.washingtonpost.com/wp-srv/politics/daily/oct98/clifford101198.htm. (accessed December 8, 2014)

Appendices

APPENDIX I

Terms

1. **NVN** stands for North Vietnam
2. **DRV** stands for Democratic Republic of Vietnam , which refers to North Vietnam
3. **NLF** stands for National Liberation Front a North Vietnamese controlled semi-entity consisting of North Vietnamese soldiers and South Vietnamese partisans, commonly referred to as the Viet Cong.
4. **GVN** stand for Government of the Republic of Vietnam, which refers to South Vietnam
5. **Viet Minh**. This term is an abbreviation of V*iệt Nam Độc Lập Đồng Minh Hội,* which literally translates as the "League for Viet Nam's Independence." Founded by Ho Chi Minh, The Việt Minh initially formed to seek independence for **Vietnam** from the **French Empire**. When the **Japanese occupation** began, the Việt Minh opposed Japan with support from the United States and the **Republic of China**. After World War II, the Việt Minh opposed the re-occupation of Vietnam by France.[1]
6. **Saigon** The capital of South Vietnam is often used to represent the South Vietnamese Government.
7. **Hanoi** The capital of North Vietnam is often used to represent the North Vietnamese Government.

---

[1] "Who Were the Viet Minh"
http://asianhistory.about.com/od/Asian_History_Terms_U_to_Z/g/Who-Were-the-Viet-Minh.htm (accessed November 21, 2014)

APPENDIX II

March Forward Line Time

5/7/1954	Geneva agreements
Early 1960s	Against Soviet advice, North Vietnamese make preparation for armed struggle and South
Early 1960s	Soviet position - avoid US confrontation
	China position confront the United States in South Vietnam
Early 1960	Hanoi declares intention to promote revolutionary struggle in South
12/20/1960	NLF formed
Spring 1962	China pressures North Vietnam for increased South Vietnam violence
Winter 1964	NVN meets with Khrushchev to get greater support- mission fails
10/14/1964	Khrushchev out of power
Winter 1965	NVN visit Soviets, Get message that they prefer settlement
Winter 1965	China opposes any settlement
Spring/65	NVN proposes four points
Spring/1965	pro-China Foreign Minister replaced in NVN Politburo in response to China obstructing supply flow from Russia
Spring1965	Moscow calls for US bombing halt to generate peace talks
Spring/1965	US short bombing halt receives negative reaction from Hanoi, bombing reinstated
Spring/1965	US air strikes increases

Spring/1965	China urges more NVN troops into the South with increased US confrontation
Winter/66	NVN leadership shifts from China to Soviet influence
	US proposes 14 points - interpreted by NVN as an acceptance of three of their four points proposal
Feb./1966	Soviets pressure Hanoi to negotiate - this is rejected
March/1966	NVN warmly praises Moscow leadership but rejects advice to negotiate
April/1966	China rejects all negotiations and predicts war to last six to seven years
June/1966	NVN proposal, halt the bombing permanently and they will decelerate movement of troops into the South and not demand communist control over South
July/1966	Hanoi declares they're not under the thumb of China
Nov./1966	NVN politburo declares neutral stance on Soviet-Sino conflict and declares they will no longer be deterred by China from a negotiated settlement
Nov./1966	NVN declares that a US Bombing halt and recognition NLF as the South's spokesman conditions for negotiation
Dec./1966	Hanoi attacks the validity of Mao's cultural Revolution
Winter/1967	NVN Premier Pham Van Dong goes to Moscow gets support for military effort and negotiating efforts. Dong visits China who strongly oppose negotiation and advocate fighting five to seven more years
Winter/1967	Sources state that bombing of North Vietnam is having an effect
Winter/1967	Permanent language disappears from requests for unconditional bombing halt
24504	Hanoi privately assures the United States of their sincere intentions

2/8/1967	LBJ letter to Ho Chi Minh offering a bombing and hold on US buildup halt for promise of de-escalation a southern infiltration, February 14 given as ultimatum for response
2/8/1967	LBJ halts the bombing
2/14/1967	LBJ reinstates bombing due to lack of Hanoi response
2/15/1967	Ho Chi Minh responds out of time refusing de-escalation and demanding unconditional bombing halt
March/1967	Hanoi announces that China's influence over their policy is waning
April/1967	NVN goes to Moscow for supplies, informed that victory is not possible and pressured for negotiation
May/1967	Sources report Dong fed up with war
July/1967	NVN Militant minister Thinh dies
8/25/1967	LBJ sends note to Hanoi -- US will stop bombing if assure prompt discussion and Hanoi not to take military advantage. Question of assume or assured remains unclear
9/10/1967	Hanoi responds that they will negotiate only if there are no reciprocal conditions and that the front is recognized as an entity, but need not be recognized as the sole representative for South Vietnam. Russia endorses plan -China strongly opposes
9/1/1967	Hanoi drops demand for "permanent" cessation of bombing
9/29/1967	LBJ San Antonio speech similar to Hanoi note but uses "assume" language for North Vietnamese response
9/29/1967	Hanoi rejects San Antonio plan
10/1/1967	Hanoi optimistic as to victory

12/1/1967	Sources reveal North Vietnamese are being hurt by US air strikes
1/1/1968	LBJ redefines San Antonio speech to require North Vietnamese assurances instead of United States assumptions
1/1/1968	Hanoi implies that they will not take advantage of the US bombing halt
1/30/1968	Tet offensive
2/1/1968	Hanoi rejects again the San Antonio plan and request United States to "demonstrate the reality of a bombing halt"
6/2/1968	Kosygin letter to LBJ
6/13/1968	Soviet letter to NVN
7/13/1968	NVN responds the Soviet letter
8/20/1968	Soviets invade Czechoslovakia
9/17/1968	Harriman and Vance report positive movement at talks
9/21/1968	Oberemko and Vance discuss the importance of Saigon participation in negotiations as well as misinterpretations as to "could be" "would be" language
10/9/1968	North Vietnamese negotiators indicate to Harriman and Vance that they would not oppose Saigon participation at negotiations
10/10/1968	Oberemko delivers message that Moscow endorses facts of life in Saigon participation however LBJ wants official approval from Moscow
10/13/1968	Moscow produces official approval of the United States plan
10/22/1968	All Parties agree to participation of four powers (U.S, NVN, NLF and GVN)
10/25/1968	Kosygin letter to LBJ -- Soviets want peace- timing is good
10/27/1968	Harriman and Vance report to LBJ that the North Vietnamese have dropped all unreasonable demands
10/28/1967	Bunker meets with Thiệu and Ky and reports they are in agreement with US plans

10/16/1968	LBJ informs Nixon of Humphrey about the peace initiative and warns Nixon not be counterproductive
10/27/1968	LBJ wants Soviet assurances of facts of life recognition
10/28/1968	Soviet supply assurances on facts of life recognition
10/29/1968	Thiệu Speech he needs more time
10/29/1968	LBJ instructs Bunker to pass on his strong concerns to Thiệu
10/31/1968	LBJ speech

APPENDIX III

Time Conversion Chart

Vietnam		Washington D.C.	
12:00:00 midnight	Thursday, October 31, 1968	1:00:00 PM	Wednesday, October 30, 1968
1:00:00 AM		2:00:00 PM	
2:00:00 AM		3:00:00 PM	
3:00:00 AM		4:00:00 PM	
4:00:00 AM		5:00:00 PM	
5:00:00 AM		6:00:00 PM	
6:00:00 AM		7:00:00 PM	
7:00:00 AM		8:00:00 PM	
8:00:00 AM		9:00:00 PM	
9:00:00 AM		10:00:00 PM	
10:00:00 AM		11:00:00 PM	
11:00:00 AM		12:00:00 midnight	Thursday, October 31, 1968
12:00:00 PM		1:00:00 AM	
1:00:00 PM		2:00:00 AM	
2:00:00 PM		3:00:00 AM	
3:00:00 PM		4:00:00 AM	
4:00:00 PM		5:00:00 AM	
5:00:00 PM		6:00:00 AM	

6:00:00 PM		7:00:00 AM
7:00:00 PM		8:00:00 AM
8:00:00 PM		9:00:00 AM
9:00:00 PM		10:00:00 AM
10:00:00 PM		11:00:00 AM
11:00:00 PM		12:00:00 AM
12:00:00 midnight	Friday, November 01, 1968	1:00:00 PM

APPENDIX IV

New Jersey Model Jury Charge

5.36   MEDICAL NEGLIGENCE

Pre-Existing Condition - Increased Risk/Loss of Chance – Proximate Cause (12/02)

Introductory Note to Judge:

In a series of cases, including *Fosgate v. Corona*, 66 *N.J.* 268 (1974); *Evers v. Dollinger*, 95 *N.J.* 399 (1984); *Scafidi v. Seiler*, 119 *N.J.* 93 (1990); *Gardner v. Pawliw*, 150 *N.J.* 359 (1997), and most recently *Reynolds v. Gonzales*, 172 *N.J.* 266 (2002), the New Jersey Supreme Court has established a modified standard of proximate cause for use in certain medical negligence cases. The following charge is to be used in cases where it is alleged that the plaintiff has a preexisting condition which creates a risk of harm and the defendant's negligence increases the risk of harm by depriving the plaintiff of a chance of recovery. Furthermore, in *Reynolds, supra*, the Supreme Court held that failure to specifically explain the charge in the context of the facts of the case was reversible error. Therefore, to assist trial judges and practitioners this Model Charge uses typical medical negligence theories as illustrative examples.

Additionally, in cases involving an allegation that the failure to perform a diagnostic test increased the risk of harm from a preexisting condition, the trial court must also give that portion of the charge derived from *Gardner, supra*, as indicated below.

In this case, [insert here a detailed factual description of the case] If you determine that the defendant was negligent, then you must also decide what is the chance that: [(1) the plaintiff would not be dying of cancer; or (2) the plaintiff's husband would not have died of the heart attack et cetera], if the defendant had not been negligent. Thus, if you decide that the defendant was negligent, then you must decide to what extent were the plaintiff's injuries caused by the preexisting medical condition and to what extent were the injuries caused by the defendant's negligence.

When the plaintiff came to the defendant, he/she had a preexisting condition [*here describe the condition, e.g., breast cancer; heart attack et cetera*] which by itself had a risk of causing the plaintiff the harm he/she ultimately experienced in this case. However, the plaintiff claims that the defendant's negligence increased that risk of harm and contributed to the ultimate injury [*here describe the ultimate harm*]. To establish that the defendant's negligence was a cause of his/her injuries or damages, the plaintiff must first prove that the defendant's negligence increased the risk of harm posed by plaintiff's preexisting condition.

Second, the plaintiff must prove that the increased risk was a substantial factor in producing the ultimate harm or injury. If the negligent act was only remotely or insignificantly related to the ultimate harm or injury, then the negligent act does not constitute a substantial factor. However, the defendant's negligence need not be the only cause, nor even a primary cause, of an injury for the negligence to be a substantial factor in producing the ultimate harm or injury. Whether the increased risk was a substantial factor is to be reflected in the apportionment of damages between the increased risk and the preexisting condition. If under all of the circumstances here [*here insert specific circumstances such as the delay in the diagnosis of the breast cancer or the heart attack*] you find that the plaintiff may have suffered lesser injuries if the defendant was not negligent, then the defendant is liable for the plaintiff's increased injuries. On the other hand, if you find that the plaintiff would have suffered the same injuries even if the defendant was not negligent, then the defendant is not liable to the plaintiff.

If you determine that the defendant was negligent in not having a diagnostic test performed, in this case [*here indicate the test(s)*], but it is unknown whether performing the test would have helped to diagnose or treat a preexistent condition, the plaintiff does not have to prove that the test would have resulted in avoiding the harm. In such cases the plaintiff must merely demonstrate that the failure to give the test increased the risk of harm from the preexistent condition. A plaintiff may demonstrate an increased risk of harm even if such tests are helpful in a small proportion of cases.

If you find that the plaintiff has proven that the defendant was negligent, the plaintiff is not required to quantify or put a percentage on the extent to which the defendant's negligence added to all of the plaintiff's final injuries. In cases where the defendant's negligence accelerated or worsened the plaintiff's preexisting condition, the defendant is responsible for all of the plaintiff's injuries unless the defendant is able to reasonably apportion the damages. If the defendant claims that all or part of the plaintiff's injuries would have occurred anyway, then the defendant, and not the plaintiff, has the burden of proving what percentage of the plaintiff's injuries would have occurred even if the defendant had not been negligent. If the injuries can be so apportioned, then the defendant is responsible only for the amount of ultimate harm caused by the negligence.

For example, if the defendant claims that: [(1) the plaintiff would still have suffered the spread of her cancer even if the diagnosis had been made in January 2001; or (2) that the plaintiff's husband still would have died of a heart attack even if treated earlier], and if the defendant can prove that an apportionment can be reasonably made, separating those injuries the plaintiff would have suffered anyway, even with timely treatment, from those injuries the plaintiff suffered due to the delay in treatment, then the defendant is only liable for that portion/percentage of the injuries the defendant proves is related to the delay in treatment of the plaintiff's original condition. On the other hand, if you find that the defendant has not met the defendant's burden of proving that plaintiff's injuries can be reasonably apportioned, then the defendant is responsible for all of the plaintiff's harm or injury.

When you are determining the amount of damages to be awarded to the plaintiff, you should award damages for all of the plaintiff's injuries. Your award should not be reduced by your allocation of harm. The adjustment in damages, which may be required, will be performed by the Court.

APPENDIX V

Jury Verdict Sheet

1. Do you find that the critical parties (The US, the North Vietnamese, the South Vietnamese and their allies) to the Paris Peace talks were sincere in their peace efforts in October 1968
   YES____   NO_____
   If you answered YES, proceed to answer question #2. If you answered NO, then stop your deliberation at this point

2. Do you find that Richard Millhouse Nixon conspired, planned or plotted to prevent the South Vietnamese Government from attending the November Paris Peace talks
    YES____   NO_____
    If you answered YES, proceed to answer question #2. If you answered NO, then stop your deliberation at this point

3. Applying the law of causation as charged by the Judge, I hereby find that the acts of defendant Nixon **were a legal cause** of the ultimate act of the South Vietnamese failing to timely attend the peace conferences.

    YES____   NO_____
    If you answered YES, proceed to answer question #3. If you answered NO, then stop your deliberation at this point.

4. Do you find that Nixon's actions increased that risk of the peace conference's failure and that increased risk was a substantial factor in actually producing the conference failure?

    YES____   NO_____
    If you have answer, of the above questions YES, then you have pronounced Richard Millhouse Nixon liable for the lives lost, lives destroyed by physical and/or psychological injury and the economic cost of the continuation of the Vietnam War past 1968.

(Please make sure the circle your choice before handing it to the court clerk)

INDEX

A

14 point statement, 22
Abrams, 36, 56, 58, 137
Agnew, 109, 111, 112, 113, 114, 115, 183
Agnew's, 112, 114, 115, 183
Aitken, 8, 9, 75, 135, 138, 139, 145
Albuquerque, 109, 110, 111, 112, 113, 114, 115, 124, 126, 146
Allen, 76
Ambrose, 9, 65, 94, 120, 126, 134, 148, 152, 160, 179

B

Ball, 40, 43, 46
Ball Rule of Power, 43
Berman, 60, 158
Bernstein, 66
Bjola, 172
Bobby Kennedy, 5
bombing halt, xii, 1, 8, 12, 21, 22, 23, 24, 25, 26, 30, 33, 48, 52, 53, 56, 78, 81, 86, 89, 97, 132, 134, 137, 139, 153, 154, 156, 174, 179, 188, 191
Box 13 incident, 6
Brezhnev, 49
Bundy, 46, 72, 76, 88, 89, 90, 94, 108, 121, 135, 141, 142, 145, 157, 158, 160, 178, 179, 180, 183
Bunker, 27, 43, 78, 79, 80, 82, 94, 95, 96, 97, 99, 103, 104, 105, 106, 107, 115, 119, 133, 134, 137, 153, 154, 161, 191, 192

C

Califano, 3

Camp David, 40, 41, 46, 48
Caro, 4, 5, 6
causation, 164, 165, 166, 196
Chennault, xii, xiii, xv, xvi, 11, 38, 63, 66, 67, 68, 69, 70, 71, 72, 73, 74, 75, 76, 77, 83, 84, 85, 86, 87, 88, 91, 92, 93, 100, 101, 102, 103, 107, 108, 109, 111, 112, 113, 114, 115, 116, 117, 118, 120, 121, 122, 123, 124, 125, 126, 127, 128, 129, 130, 131, 132, 135, 136, 138, 139, 140, 141, 142, 144, 145, 146, 147, 148, 149, 150, 152, 154, 159, 160, 162, 163, 182, 183, 184, 186
Chicago Convention, 8, 174
China lobby, xii, 72, 121
Chotimer, 66, 150
CIA, xix, 9, 14, 18, 19, 20, 21, 22, 23, 26, 27, 28, 30, 31, 36, 39, 45, 47, 106, 162
Cialdini,, 175
Clark, xii, xvi, 2, 5, 27, 28, 37, 38, 42, 46, 47, 83, 84, 92, 120, 134, 135, 154, 155, 170, 186
Cleary, 170, 172, 176, 177
Clifford, xii, xvi, 2, 5, 7, 8, 9, 10, 27, 28, 31, 36, 37, 38, 39, 40, 41, 42, 43, 44, 45, 46, 47, 48, 57, 78, 80, 88, 92, 93, 95, 96, 104, 115, 116, 119, 120, 129, 130, 131, 134, 135, 136, 154, 155, 160, 170, 172, 186
coalition, 28, 71, 72, 77, 107, 116, 129, 159, 163, 179
cognitive dissonance, 175
Connolly, 11
Corcoran, 100, 101, 102, 135, 140, 141, 145
Crane, 112, 114
Cronkite, 29, 174
Cultural Revolution, 23, 34

CPSIA information can be obtained
at www.ICGtesting.com
Printed in the USA
LVOW11s0034070318
568947LV00004B/309/P